Reimagine Remote Working with Microsoft Teams

A practical guide to increasing your productivity and enhancing collaboration in the remote world

Sathish Veerapandian

Harsharanjeet Kaur

Ashok Madhvarayan

Sriram Rajamanickam

BIRMINGHAM—MUMBAI

Reimagine Remote Working with Microsoft Teams

Associate Group Product Manager: Pavan Ramchandani
Publishing Product Manager: Bhavya Rao
Senior Editor: Sofi Rogers
Content Development Editor: Feza Shaikh
Technical Editor: Shubham Sharma
Copy Editor: Safis Editing
Project Coordinator: Manthan Patel
Proofreader: Safis Editing
Indexer: Tejal Daruwale Soni
Production Designer: Ponraj Dhandapani

First published: November 2021

Production reference: 1101121

Published by Packt Publishing Ltd.
Livery Place
35 Livery Street
Birmingham
B3 2PB, UK.

978-1-80181-416-4

www.packt.com

To my mother, Baljinder Kaur, and father, Daljeet Singh, who always encouraged me to be the best version of myself, and to my husband and siblings for their unceasing support.

– Harsharanjeet Kaur

Contributors

About the authors

Sathish Veerapandian is a Certified Microsoft Infrastructure/Cloud Architect with 14 years of International large scale hands-on experience in Planning, Designing, Execution, IT Management of Messaging Platforms such as Microsoft Teams with Telephony, Skype for Business Voice, Microsoft Exchange, Intune Deployment, Microsoft Azure and Microsoft Security Implementations.

His dedication to serve the technical community has earned him the title of Microsoft MVP for the past 7 years, and he shares his technical knowledge and skills through Local Meetups, blogs (`https://ezcloudinfo.com`), and participates in Microsoft Ignite sessions. He is well known in the community for his contributions in Office 365, Microsoft Teams and Security platforms.

Harsharanjeet Kaur's skill set has allowed her to wear many hats during her career, including being a blogger, a Microsoft Certified Trainer for more than 5 years, a cloud consultant and architect, and a PowerShell automation expert. She has experience in various technologies, such as Azure IaaS, DevOps, Microsoft Teams administration, Identity and Access Management, Microsoft Intune, and perimeter security, and has worked with various government and corporate clients across the US, the UK, Asia-Pacific, and many other regions

Harsharan lives in Central India with her husband and loves to volunteer for social causes. You can reach out to her on Twitter (`@harsharanjeet`) or Linkedin (`linkedin.com/in/harsharanjeet/`) and she also has a website at `www.harsharanjeet.com`.

Ashok Madhvarayan is a Microsoft Certified Professional, blogger, and author at Cloud Exchangers, and makes real-world technical contributions via Microsoft communities (Q&A). Extensive knowledge and experience in messaging (Microsoft Exchange Server), the cloud (Microsoft Azure, Microsoft 365, Enterprise Mobility & Security), and services including infrastructure (Windows Server, Active Directory, ADFS, ADCS, file servers, System CenterConfiguration Manager), unified communication (MS Teams, Skype for Business, video conferencing room systems, Surface Hub), virtualization (Hyper-V), and databases (SQL).

Sriram Rajamanickam is a Microsoft Certified consultant with proven experience in Microsoft cloud technologies specialized in Microsoft 365, Azure, Intune, Azure Information Protection, Windows domains, Microsoft Exchange Server, Windows Server, and Windows virtualization. He is a senior specialist currently working with a government entity responsible for operating government shared services with respect to Microsoft technologies and their successful cloud journey.

About the reviewers

Peter Rising is a Microsoft MVP in Office apps and services. He has worked for several IT solutions providers and private organizations in a variety of technical roles focusing on Microsoft technologies. Since 2014, Peter has specialized in the Microsoft 365 platform, more recently shifting his focus to security and compliance. He holds several Microsoft certifications, including MCSE: Productivity, MCSA: Office 365, Microsoft 365 Certified: Enterprise Administrator Expert, Microsoft 365: Security Administrator Associate, and Microsoft 365 Certified: Teams Administrator Associate. He is also the author of the Packt Microsoft MS-500 exam guide, and the coauthor of the Microsoft MS-700 exam guide.

Steven Van Houttum is an independent consultant and trainer specialized in Microsoft Unified Communications. He is a **Microsoft Certified Trainer (MCT)**, **Certified Information Systems Security Professional (CISSP)**, and has been awarded **Microsoft Most Valuable Professional (MVP)** from 2006-2010 for Exchange and since 2011 for Lync (now Office Apps and Services).

He is a frequent speaker on Microsoft Teams and Skype for Business Server, at Microsoft events and at community events.

Table of Contents

3

Workforce Management in Teams

Section 2 – Collaboration, Events, and Communication

4

Managing Collaboration in Teams

5

Managing Communication in Teams

6

Organize Virtual Events

Section 3 – All about Security, Client Automation, Teams Etiquette, and Tips and Tricks

7

User and Data Security

8

Teams Etiquette and Best Practices

9

End User Automation

10

Productivity Tips and Tricks

Other Books You May Enjoy

Index

Preface

The breakout of the pandemic has forced the world to embrace remote working and the modern style of virtual business. However, end users may find it challenging to cope with this sudden change in working style, not aware of all the features and remote working tools available to make their life easy. Microsoft Teams is an exceptional platform, adopted by many organizations for unified communication and collaboration, and this book will help you to make the most of its capabilities.

Complete with step-by-step explanations and screenshots, this book guides you through the topics that you'll find useful in your daily use of Teams. You'll learn how to manage your teams and projects with Microsoft Teams in a structured and organized way. The book provides hands-on information with a focus on the end user side to help corporate users to increase productivity and become Microsoft Teams superusers. Finally, you'll explore the most effective ways of using the app with best practices and tips and tricks for making the most of the features available for your scenario.

By the end of this Microsoft Teams book, you'll have mastered Microsoft Teams and be fully equipped as a modern collaboration end user to effectively increase your remote working productivity.

Who this book is for

This book is for anyone who wants to improve their day-to-day productivity using Microsoft Teams. Anyone with access to Office 365 apps will find this book useful irrespective of their designation. Fundamental knowledge of Microsoft Office 365 applications is required.

What this book covers

Chapter 1, *Managing Meetings in Teams*, introduces Microsoft Teams as a hub for teamwork in Office 365. A key part of being successful in collaborative work is to stay on top of all meeting schedules and manage them promptly without any overlap. In this chapter, we will cover the key features that are available in Microsoft Teams for managing and organizing meetings.

Chapter 2, *Project Management in Teams*, looks at Microsoft Teams' unified collaboration capabilities, putting all of the key aspects of project management together in one place. In this chapter, we'll go over the actions that will help us be more efficient with Microsoft Teams for project management. This chapter will show us all of the project management options that are currently available in Teams.

Chapter 3, *Workforce Management in Teams*, addresses how managing the workforce is a key aspect of every organization because great employees can deliver great customer satisfaction by ensuring quality, which results in great businesses. At the end of this chapter, you will be familiar with using productivity and collaboration apps. With continuous practice, you can even go the extra mile of customizing the apps based on your organization's needs.

Chapter 4, *Managing Collaboration in Teams*, looks at one of the main aspects required for a strong team – collaboration. There are several communication solutions that are available on the market; however, Microsoft Teams is more convenient in terms of integrating with Office software such as MS Word, Excel, OneNote, and other applications. In this chapter, we will look at all options that can help us to improve collaboration with coworkers by using Microsoft Teams as a central workplace environment.

Chapter 5, *Managing Communication in Teams*, looks at how Microsoft Teams helps customers to have seamless and secure collaboration in the workplace. Teams also integrates with other Office 365 products to have effective communication, which in turn helps your employees or customers to stay on top of all information. Upon successful completion of these topics and getting hands-on with a few practice scenarios, you will be fully comfortable in managing your communication effectively with these tools.

Chapter 6, *Organize Virtual Events*, addresses how virtual events are now extremely popular in this new era of remote working. These events are not limited to the geographical location of the attendees as they happen over the internet. Virtual events could include webinars, training, conferences, live events, and much more. By the end of this chapter, you will be able to organize virtual events for your organization.

Chapter 7, *User and Data Security*, covers how security becomes essential when business data or information is shared among users. Keeping track of basic data operations such as read or modify is vital for compliance auditing. In this chapter, we will discover best practices to provide security to users and shared data. We will also discover advanced security features to prevent both malicious attacks and accidental data loss.

Chapter 8, Teams Etiquette and Best Practices, looks at how, in the world of remote working and working from home, it is inevitable to not to deviate from professional courtesy. So much so, that at times we overlook the presence of individuals whom we interact with every single day. In this chapter, we will learn about online meeting etiquette as well as recommendations for using Teams.

Chapter 9, End User Automation, covers business process automation – a basic aim that every company aspires to achieve. If your organization is already using Office 365, then you already have a few sets of tools that can help you to achieve business process automation. In this chapter, we will go through a list of end user automation tools that are available and that can be integrated with Microsoft Teams.

Chapter 10, Productivity Tips and Tricks, goes through the module that will help us in going around Microsoft Teams Tips and Tricks. Every week, Microsoft releases tips and shortcuts to help you be more productive and efficient with this powerful tool.

To get the most out of this book

A basic understanding of using the Teams application and Microsoft 365 applications as an end user for meetings and collaboration is required.

Software/hardware covered in the book	Operating system requirements
Microsoft Teams and collaborative Microsoft 365 apps	To get started with our practice, we recommend signing up for Microsoft 365 trial subscription E3 or E5.

All Microsoft 365 applications must be enabled by your administrator. Activation of the E3 or E5 license is recommended to get the best out of this book.

Download the color images

We also provide a PDF file that has color images of the screenshots and diagrams used in this book. You can download it here:

`https://static.packt-cdn.com/downloads/9781801814164_ColorImages.pdf`

Conventions used

There are a number of text conventions used throughout this book.

`Code in text`: Indicates code words in text, database table names, folder names, filenames, file extensions, pathnames, dummy URLs, user input, and Twitter handles. Here is an example: "So, in our example, we have entered `I can help with questions related to time off`."

Bold: Indicates a new term, an important word, or words that you see onscreen. For instance, words in menus or dialog boxes appear in **bold**. Here is an example: "To access the previous version, go to **Files | Open in SharePoint**."

> **Tips or important notes**
> Appear like this.

Get in touch

Feedback from our readers is always welcome.

General feedback: If you have questions about any aspect of this book, email us at `customercare@packtpub.com` and mention the book title in the subject of your message.

Errata: Although we have taken every care to ensure the accuracy of our content, mistakes do happen. If you have found a mistake in this book, we would be grateful if you would report this to us. Please visit `www.packtpub.com/support/errata` and fill in the form.

Piracy: If you come across any illegal copies of our works in any form on the internet, we would be grateful if you would provide us with the location address or website name. Please contact us at `copyright@packt.com` with a link to the material.

If you are interested in becoming an author: If there is a topic that you have expertise in and you are interested in either writing or contributing to a book, please visit `authors.packtpub.com`.

Share Your Thoughts

Once you've read *Reimagine Remote Working with Microsoft Teams*, we'd love to hear your thoughts! Scan the QR code below to go straight to the Amazon review page for this book and share your feedback.

https://packt.link/r/1801814163

Your review is important to us and the tech community and will help us make sure we're delivering excellent quality content.

Section 1 – Managing Your Meetings, Projects, and Workforce

Once you complete this part, you will be fully competent in managing your meetings, tracking your projects, issues, and tasks, and easily managing your workforce from Teams teams and channels. We highly recommend using these features and functionalities only from the Teams desktop client for a full-featured experience.

In this part, we cover the following chapters:

- *Chapter 1, Managing Meetings in Teams*
- *Chapter 2, Project Management in Teams*
- *Chapter 3, Workforce Management in Teams*

1
Managing Meetings in Teams

Microsoft Teams is a hub for teamwork in Office 365. A key part of being successful in collaborative work is to stay on top of all meeting schedules and manage them promptly without any overlap. Microsoft Teams helps you to meet in a smarter way and to have focused meetings, which can eventually increase users' productivity.

Microsoft Teams delivers a unique end-to-end meeting experience that features the human element of face-to-face interaction, while helping people stay focused before, during, and after meetings to accomplish more together. Meetings in enterprises have changed drastically, with the majority of the workforce connecting remotely, and, in this chapter, we will cover the key features that are available in Microsoft Teams.

This chapter will cover the following main topics:

- The various meeting options available in Microsoft Teams to schedule or join meetings
- Creating surveys, polls, customer feedback, and employee satisfaction via Microsoft Forms
- Seamless document meeting notes via Microsoft OneNote
- Using the channel Calendar to stay up to date on a particular Teams channel
- How Microsoft Bookings helps in organizing meetings and appointments with stakeholders

Upon successful completion of these topics and getting hands-on with a few practice scenarios, you will be fully comfortable in managing your meetings effectively with Microsoft Teams.

Meeting options via Windows/Mac

Microsoft Teams provides various ways to schedule meetings via the Teams desktop client / Teams Web on your Windows/Mac, mobile devices, or iPad/tablet devices:

1. Log in to Microsoft Teams using your credentials. On the left side, you will see the **Calendar** button. Click on **New meeting** and schedule a meeting.

2. Click on the **New meeting** dropdown in the top-right corner and select **Schedule meeting**.

Figure 1.1 – New meeting drop-down menu

3. You have an option to modify the view of the calendar to show meetings for a day, work week, or calendar week.

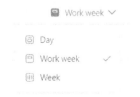

Figure 1.2 – Calendar view options

4. Add a title for the Microsoft Teams meeting that gives a quick insight into the meeting for the recipients.

5. Modify **Time Zone** if required.

6. **Require Registration** allows the meeting organizer to request participants to register for an event.

> **Note**
>
> If you require the user to register for this event, we cannot add a channel to the meeting. The registration link can be modified.

7. Add participants by typing in the first few letters of the recipients' names and Teams will pull out suggestions from the address book.

Figure 1.3 – Looking up recipients in the address book

8. You will also notice that the availability of the participants is shown automatically based on the date and time that you choose. This helps you to adjust the meeting time directly, avoiding any decline responses. This availability feature is limited to internal organization members.

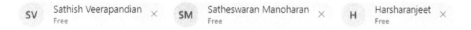

Figure 1.4 – Availability of participants

9. To invite someone outside your organization, type in their email address and they will get a link to join as a guest. You can also add optional recipients.

Figure 1.5 – Inviting a guest

10. Choose the start and end date and time from the date picker. Use the **All day** toggle bar if you wish to have the meeting for the whole day.

Figure 1.6 – Setting start and end times

11. Scheduling Assistant is a key feature with Exchange, and this is available in Microsoft Teams as it is tightly integrated with your Exchange calendar.

Figure 1.7 – Scheduling Assistant

This feature helps you to show the free/busy information of the meeting recipients and helps you to decide on a suitable time at which all participants will be able to join the meeting.

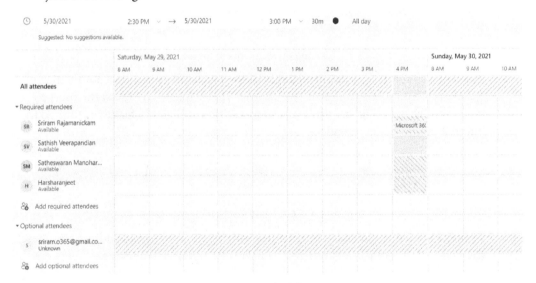

Figure 1.8 – Using Scheduling Assistant

12. There are a variety of options to choose from out of the box from Teams to set a meeting as a recurring meeting or choose a custom date.

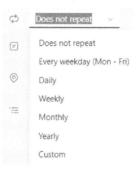

Figure 1.9 – Create a recurring meeting

Channel Meeting

Teams meetings allow you to directly add a team channel where all the members of the channel will be auto-added to the meeting request. This allows you to post the meeting link in the channel to join the meeting and to collaborate.

Figure 1.10 – Adding a Teams channel to a meeting

13. You can add a location according to your Rooms system, or by default, the meeting is created as an online meeting.

14. Finally, add the agenda in the body of the meeting for the participants to be prepared well ahead of the meeting. You can use the default word editing options, such as **Bold**, **Italics**, **Underline**, and other formatting options, for clearer content.

Figure 1.11 – Preview of the meeting request

Now all the participants who are added to the meeting should have an email with the meeting link to **Join**.

Meeting options are limited when initiating them through mobile devices; however, most of the settings are like the steps in this section.

Initiating a meeting

A Microsoft Teams meeting can be initiated from the Teams client directly, or from Outlook, as the Teams and Outlook calendars are completely integrated with each other.

> **Note**
>
> The Outlook plugin option is applicable only if it is enabled by your administrator.

To start a meeting, follow these steps:

1. Click on the **Calendar** icon in the Teams client. You will notice that the meeting item has a **Join** option at the scheduled time. Click on **Join**.

Figure 1.12 – Calendar within Teams

2. Teams allows you to configure your audio and video settings before the actual meeting starts. This option is not limited to the organizer, any participant who joins in the meeting will be allowed to choose their preferred audio and video options.

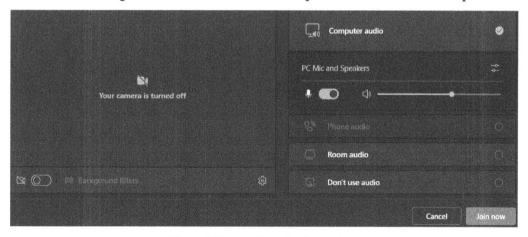

Figure 1.13 – Audio and video options

Turning video on and off

To turn video on and off and to see how to set up your preferences, follow these steps:

1. You can choose to turn your video on or off during meetings. You can simply use the toggle button to turn on your video. Microsoft Teams remembers your initial settings for your later meetings. You can always change the settings based on your needs.

Figure 1.14 – How to toggle video on

2. Once the video is turned on, you can choose from the variety of background filters that are available by clicking on **Background filters**. Microsoft Teams also allows you to add a personalized background filter (such as a company logo) to show as your background during the whole meeting.

Figure 1.15 – Background filters

3. Click on the **Settings** button and choose your audio preference. Microsoft allows you to select your computer audio for voiceovers during the meeting, or a room system if your IT team has configured any room devices in your meeting rooms. More importantly, you can join as a silent audience by selecting the option **Don't use audio**. Please feel free to select the appropriate option for your voiceover. From this screen, Teams also allows you to adjust your computer's speaker volume.

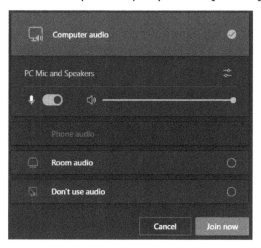

Figure 1.16 – Adjust speaker volume

Alternatively, you can open your Microsoft Outlook or Outlook Web Access, click on **Calendar**, and initiate the meeting from either of these clients.

Configuring meeting options

Once you have initiated the meeting, you can still change your audio or video preferences by clicking on the options in the top-right corner of your client.

Figure 1.17 – Options within an active meeting

Let's look at what each option icon allows you to do:

*   **Participants**: Click on the **Participants** button to display all meeting participants, including the people who are invited and are yet to join.

- **Conversation**: Select the **Conversation** button to have an overview of the chat between participants within the meeting. You also have the option of adding files, emojis, GIFs, and stickers. Emojis, animated GIFs, and stickers are a great way to add some fun and express yourself in your communication! Teams has added new emoji galleries with over 800 emojis to choose from, including some you can personalize.

- **Categorizing Messages**: This is one of the most used features, to categorize a message before sending. As you can see in the following screenshot, if you categorize the messages as **Urgent**, every participant will be notified every 2 minutes for 20 minutes, so you can bring a critical message to everyone's attention.

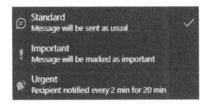

Figure 1.18 – Categorizing messages

Select the ...to configure further options such as screen recording, turning on live captions, and meeting notes.

Figure 1.19 – Further meeting options

- **Device settings**: Device settings allows you to change the audio/video options at any time in the meeting.

- **Meeting options**: Although default participant settings are determined by a company's IT admin, the meeting organizer may want to change them for a specific meeting. The organizer can make these changes on the **Meeting options** web page.

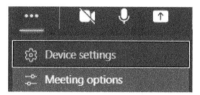

Figure 1.20 – Meeting options

- **Lobby Settings**: It is very important to know that IT admins can set default policies; however, meeting organizers can always override the settings for their particular meeting. It can be very useful when you have a meeting with management users and you do not want them to have to wait in the lobby to get into the meeting. So, you can simply choose any one of the lobby settings based on the following screenshot and table.

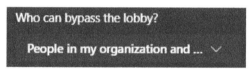

Figure 1.21 – Bypassing the lobby

Who can bypass the lobby?	What happens	Recommended when...
Only you	As the meeting organizer, only you can get into your meeting directly. Everyone else will wait in the lobby.	You want everyone else to wait in the lobby until you're ready to admit them.
People I invite*	Anyone who receives the invitation, including those to whom it's forwarded, will join the meeting directly. This doesn't include distribution lists—people must be invited individually. If you don't want people to forward the invite to others, turn off Allow Forwarding in the invitation.	You want a specific, limited group of people to join the meeting directly, and everyone else to wait in the lobby.
People in my organization	Only people within your organization can get into your meeting directly. Everyone else will wait in the lobby.	You want all guests and external people to wait in the lobby so you can approve them one by one.
People in my organization and guests	People in your organization and guests (including those who have different email domains than yours) can get into your meetings directly.	You want all external people (anyone outside your organization, except guests) to wait in the lobby so you can approve them one by one.
People in my organization and trusted organizations and guests	People in your Teams organization, external participants from trusted organizations, and guests can get into your meetings directly.	You want some external people to wait in the lobby so you can approve them one by one.

Figure 1.22 – Options for lobby settings

- **Caller Bypass**: You can allow callers who are dialing in using mobile to be auto-admitted into the meeting, thus bypassing the lobby.

Figure 1.23 – Allowing callers to bypass the Lobby

- **Notifications**: You may want to receive an alert when someone calling in by phone joins or leaves your meeting.

- **Meeting Roles**: Meetings can have participants who are internal to the organization or are external guests or vendors. It is vital for an organizer to know the roles of each participant, and Microsoft Teams allows you to preconfigure the settings once the meeting request is created. This can also be done during the meeting. There are two roles to choose from: **presenter** and **attendee**. Presenters can do just about anything that needs doing in a meeting, while the role of an attendee is more restricted. The following table outlines the abilities of an Organizer, Presenter, and Attendee:

Capability	Organizer	Presenter	Attendee
Speak and share video	Yes	Yes	Yes
Participate in meeting chat	Yes	Yes	Yes
Share content	Yes	Yes	No
Privately view a PowerPoint file shared by someone else	Yes	Yes	Yes
Take control of someone else's PowerPoint presentation	Yes	Yes	No
Mute other participants	Yes	Yes	No
Prevent attendees from unmuting themselves	Yes	Yes	No

Figure 1.24 – Capabilities of meeting roles

Managing meeting roles

Microsoft Teams allows you to change meeting roles before the meeting or during the meeting. It is always recommended that the options are configured before the meeting to avoid last-minute changes.

> **Note**
> You'll need to send out the meeting invite before you can assign roles.

The next sections will go through how to manage meeting roles depending on when they are being modified.

Before the meeting

If managing roles before a meeting has started, follow these steps:

1. Click on the **Calendar** tab on the Teams client, click on the meeting on the calendar, and click **Edit**.

Figure 1.25 – Select Edit

2. Editing the meeting allows you to add/remove recipients and change the time, location, and room systems. It also allows you to configure roles for the participants of the meeting. To modify the roles, you can click on **Meeting options**.

Figure 1.26 – Meeting options

This will open all available meeting options that you can customize. The good thing here is that you can even modify the other settings that are mentioned above in this console. In this example, I just wanted one of my colleagues to be the presenter and everyone else to be an attendee.

Figure 1.27 – Configuring Roles in a Meeting

Allowing camera and mic options for participants

Mostly all meeting conversations require bidirectional communication and face-to-face interaction allows a meeting to be more productive. However, it may cause certain inconveniences as remote working is continuing for many organizations, and sometimes participants join a meeting from a noisy environment. The Microsoft Teams client allows you to decide as an organizer to allow mic and camera for attendees. We can simply toggle the settings on/off. It also allows you to change these at any time during the meeting. To allow these options, click on the **Meeting options** icon during the meeting. When turned off, the participants' camera and mic will be grayed out.

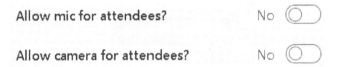

Figure 1.28 – Toggling camera and mic for attendees

We can now join the meeting and see the experience we have created by clicking on the **Join** button on the meeting item.

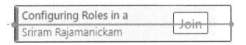

Figure 1.29 – Joining the meeting

During the meeting

All the roles options mentioned in the previous section can be modified even after the meeting is started. Once the organizer or the presenter completes the presentation, if you would like other participants to turn on their mic or camera, the organizer or presenter is able to change the settings by clicking on **Meeting options**.

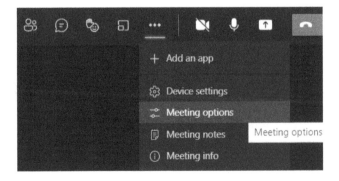

Figure 1.30 – Changing role options during a meeting

Sharing content during a meeting

As we have seen in the previous section on role configuration, you can define who is allowed to present their content during a meeting. Only the allowed participants will have **Share content** as an available option.

Figure 1.31 – Share content option during a meeting

The organizer or presenter can share their desktop, Windows, PowerPoint, or Whiteboard. The following table describes the outcome of each sharing option that is available.

Share your...	If you want to...	Great when...
Desktop	Show your entire screen, including notifications and other desktop activity.	You need to seamlessly share multiple windows.
Window	Show just one window, and no notifications or other desktop activity.	You only need to show one thing and want to keep the rest of your screen to yourself.
PowerPoint	Present a PowerPoint file others can interact with.	You need to share a presentation and want others to be able to move through it at their own pace.
Whiteboard	Collaborate with others in real time.	You want to sketch with others and have your notes attached to the meeting.

Organizers are allowed to include their computer audio when they present any audio files where all the participants in the meeting can hear the video and audio buffer from the organizer's computer.

Figure 1.32 – Include computer sound

If you choose to present your windows, Teams will show all the tools and files that are open on your system, and you can choose the desired one to present.

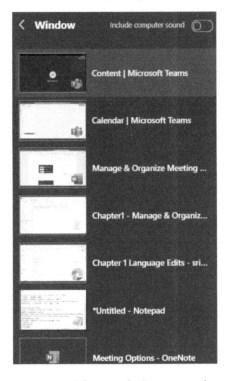

Figure 1.33 – Selecting which screen to share

If you choose to present a PowerPoint slide, Teams allows you to choose files from your computer or OneDrive.

Figure 1.34 – Presenting files from different locations

Presenter mode

The meeting organizer can customize the presenter mode by choosing whether they would like to present **Content Only** or **Standout**.

> **Note**
>
> Presenter mode is relatively new and Microsoft will be rolling out this option to tenants, so if it is not available in your organization, an IT admin should be able to guide you on the timeline of this option becoming available to end users.

- **Standout mode** shows the presenter in front of the content.
- **Reporter mode** displays content above the presenter's shoulder.
- **Side-by-side mode** has the content and the presenter displayed side by side.

Breakout rooms

Breakout rooms allow the organizer of the meeting to bring participants into smaller groups for lively brainstorming sessions. At times, it may be difficult to have a productive meeting, especially when you have a large audience with different areas of expertise in a single meeting. Breakout rooms easily create subgroups, and Teams allows you to add participants manually or automatically to these subgroups. We can set a timeline for each group, promote collaboration within groups, interact with participants, broadcast a message to the subgroups, and finally, close the breakout rooms.

> **Notes**
>
> These features are not currently available in breakout rooms:
>
> Call me
>
> Adding people to the meeting from the participants panel
>
> Adding additional people to the meeting chat
>
> Copying the Join meeting info

Let's see breakout rooms in action.

Creating breakout rooms

To create breakout rooms, a meeting should be initiated. In the top-right corner, you will have a **Breakout rooms** option.

Figure 1.35 – Enabling breakout rooms

Select the option to manually or automatically create breakout rooms. Automation will allow Microsoft Teams to auto-split the users based on the number of rooms selected.

> **Note**
>
> If automatic selection is selected, breakout rooms cannot be edited or modified, so it is recommended to go with manual selection and click **Create rooms**.

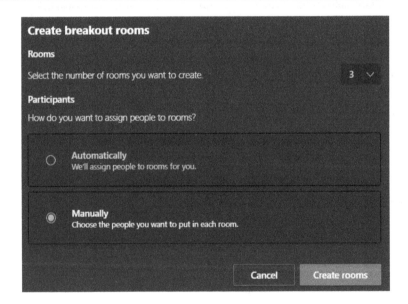

Figure 1.36 – Creating Breakout Rooms

Assigning people to breakout rooms manually

Based on the number of rooms selected on the previous screen, Teams will create the rooms and allow you to select participants to add to breakout rooms.

You can rename the rooms as per the logical naming convention that you would like to use.

Click on the **Assign participants** option and select users to add them to the room.

Figure 1.37 – Assign participants

Select the participants and click the **Assign** button to assign the users to the renamed group. The organizer can always assign members to different groups.

> **Note**
>
> Currently, participants who joined the meeting via PSTN or Teams devices cannot be assigned to rooms. We suggest using the main meeting as a breakout room for these people.

Figure 1.38 – Not all participants can be assigned to rooms

The organizer can join any room, which will allow them to interact in the respective breakout rooms.

Figure 1.39 – Joining a room as the organizer

Sending announcements to breakout rooms

You may want to send announcements to give time updates, for example, or share discussion prompts. So, all individual rooms get a message labeled with the **Important** category, click on the 🗨 **Announcement** button:

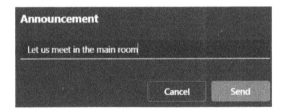

Figure 1.40 – Sending an announcement

The organizer can navigate to the chat space on the Teams client and navigate to any breakout room that is created and collaborate normally, like in a Teams channel.

Figure 1.41 – An announcement across all rooms

Click on the **Close room** option on the breakout room to close all rooms to get back into the original meeting.

> **Note**
>
> Each and every breakout room will have an attendance report available for download so you can see the time spent in each room.

Once the meeting rooms are closed, the room members can no longer send any messages or collaborate further.

You now have a better understanding and have become familiarized with different options available in a Teams meeting. In the upcoming section, we will cover the highlights of channel meetings and channel notes.

Channel meetings and notes

We understand everyone who is using Microsoft Teams will already have multiple channels created by the organization's IT team or a user. We would like to give an overview of Teams channels to explain channel meetings and notes better.

Channel meetings and notes help in ad hoc meetings and provide a better collaboration experience. Channels are dedicated sections within a team to keep conversations organized by specific topics, projects, disciplines—whatever works for your team! Files that you share in a channel (on the **Files** tab) are stored in SharePoint. Channels are places where conversations happen and where the work gets done. Channels can be open to all team members or, if you need a more selected audience, they can be private. Standard channels are for conversations that everyone in a team can participate in and private channels limit communication to a subset of people in a team. Channels are most valuable when extended with apps that include tabs, connectors, and bots that increase their value to the members of the team.

Channel meetings are useful when you would like to have an ad hoc call immediately with all the stakeholders working on a project. The stakeholders will be added as part of the Teams channel that you have explicitly set up for the project, which can be private or public.

If you would like to schedule a meeting with the entire team, please remember to add the meeting channel when you create a meeting request via the Teams calendar, which will do the following in the backend:

- It will create a meeting link and post it in the channel so the channel members can directly add it to their calendar.
- It will send an email notification with the Team calendar info.

- Participants who accept or reject the meeting are automatically updated in the tracking, which can be accessed by the organizer.

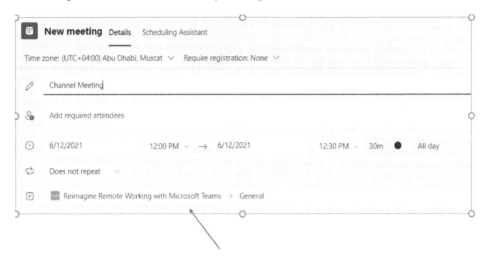

Figure 1.42 – Creating a new channel meeting

- A link is automatically added to the channel where the participants can click on **Join**:

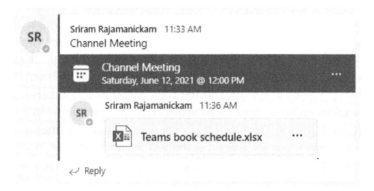

Figure 1.43 – Channel meeting join options

Ad hoc meeting in a channel

In the top-right corner of every team, you will find the option to meet or schedule a meeting. When you click on **Schedule a meeting**, Teams automatically adds all channel participants to the meeting:

- When you would like to make an important announcement on a project and would like to immediately meet the team, you can use the **Meet now** option, which will immediately add all users to the meeting and will prompt the users to join.

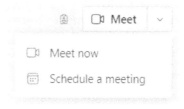

Figure 1.44 – Scheduling ad hoc meetings from a channel

- The **Meet now** option allows the organizer to copy the meeting link for sharing with other external participants.

- Start typing the name or phone number of someone you want to invite in the box under **People** at the top right. Select them when they appear in the list, and they'll get a call right away.

- Share the meeting via email.

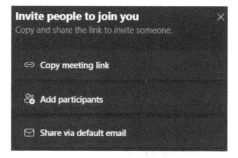

Figure 1.45 – Extending the meeting to additional participants who are not in the channel

> **Note**
> These options are extremely useful if you don't have an Outlook client installed and would like to set up professional meetings.

Meeting notes

Meeting notes are a great place to capture and share notes before, during, and after a Teams meeting. Meeting notes are very important when it comes to making meetings productive.

The following are the most important reasons to have meeting notes:

- Organizers and participants have a guide for reference.
- They serve as a reminder.
- They're a reference for participants who missed the meeting.
- They're time-saving.
- Corporate defense.

A few important things to remember

- Only people in the same organization as the meeting organizer will be able to start or access meeting notes.
- Meeting notes are available in meetings with up to 100 people.
- Only people who are invited to a meeting before notes are created will have access to them initially. Others can request access, and the owner of the notes will be notified via email.

Before a meeting

- Microsoft Teams allows you to edit meeting notes before a meeting is kicked off.
- To edit meeting notes, select **Calendar** in the Teams client, click on the meeting item, and then **Edit**. This takes to you to the **Meeting Edit** options.
- Notes will now be visible to all participants in the meeting for them to be prepared.

During and after a meeting

1. Meeting notes are available to all the participants of the meeting during the actual meeting.
2. The organizer and participants can click on the three dots in the top-right corner and access meeting notes anytime during and after the meeting by navigating to the meeting chat or channel chat window that is created.

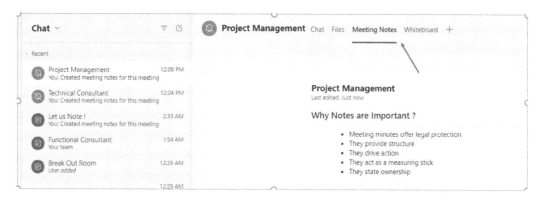

Figure 1.46 – Adding notes during and after a meeting

You now have a better understanding and have familiarized yourself with the various options for Teams channel meetings.

In the upcoming section, you will gain insights into the channel calendar, which is a new add-on in Microsoft Teams. The channel calendar helps you to organize the calendar of a Teams channel.

The channel calendar

Microsoft announced this feature as part of their Teams roadmap, and it was released in January 2021. The channel calendar allows you to add a calendar specifically to a channel. It was released to have more organized meetings by showing the calendar that is specific to a channel. The channel calendar was always available behind the scenes, but Microsoft decided to make it visible to all channel members. Setting up the channel calendar has the following benefits:

- The channel calendar allows team members to access channel meetings in the calendar grid.

- The channel calendar allows you to easily add a calendar item to the channel and shows it as a feed in the channel with the meeting link.

- Meetings created by adding the channel will be available and will show up in the channel calendar.

- When a meeting is created via channel meetings by adding a channel to a meeting, meeting requests only show up in the organizer's calendar. When we use **Channel calendar**, it is available to all users.

- When an event is created using the channel calendar, you are not able to remove the channel and it is grayed out, which makes sense as you want all the participants of the channel to be aware of the meeting.

The following steps add a channel calendar on Teams:

1. To add a channel calendar, navigate to **Teams Channel** and click on the (+) symbol to add the channel calendar from the applications:

Figure 1.47 – Adding a channel calendar

2. Search for channel calendar in the apps search box and select **Channel calendar**. You will be prompted to change the name if required, so the calendar name is logical. You can then post the calendar to the group.

Figure 1.48 – Searching the channel calendar

3. Once the channel calendar is added, provide a logical name for the calendar tab, which will be visible on your Teams client.

Figure 1.49 – Name the channel calendar

4. The organizer can use the channel calendar on the Teams client and create a calendar request on the channel, which will be reflected on the channel calendar.

Figure 1.50 – Creating a calendar event

5. The organizer can use the New Event directly on the channel calendar to create a calendar item:

Figure 1.51 – Add new event

Important limitations – channel calendar

Channel members will not receive a direct invite unless you add their names individually.

This is an important thing to note, as most users depend on the Outlook calendar. So, it is the organizer's responsibility to add the recipients explicitly to the meeting if they wish them to get an email notification and add the meeting to Outlook. Not doing this can sometimes mean a meeting is missed. The following limitations are to be remembered while using the Teams channel calendar:

- There is no private channel support.
- There can be only one calendar per channel.
- There is no guest access.
- There is no Outlook integration.
- There is no SharePoint calendar integration.
- Each time you schedule an event, it will create a post in the channel with a summary of the event details.
- Only members who have turned on notifications for that channel will receive a notification that an event was created.
- Only teams created before May 2018 can be added to an invite. If your team was created after May 2018, you can only add channels, Outlook groups, and individuals to an invite.

You now have a better understanding of, and are familiarized with, the various options on a Teams channel calendar.

In the upcoming section, you will learn about Microsoft Bookings, which is a powerful tool for businesses to manage customer bookings and schedules.

Microsoft Bookings

In this section, we will get a deep insight into Microsoft Bookings. As an overview, Microsoft Bookings provides individuals and businesses an end-to-end scheduling assistant and an appointments management system. Bookings are integrated into the Outlook calendar, which gives customers or business users the flexibility to book a time that is best suited for both parties:

- Automated email notifications reduce no-shows and improve customer satisfaction.

- Microsoft Bookings is highly customizable, which helps customers to book efficiently and allows business owners to be prepared before meetings.

- Bookings is integrated into the Office 365 suite of products, which means business owners can effectively use the powerful Microsoft Teams to virtually meet customers. Customers get a unique meeting link to the email address that they enter upon booking, which they can click on and join the meeting.

> **Note**
> It is not necessary for the customer to have an Office 365 identity; they are free to use their Gmail or AOL (and other) accounts to join.

There are three primary components of Bookings:

- A booking page where your customers and clients can schedule appointments with the staff member who is providing the service or running the appointment. This web-based scheduling page can be shared via a direct link, your Facebook page, and even through link embedding within your website.

- A web app that contains a set of web-based, business-facing pages where Bookings calendar owners and administrators within an organization can define appointment types and details, manage staff schedules and availability, set business hours, and customize how appointments are scheduled. These pages allow for versatility and the ability to customize a Bookings calendar to fit the diverse needs of the person or organization.

- A business-facing mobile app where Bookings calendar owners and administrators can see all their appointments, access customer lists and contact information, and make manual bookings on the go.

Licensing requirements

Bookings is available and active by default for Microsoft 365 Business Premium, Microsoft 365 Business Standard, A3, A5, E3, and E5 customers worldwide. Bookings is also available in Office 365 operated by 21Vianet.

> **Note**
>
> Before proceeding with Bookings, please ensure that your IT team has enabled the service for you. If you are the global administrator of your own tenant, and if you have any of the aforementioned licenses assigned, Bookings will work for you.

Client requirements

Bookings is an online service, so you do not need to download any client. Just go to the app launcher within the Microsoft 365 web experience. Administrators can also use the Bookings companion app to stay current with the latest information about customers and their appointments.

Let's get started with Bookings:

1. To onboard yourself and set up Bookings, please visit the following onboarding URL

    `https://outlook.office.com/bookings/onboarding`

2. Since this is first-time onboarding, it will prompt you to add a Bookings calendar with a few details about the business. For this demo, we can add a Bookings calendar name such as `DevOps Enterprise Support` and select the business type.

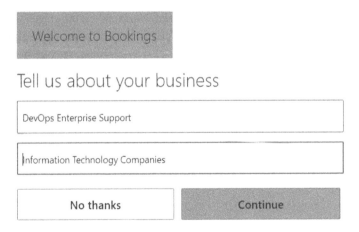

Figure 1.52 – Naming the business

3. You are now ready to set up Bookings for your organization. In the left-hand pane, you have all the configurable items to have a seamless Bookings solution for your organization.

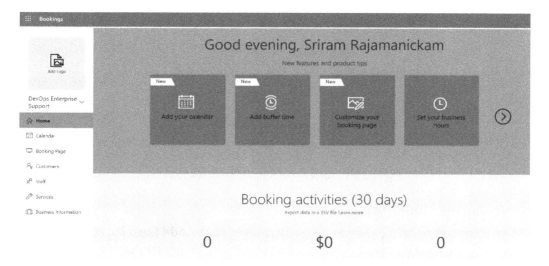

Figure 1.53 – Welcome page on Bookings

4. Once the calendar is added for the first time using the onboarding link, you can use the direct URL:

`https://outlook.office.com/bookings/homepage`

5. As an alternate approach, you can use the default Office 365 login, `https://login.microsoftonline.com`, select **All apps**, and click **Bookings**.

Follow these steps to add Bookings to the Teams client:

1. Click on the three dots (…) on the Teams client.
2. Search for the **Bookings** app in the search window.
3. Click on the app and add the widget to your Teams client.

4. The Bookings app will be available for quick access when you launch the Teams client every time.

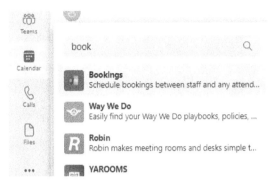

Figure 1.54 – Adding Bookings to your Teams client

Customizing Bookings

Let's start by setting up the company logo by clicking on the **Add Logo** tile in the top-left corner of your **Bookings** page. Select an image from your computer that is appropriate for the business. Once the logo is updated, it will allow you to choose a theme for the background color.

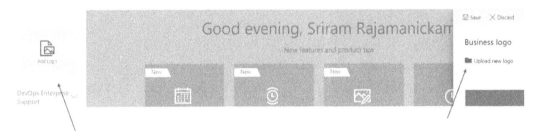

Figure 1.55 – Adding an organization logo

Business information

In Microsoft Bookings, the **Business information** page within the web app contains all the details that you would typically find on a business' "About us" page. These details include the relevant name, address, phone number, website URL, privacy policy URL, logo, and business hours.

The information you provide here will be displayed on the page customers and clients use to book appointments (known as the booking page) and in messages and reminders sent to them by Bookings. An example of this information on the booking page is highlighted here.

In Microsoft 365, select **App launcher** and then select **Bookings**.

1. In the navigation pane, select **Business Information**.

2. Enter a name suitable for the business and the phone number that you will need for the Bookings calendar.

3. Type in the email address where you would like to get notifications in the **Send customer replies to**.

4. For the website URL, please type the URL that is the home page of your business.

5. You can mention the privacy policy and terms and conditions of your business.

6. Finally, set the currency type for the service offering and click on **Save**.

Business hours

*   By default, in the Microsoft Bookings app, business hours are set to 8 a.m. to 5 p.m. with 15 mins increments; however, you can tweak this as per the business needs.

*   On the **Business information** page, under **Business hours**, use the dropdowns to select start and end times for each day.

*   Click + or - to set the start and end times for **Business hours**.

Figure 1.56 – Editing Business information

Setting off hours

The business needs to have **off hours** to take care of internal processes such as staff meetings and updating inventory. Bookings allows you to add *off* hours, where customers will not have time slots available for booking.

For example, if you have staff meetings every Thursday from 13:00 to 14:00 and want to block out that time so all your staff members can attend, you can do this:

Figure 1.57 – Editing Business hours

To configure off hours, please follow these steps so customers don't see these times for booking appointments:

1. On the **Business information** page, under **Business hours**, select a start and end time during which time staff can do their internal processes.

2. Select + to create a new row for Thursday.

Configuring service details

- **Service name**: Enter the name of your service. This is the name that will appear in the drop-down menu on the calendar page.

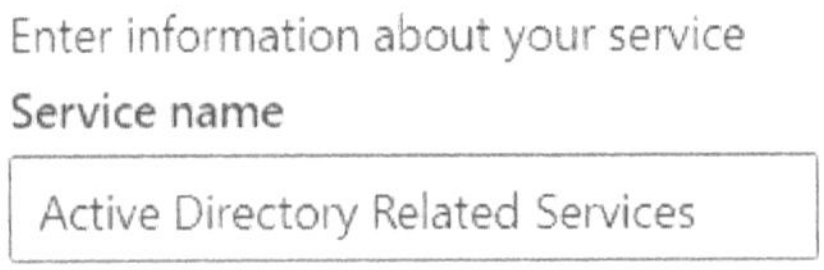

Enter information about your service

Service name

Active Directory Related Services

Figure 1.58 – Editing Service name

- **Description**: It is good to give a description of the service offering, which will help the customer to pick a suitable service.

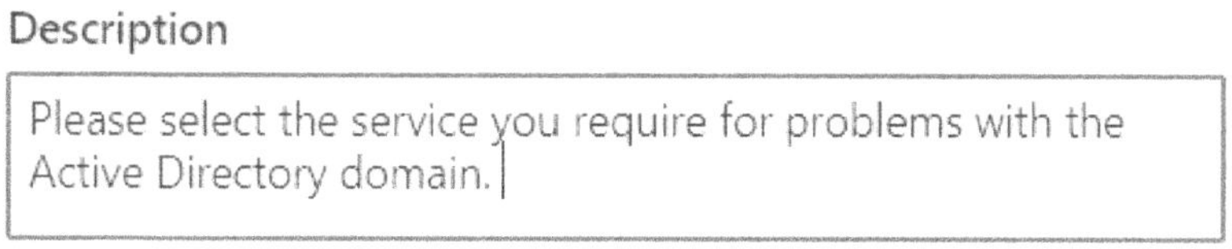

Description

Please select the service you require for problems with the Active Directory domain.

Figure 1.59 – Modifying the service description

- **Default location**: This location will be displayed on confirmation and reminder emails for both staff and customers, and it will be displayed on the calendar event created for the booking.

Default location

Our office address

Figure 1.60 – Modifying the service location

- **Add online meeting**: Online meetings allow you to have a meeting online with Microsoft Teams. You can click on the toggle bar to adjust the settings.

Add online meeting ⓘ

Figure 1.61 – Enabling online meetings

- **Default Duration**: This helps to book the staff calendar for a time. In this case, we have selected 1 hour when the staff calendar won't be available during this time slot for other meetings.

Default Duration

Days 0 ∨   Hours 1 ∨   Minutes 0 ∨

Figure 1.62 – Duration to block the staff calendar

- **Buffer time your customers can't book**: Buffer time helps your staff with extra time for every appointment. It will help staff to cover internal processes.

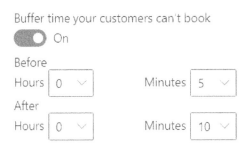

Figure 1.63 – Buffer time for staff

- **Maximum attendees per event**: This setting allows you to create services that require the ability for multiple people to book the same appointment time and the same staff (such as a fitness class). The appointment time slot for the selected service, staff, and time will be available to book until the maximum number of attendees, specified by you, has been reached. The current appointment capacity and attendees can be viewed in the **Calendar** tab in the Bookings web app.

- **Default price**: This is the price that will be displayed on the **Self-Service** page. If **Price not set** is selected, then no price or reference to cost or pricing will appear.

Figure 1.64 – Buffer time for staff

- **Notes**: This field appears in the booking event for booked staff, as well as on the event that appears on the **Calendar** tab in the Bookings web app.

- **Custom Fields**: This section allows questions to be added, or removed, if the customer needs to answer any questions to successfully book.

- **Customer email**, **phone number**, **address**, and **notes** are non-removable fields, but you can make them optional by deselecting **Required** beside each field.

- You can add a multiple-choice or text-response question by selecting **Add a question**.

- Custom fields can be useful when collecting information that is needed every time a specific appointment is booked. Examples include insurance provider prior to a clinic visit, loan type for loan consultations, major of study for academic advice, or applicant ID for candidate interviews.

Figure 1.65 – Mandatory information to be provided by a customer

- **Reminders and Confirmations**: Both types of emails are sent out to customers, staff members, or both, at a specified time before the appointment. Multiple messages can be created for each appointment, according to your preference.

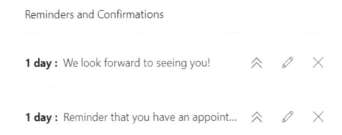

Figure 1.66 – Reminder and confirmation to customer

- **Enable text message notifications for your customer**: If selected, SMS messages are sent to the customer, but only if they opt in. Note that SMS notifications are currently only available in North America.

- **Publishing options**: Choose whether to have this service appear as bookable on the **Self-Service** page or to make the service bookable only on the **Calendar** tab within the Bookings web app.

Publishing options

☑ Show this service on the booking page

Figure 1.67 – To show the service on the booking page

- **Scheduling policy**: This setting determines how appointment times are viewed, and the time during which bookings can be made or canceled.

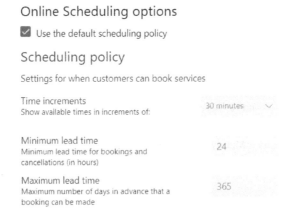

Figure 1.68 – Managing the Scheduling policy

- **Email notifications**: Sets when emails are sent to organization staff and to customers or clients.

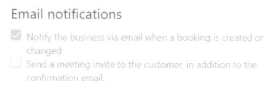

Figure 1.69– To get the internal team notified about the booking

- **Staff**: Selecting this checkbox allows customers or clients to choose a specific staff member for their appointment.

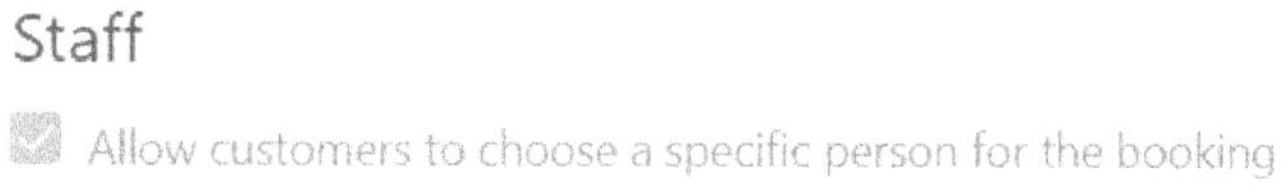

Staff

Allow customers to choose a specific person for the booking

Figure 1.70 – To allow customers to choose their preferred staff

- **Enabled**:

  - Customers can choose from all staff assigned to the appointment when booking on the **Self-Service** page. Selecting the option of **Anyone** will make Bookings choose an available staff member at random to assign to the appointment.

- **Disabled**:

  - Customers booking via the **Self-Service** page can select a service and a time and date. The available staff will be booked at random. Note that specific staff can still be selected when booked through the **Calendar** tab in the Bookings web app.

- **Availability**: The following options determine when the service can be booked:

  - **Bookable when staff are free**: The service maintains availability based on when staff are free within business hours, with no extra time restrictions.

  - **Custom hours (recurring weekly)**: The service has an added layer of availability that can be further restricted (in addition to restricting by business hours or staff hours). Use this option when your service can only be provided or performed at a specific time.

- **Set different availability for a Date Range**: This setting impacts availability at a specific point in time, instead of on a recurring basis. For example, this could be used when a machine that is needed for the service is temporarily being serviced and unavailable, or when an organization is closed for a holiday.

- **Assign Staff**: Select the staff (provided you have added staff members to the **Staff** tab) who will be bookable for that specific service. Selecting no individual member of staff will result in all staff being assigned to the service.

- **Manage staff**:

  - Go to the **Manage staff** page and select **Add staff** button.

  - When adding staff from within your organization, type their name in the **Add people** field and select them when they appear in the drop-down menu. The other fields will automatically populate.

  - Administrators can edit all settings, add and remove staff, and create, edit, or delete bookings.

  - Viewers can see all the bookings on the calendar, but they cannot modify or delete them. They have read-only access to settings.

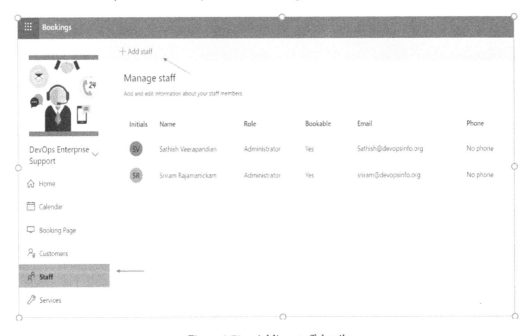

Figure 1.71 – Adding staff details

Figure 1.72: Updating the staff details

- **Booking Page**:

  Click on **Booking Page** on the left side to configure booking controls.

  - If you select **Require a Microsoft 365 Account** for booking, other customers with Gmail or an AOL ID won't be able to book.

Figure 1.73 – Booking page access control

  - **Booking page access control**: Selecting **Disable direct search engine indexing of booking page** prevents your booking page from appearing in the search results of Google or other search engines.

- **Customer data usage consent**: When selected, text requesting the user's or customer's consent for your organization to use their data will appear on the **Self-Service** page. The box will have to be checked by the user in order to complete the booking.

- **Availability**: Availability helps you to customize the time ranges when the service is available; otherwise, it is restricted to the configured business hours.

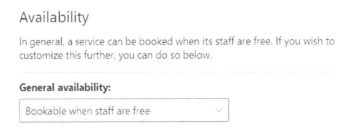

Figure 1.74 – Configuring Availability

- **Customize your page**: Choose colors and logos that appear on the **Self-Service** page for brandling.

- **Region and time zone settings**: Set your local time zone, which converts the time zone to the customer's time zone automatically whenever booking a meeting. For example, if an appointment is available at 5:00 p.m. GST, someone in IST will see the available time displayed as 6:30 p.m. IST.

Figure 1.75 – Time zone adoption

Publish/Unpublish

After configuring the settings, click on Publish/**Unpublish** at the top of the page to allow external parties to book meetings.

Figure 1.76 – Publishing the configuration

Staff calendar

As the business owner, you can have a quick glance at all your staff members' calendars to see their availability.

Figure 1.77 – Checking the staff calendar

Booking page for customers

As we have created a booking page, you can share this URL or embed this URL on the public website or Facebook feeds to have seamless booking for your customers:

```
https://outlook.office365.com/owa/calendar/
DevOpsEnterpriseSupport@devopsinfo.org/bookings/
```

Figure 1.78 – Final look of the booking app

> **Note**
>
> Admins can use the Microsoft Bookings app on their Android/iOS platform to have a quick overview of all their booked sessions and be prepared to serve.

With remote working increasing, Microsoft Bookings helps small businesses to set up an easy solution for customers using Microsoft collaboration tools to connect with customers.

You now have a better understanding of, and are familiar with, the various options on Microsoft Bookings.

In the upcoming section, you will learn about Microsoft Forms, which is a powerful tool for corporate surveys or quizzes, to collect reports from staff or customers.

Microsoft Forms

In this section, we will cover an overview of Microsoft Forms. Microsoft Forms can be used as a corporate survey solution. The solution allows users to customize questions, with options such as getting the user's opinion on a product the organization is working on, HR-based surveys, and a lot more. It can also be used for creating corporate quizzes. Microsoft Forms is a free tool that does not require any licenses.

Accessing Forms

1. Log in to Microsoft Online Services at `https://login.microsoftonline.com` using your corporate email address and password.

2. Select **All app** launcher in the top-left corner of the web browser and click **Forms**.

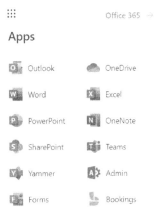

Figure 1.79 – Accessing Microsoft Forms

3. You will be redirected to the Forms welcome page, where you can start customizing the survey questions or quiz.

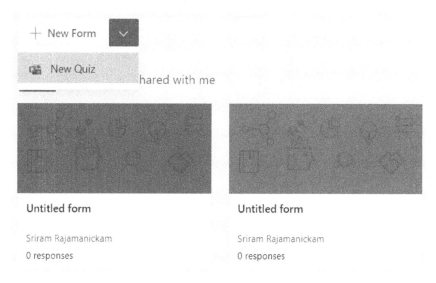

Figure 1.80 – Forms welcome page

Customizing Forms

1. Click on **New Form**, which will allow you to create your own form. The first thing to do here is to set up a suitable title for your survey:

Figure 1.81 – Title for the survey

2. In the top-right corner of this page, click on the three dots to go to the Forms **Settings** console.

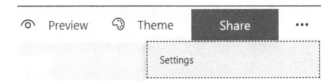

Figure 1.82 – Forms Settings

3. Select the targeted audience who can fill in the survey:

    -   **Anyone can respond** will be an anonymous survey where anyone with the link can fill in the survey.

    -   **Only people in my organization can respond** will allow only people who have signed in using their corporate identities to fill in the survey. Optionally, you can record a participant's name and allow only one response per person. Based on the requirement, these options should be carefully selected.

    -   **Specific people in my organization can respond** is targeted at a particular set of people who can fill in the survey.

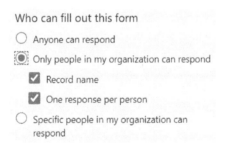

Figure 1.83 – Survey audience options

4. We can customize survey response options:

    -   **Accept responses**: This can be unchecked when the survey requires tweaking questions. Once checked, the intended recipients can start filling in the survey.

    -   **Start date** and **End date**: You can set up a start date and end date to lock down the survey start and end date. This allows you to close the survey or start the survey at the intended time.

    -   **Shuffle questions**: This can be turned on when you want to have the questions shuffled by the Forms engine automatically. By default, shuffling is turned off and a question order will be in place.

- **Customize thank you message**: You can send a customized message when the audience takes the survey.

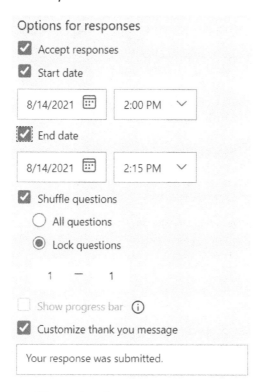

Figure 1.84 – Survey response options

5. **Response receipts**: This allows you to inform the audience that their response has been recorded.

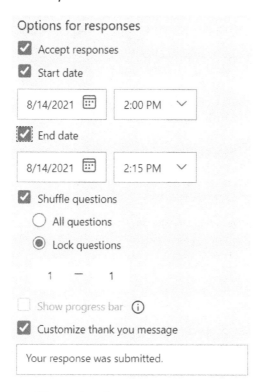

Figure 1.85 – Survey Response receipts options

6. Microsoft Forms allows you to add survey questions in other languages. From the settings, you have an option to select **Multilingual** and add a primary language.

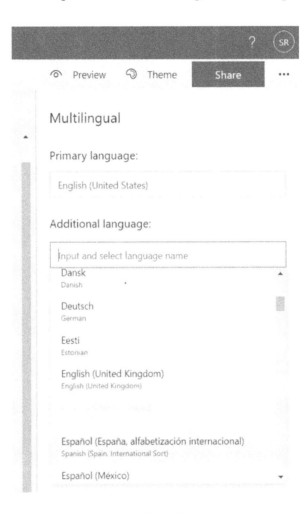

Figure 1.86 – Adding other languages

Configuring themes

Forms allows you to choose from the inbuilt theme which is built on this product by default. It does not restrict you to using the inbuilt themes. You can search Bing, upload your own theme, or search from your OneDrive location:

1. In the top-right corner, you will see **Theme**, which will allow you to configure the theme for the survey.

Figure 1.87 – Configuring a theme

Figure 1.88 – Inbuilt themes

2. Click on the (+) symbol to upload a customized theme from the following location:

Figure 1.89 – Uploading custom themes

Configuring questions for a survey

Forms allow you to add multiple question types based on the business needs and the variety of answering options allowed.

1. Click on the + symbol and add a question type.

Figure 1.90 – Adding survey questions

2. Click on the + symbol, add a question type, and type in the question. The Forms engine will give suggestions based on the question you type. You can discard them and use your own.

3. **Multiple answers** allows you to select multiple options for a question.

4. **Required** makes the question mandatory, so the user cannot skip it and move on to the next question.

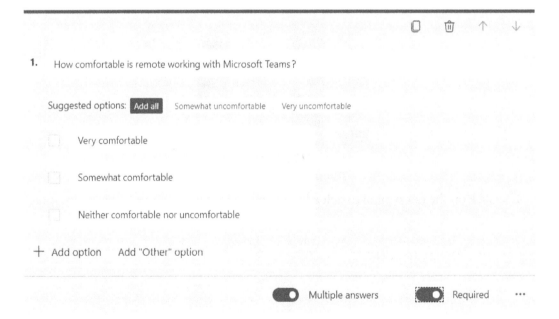

Figure 1.91 – Customizing a survey question

5. Similarly, you can create multiple question types within a single survey. The following are some examples of this.

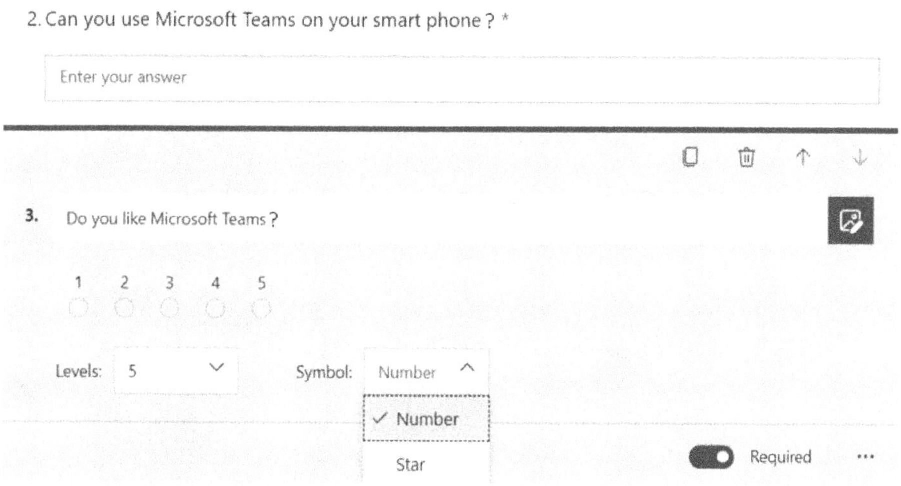

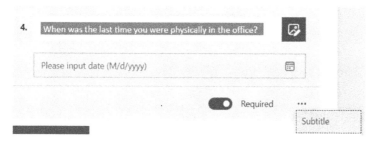

2. Can you use Microsoft Teams on your smart phone ? *

Enter your answer

3. Do you like Microsoft Teams ?

    1   2   3   4   5

    Levels: 5   Symbol: Number

                                  ✓ Number

                                  Star   Required   ...

Figure 1.92 – Customizing a survey question

6. You can add a subtitle to each question to provide a description of the question.

4. When was the last time you were physically in the office?

    Please input date (M/d/yyyy)

                                          Required   ...

                                                     Subtitle

Figure 1.93 – Adding a subtitle

Configuring branching

In this section, we will cover the branching options of Forms, which allow you to directly bypass a question and go to the next section. One of the real use cases we recently came across was that our organization planned to provide Microsoft training for all cloud technologies. The list of technologies was from basic to expert level, so we used the branching logic to allow users to select their preferred training session and to book their training slots. Let's see branching in action:

1. To create branching, go to questions and select **Add branching**.

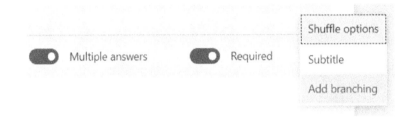

Figure 1.94 – Adding branching

2. As you can see in the following screenshot, you can configure a question so that you can directly bypass it and go to another question based on the selection.

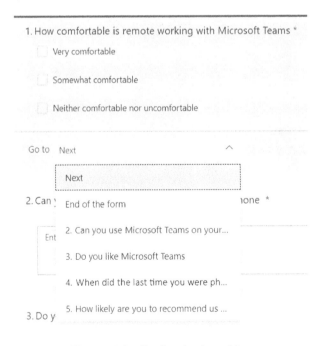

Figure 1.95 – Configuring branching

3. You can reset the branching if you have challenges with grouping by clicking in the top-right corner of the branching page.

Figure 1.96 – Reset branching

4. Finally, you can preview the survey form and publish it.

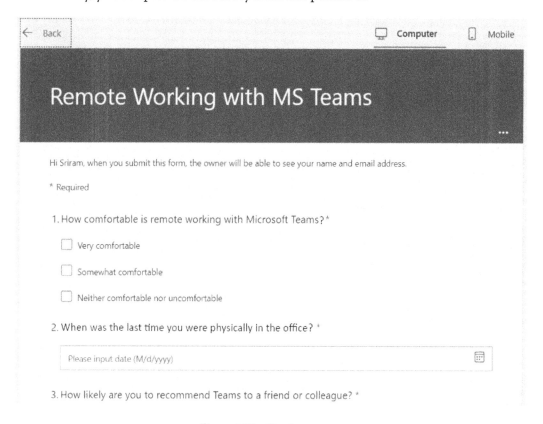

Figure 1.97 – Preview survey

Tracking responses

Once the survey is filled in, the survey creator will be notified of the responses and can log in to their portal and track the responses and export them into Excel to collect the required data.

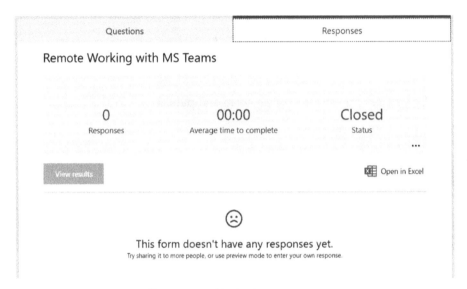

Figure 1.98 – Reviewing responses

You now have a better understanding of, and are familiar with, how to configure Microsoft Forms for your corporate surveys.

Summary

In this chapter, we have taken a deep dive into organizing Microsoft meetings, channel calendars, channel meetings, meetings notes, Microsoft Bookings, and Microsoft Forms. By practicing on your own Teams client, you should be able to get hands-on experience for the targeted topics. The way organizations work has drastically changed in recent years, and remote working is being adopted by many organizations. With the powerful tools in Microsoft Teams and the Office 365 stack, you will be able to organize your daily tasks and meeting schedules seamlessly. Microsoft Teams is a state-of-the-art tool that is currently available on the market for collaboration, so please read through the upcoming chapters for a lot of amazing features that can ease your day-to-day tasks.

In the upcoming chapter, we will learn about the project management tools that are available on the Office 365 stack and integration with Microsoft Teams.

2
Project Management in Teams

We feel more at ease following up with teammates, detecting barriers, updating our projects, and keeping track of our projects when we have a proper project management mechanism in place. Project management also serves as a fundamental criterion for defining stakeholders, adding connected workforces, classifying budget allocation, permissions, and other aspects that are required for any new requirements to be successfully met.

The Microsoft Teams unified collaboration capabilities put all of the key aspects of project management together in one place. Having scheduled/instant meetings, coauthoring in a single file, communication between project members, and inviting external vendors/partners are all possible, which makes Microsoft Teams one of the best project management tools to come along with the Microsoft 365 suite of products, with no additional cost.

In this chapter, we'll go over the actions that will help us be more efficient with Microsoft Teams for project management. This chapter will show us all of the project management options that are currently available in Teams. For a project that has already begun, it is recommended to pick one strategy and stick with it. The appropriate solution can be picked based on convenience.

We will have the following learning objectives in this chapter:

- How Microsoft Tasks helps businesses to keep track of projects
- The Milestones app and Teams as a superior option for project management
- Using the Project and Roadmap apps to keep track of your projects
- Creating lists and following up on projects
- Familiarizing yourself with Azure Boards and utilizing it for projects

Upon successful completion of these topics and getting hands-on with a few practical scenarios, you will be fully comfortable in managing your projects effectively from Microsoft Teams.

Technical requirements

To get started with our practice, we recommend signing up for an Office 365 trial E3 subscription, following the steps that are mentioned in our main index. All Microsoft applications must be enabled by your administrator.

How Microsoft Tasks helps businesses to keep track of the projects

Tasks is one of the newest apps in Microsoft Teams, launched less than a year ago. Tasks is a replacement for the Microsoft Tasks by the **Planner** and **To Do** apps. With Microsoft Tasks, you can track individual tasks, as well as your shared tasks within a team, easily.

All the tasks that are associated with any project can be created and shared within the team. The best part is we can define timelines in Microsoft Tasks, which will help us to complete tasks on time and keep track of them.

1. To get started with Tasks, log in to your Teams client: choose the team where you want to add the task.

Figure 2.1 – Look up the correct team

2. Navigate to **Tabs**, click on the + sign, and search for `tasks`.

Figure 2.2 – Adding a tab to Teams

3. Once the task tab has been added, and you have provided a name for it based on the project, it is ready to go for distributing tasks to the team. In the following example, we have named the tab **DevopsInfo Tasks**. Don't worry if you need to rename the tab later, as we have the option to rename them.

Figure 2.3 – Renaming the task tab

4. After adding the task tab, make sure you select the option **Group by Bucket**. You can start adding new **buckets** based on the task types. Click on **Add new bucket**:

Figure 2.4 – Navigating to the Board tab

5. When a new bucket is selected, Teams suggests adding a name. In this example, let's group the tasks based on the resources. Therefore, we have given the technical reviewer's name as one bucket.

Figure 2.5 – Give a name for the bucket

6. The new bucket is created now, so we can add a task, give the task a name, set a due date, assign people to the task, and finally click on **Add Task**.

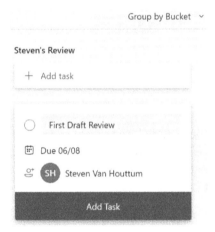

Figure 2.6 – Click on Add Task to complete task creation

7. After the task has been created, we have the option to add granular information to this task. For instance, you can label your task based on priority with colors, choose the priority of tasks, select the progress (**Started**, **In progress**, **Completed**), and choose the actual start date.

8. We can also add notes and select the option **Show on card**, which will help to track our activities when having a quick glance at the tasks.

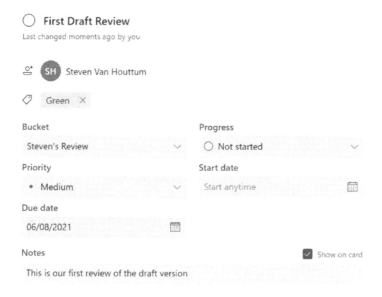

Figure 2.7 – An overview of the created task

9. Moreover, we could add a checklist like the one shown in the following screenshot. One more point to note here is that **Show on card** can be shown either as notes or a checklist. The checklist can be added as shown in the following screenshot, with the option **Add an item**. We can modify or remove items later, based on our requirements.

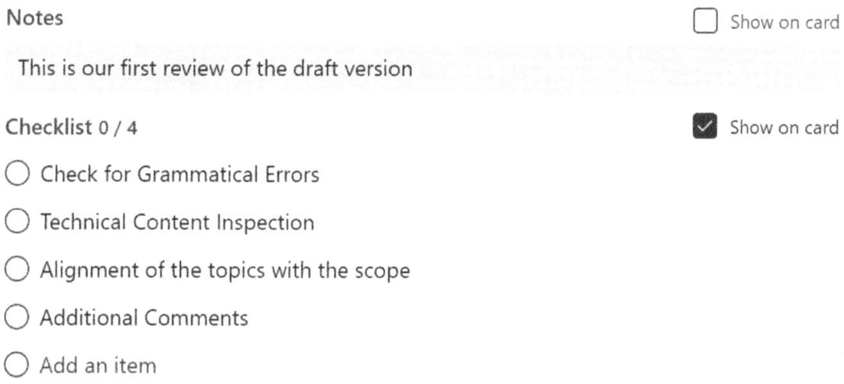

Notes   ☐ Show on card

This is our first review of the draft version

Checklist 0 / 4   ☑ Show on card

◯ Check for Grammatical Errors

◯ Technical Content Inspection

◯ Alignment of the topics with the scope

◯ Additional Comments

◯ Add an item

Figure 2.8 – Option to add notes

10. Finally, we have the option to add an attachment that is associated with the task. There are three options to add attachments: directly from the local file on your PC, a link, or a SharePoint site.

Figure 2.9 – Adding attachments

11. After adding attachments, we can see the attachments showing directly in the task (if we add them directly) or linked to a SharePoint site. We have the option to comment and send a notification to the owner of the task. On scrolling down to the bottom, we can also see who created the task, along with the date and time stamp.

Figure 2.10 – Adding comments to the task

You have now learned how to create a task and assign it to a person.

Tasks can be added based on projects and the associated tasks present in them. In this example, we are using the method of creating tasks based on the number of people working on the project. There can also be tasks added that are generic tasks for the whole team, which require attention from everyone working on the project. So, based on this example, we have created tasks as shown in the following screenshot, where we can see the tasks assigned to individual people and their current tasks. This screen shows us all the tasks in a board view. We have other view options to show our tasks, and we will look at them shortly.

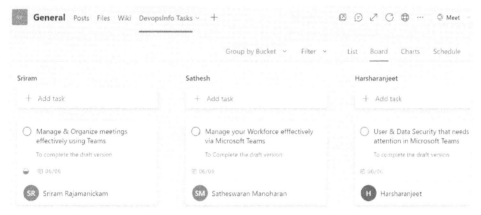

Figure 2.11 – Adding a tab to Teams

We can use the options **Group by Bucket**, **Assigned to**, **Progress**, **Due date**, **Labels**, and **Priority**. We do have the option of filtering by the parameters shown in the next screenshot. This is really helpful for any team where we have a high number of tasks assigned.

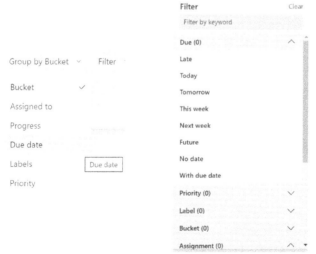

Figure 2.12 – Grouping and filtering tasks by your choice

There's also a more visually appealing way to see our Team tasks. Selecting **List** would show the view in the next screenshot. This view gives us a condensed look at **Task title**, **Assigned to**, **Priority**, due date, and which bucket it has been assigned to.

Task title	Assigned to	Priority	Due	Bucket ↓	
Manage & Organ...	Sriram Rajamanickam		6/6	Sriram	...
Manage your Workf...	Satheswaran Manoha..		6/6	Sathesh	...
User & Data Securit...	Harsharanjeet		6/6	Harsharanjeet	...
Lead Projects Easily f...	Sathish Veerapandian		6/6	Sathish	...
Book Review			5/27	Packt General Tasks	...
First Dr...	Steven Van Houttum		6/8	Steven's Review	...
Review the Packt Guidel...			6/2	Packt's Generic Tasks	...
Bi-Weekly Standup			6/10	Ongoing Obstacles	...

Figure 2.13 – List the tasks

When selecting the **Charts** view option, we see the pie chart window, as shown in the next screenshot:

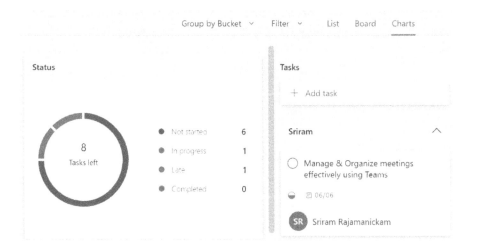

Figure 2.14 – Charts view option of tasks

A graphical view of the tasks can be seen based on their priority.

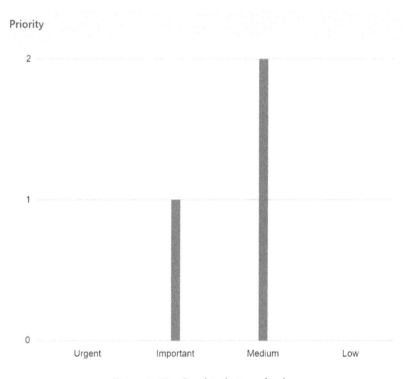

Figure 2.15 – Graphical view of tasks

The number of tasks and their priority for each individual member can be seen.

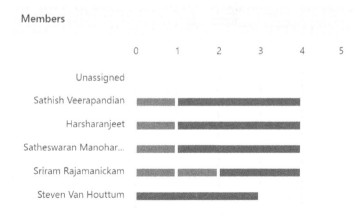

Figure 2.16 – Tasks based on members

When we click on **Schedule**, there is a good overview of the timelines of the tasks per person shown on the screen.

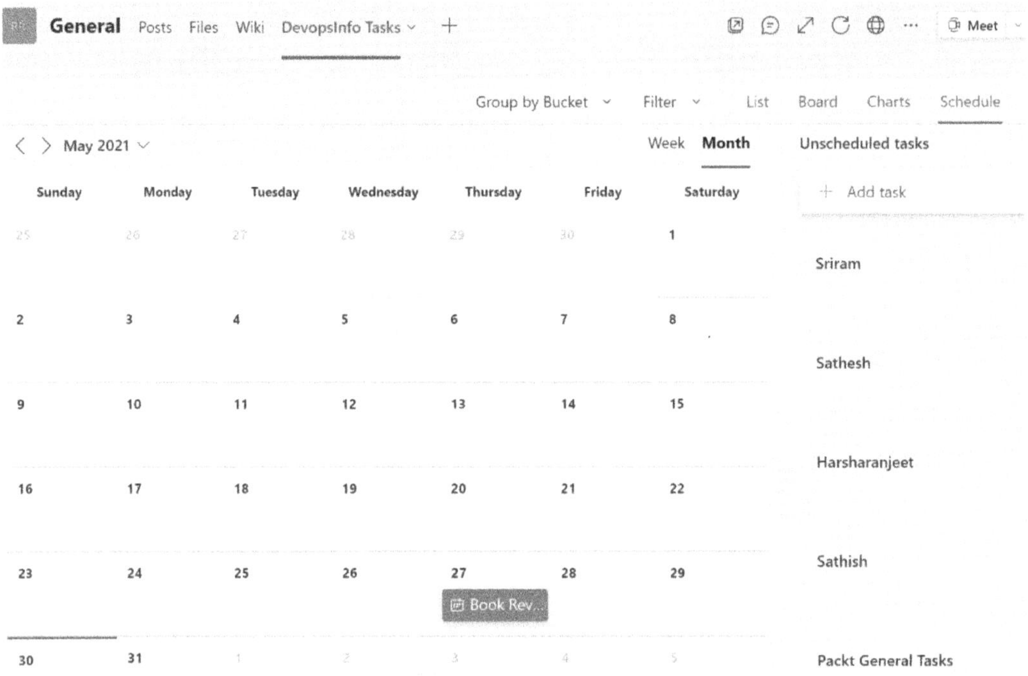

Figure 2.17 – Overview of timelines per person

We have now completed the first module in this chapter on how to effectively utilize Tasks for managing projects within Teams in an efficient manner. It's highly recommended that you use this function in a real-world scenario, such as working on your current projects, to ensure that you have complete control over your projects and that they are completed on time.

Using the Milestones app and Teams for superior project management

With the **Milestones** app in Microsoft Teams, we can incorporate our project management within Teams. The features and functionalities of Milestones are similar to those seen in Tasks and Planner. As mentioned earlier, we will be exploring all the project management methodologies that are present in Teams, and we will be using the preferred method based on each project type. A huge benefit of using Milestones is that it stands unique due to the fact that it was built using the **Power Apps Dataverse platform**. This low-code data platform enables admins to provide the best customized view from top to bottom.

To get started, navigate to the **Apps** section and search for *milestones*.

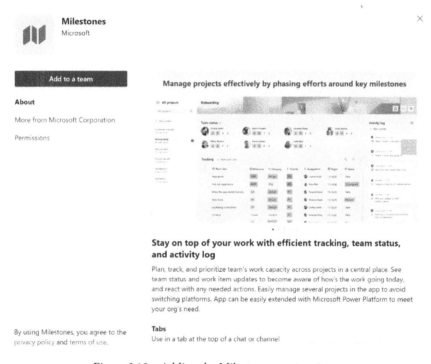

Figure 2.18 – Search for the Milestones app

On the next screen, we will see the option **Add to a team** and a summary of the look and feel of Milestones once utilized properly. Here, we have to choose the option **Add to a team** to begin with Milestones.

Figure 2.19 – Adding the Milestones app to a team

On the next screen, we will be prompted to select a team or channel name.

Set up Milestones for a team

Milestones will be available for the entire team, but you can start using it in the channel you choose.

Type a team or channel name

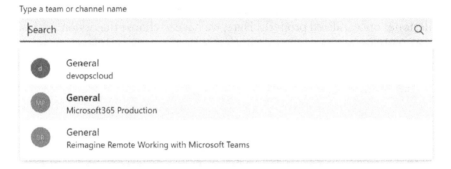

Figure 2.20 – Choosing the team or channel

In our example, we have chosen one of our team names.

Set up Milestones for a team

Milestones will be available for the entire team, but you can start using it in the channel you choose.

Type a team or channel name

Microsoft365 Production > General   ✕

‹ Back   Set up a tab

Figure 2.21 – Choosing the team

Once we click on **Set up a tab**, the project management app is built for the team. We will get the information on the next screen, and an option to post this information on the channel about the Milestones app.

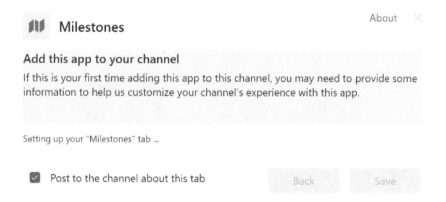

Figure 2.22 – Final setup of the Milestones app for the team

Once we navigate to the associated channel tab, we can see that the installation is in progress with the following message.

Installing the app to the channel...

This might take a while. We'll notify you when the app is installed.

Figure 2.23 – Installation progress

After installation, the Milestones app will be installed and will ask us the following consent question. This permission is only for your channel, and we can go ahead and simply click **Allow**.

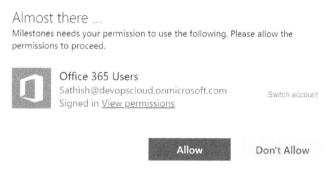

Figure 2.24 – Granting authorization

Once we click on **Allow**, we reach the following introduction page.

Figure 2.25 – Introduction page

After clicking on **Continue**, we will land on a sample template that gives us an idea of how efficiently we can utilize the Milestones app. Hover your mouse over the **All Projects** pane on the left and you will see there is an option to customize them, shown as **Click to customize**. If any existing project suits your new task, then I would recommend customizing this template.

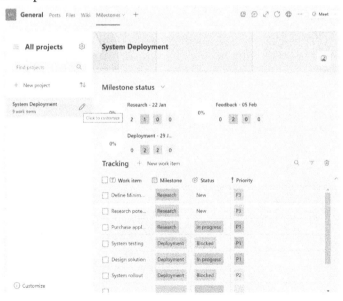

Figure 2.26 – Sample template

On clicking on the dropdown, we can change the look of the project to either **Team status** or **Milestone status**. When clicking on **Team status**, we can see the team members who are part of the team.

Figure 2.27 – Team members view from the Milestones app

Clicking on **New project** also does the same job and can show a similar tracking system to the one that we saw in the previous screenshot. More importantly, when we click on the gear icon, it navigates us to the **Global settings** screen.

Figure 2.28 – Settings option

We have three options that may be customized within **Global settings**. These are **Category**, **Priority**, and **Status**. We can add extra entries to each of the breakdowns shown in the following screenshot, as per our requirements.

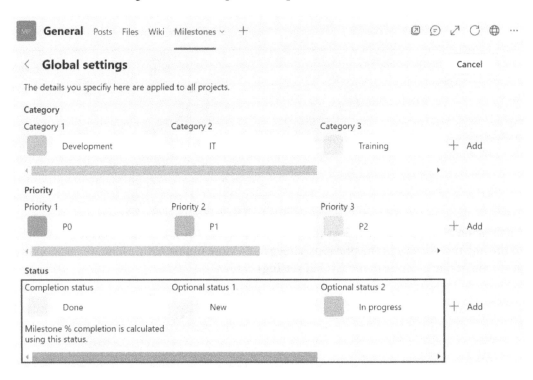

Figure 2.29 – Customization in Global settings

That's all on this topic and our quick tutorial on how to utilize Milestones. If you are familiar with using Tasks, you'll find using Milestones easy. Milestones is known as a **sample app** since Microsoft has launched this app recently, and it is built on top of the Power Platform. It's completely your choice to pick the right project management app between Tasks and Milestones. Milestones can be a perfect customized project management tool that can help us to run our project by following our timeline. Don't miss out on trying out this remarkable project management app that comes at no extra cost if you have Teams enabled on your account. Now we've completed exploring the Milestones app, we can look into our next subject on the options that are available in the Project and Roadmap apps.

Using the Project and Roadmap apps as a better way to keep track of your projects

Microsoft released the **Project** and **Roadmap** apps in Microsoft Teams in November 2020. These apps make it easier to manage, track, and collaborate on group projects. The Project and Roadmap apps can be added as tabs in any channel by selecting the + icon at the top of a channel. The Project app is really an enhanced version of the Planner app, and we can expect more enhancements to be made in the future. Being as this is a Project web app, we can expect that it will replace the Planner app in the future.

With the Microsoft Project app, we can connect to the project directly from Microsoft Teams. The best part is that team members can create new projects or open existing projects from within Microsoft Teams.

Having said that, let's use a real demonstration to see how the Project app can impress us by adding this as a tab to an existing team and see the results.

> **Note**
>
> Everyone at your organization who has Office 365, including Office 365 E5, can only view projects and roadmaps that have been shared with them. People who need to edit projects and roadmaps need a separate license. Project Plan 1 will be sufficient to collaborate from Teams with Project. A Project Plan 3 or Project Plan 5 subscription user can create and edit in the Project and Roadmap apps.

The first step is to look for Project and Roadmap apps and add them.

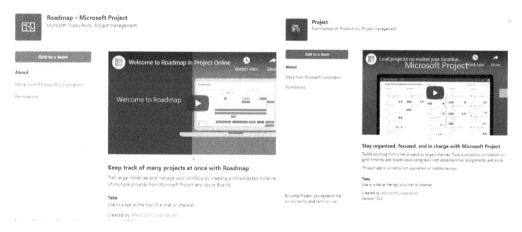

Figure 2.30 – Search for Microsoft Project

Next, we need to select the team that requires the Project and Roadmap apps.

Figure 2.31 – Adding the Project and Roadmap apps to a team or channel

Microsoft Project is the right starting point for individuals and teams collaborating on tasks.

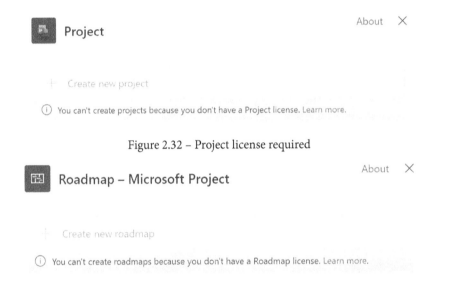

Figure 2.32 – Project license required

Figure 2.33 – Roadmap license required

Most importantly, we will not be able to add Project or Roadmap to a Teams channel if we do not have at least a Project Plan 1 license. Ideally, one person will have edit access with the license, and others with a normal Office 365 subscription can view the projects.

The Project app integrates with Project for the web and therefore allows you to add projects created using Project for the web as a tab. It does not support projects created on **Project Web App (PWA)** or **Project client (MPP files)**.

To conclude, Project and Roadmap remain the best solutions for existing tasks that are already configured on Project, and people who already have a license can use this app completely free on Microsoft Teams. Having said that, let's hop on to the Lists app to see the best options that can help us in project management.

Creating Lists and following up with projects

Microsoft Lists is an evolution of traditional **SharePoint Lists** with lots of new upgrades. We now have the option to create personal lists for following up on our own tasks. It also has lots of pre-built templates for asset management, tasks, events, recruiting, and so on. This is a huge help in managing our projects. Earlier, we were able to manage **lists** separately from the browser or even a mobile app. Now, we have an easier option to use them within Microsoft Teams by creating a new list or even opening an existing list. It's the same process as we follow for Tasks and Milestones, so the Lists app needs to be searched for in the app store and then installed, as shown in the following screenshot:

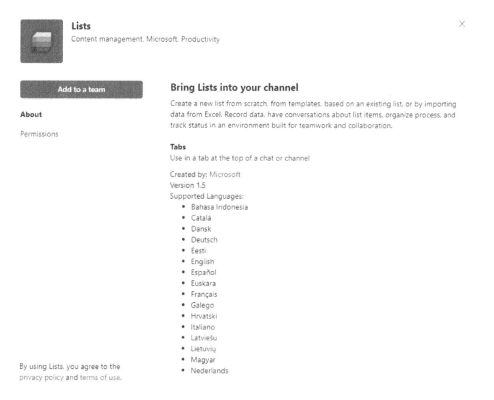

Figure 2.34 – Search for Lists in the app store

After **Lists** has been installed, we need to add it to a channel.

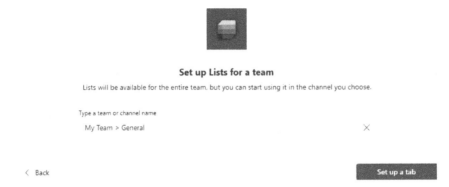

Figure 2.35 – Choosing the correct channel

After we click on **Set up a tab**, we can see that Lists is added to the selected team channel and is ready to use. We could create a new list, or even add an existing list from the lists that have been created already.

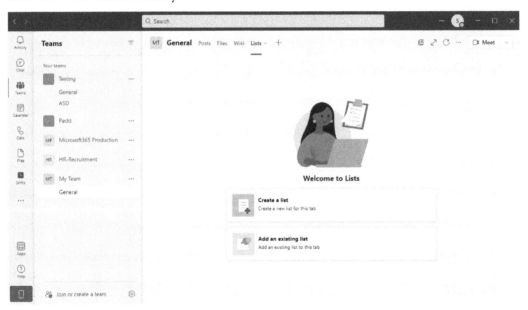

Figure 2.36 – Choosing to use Lists

For the purpose of our example, let's have a look at creating a **New List**. When we create a new list, it provides us with an option to create it from a blank list, from an existing list, and an option to import one from an Excel file.

In addition, it's also nice to see that there are lots of additional, cool Microsoft **Built-in Templates**.

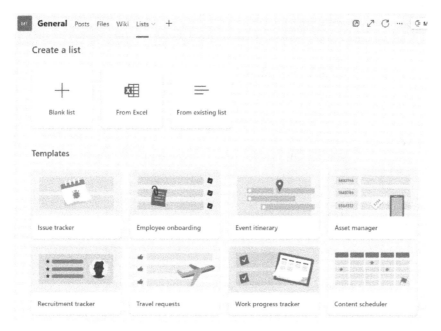

Figure 2.37 – Samples of default templates available

Having these default templates can be beneficial in most normal business operations. We will have a look at the **Recruitment tracker** option that is shown here by default.

Upon choosing **Recruitment tracker**, we can see that there are examples like the following screenshot, with the item types. Click on the **Use template** option.

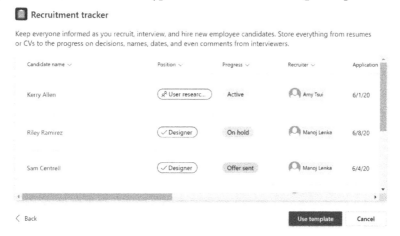

Figure 2.38 – Example view of Recruitment tracker

Upon moving to the next screen, there is an option to change the name, provide a description, and choose a color and a designated icon of our own. At this moment, as is also the case with Power Apps, there is no option to import a custom image. Click on **Create**.

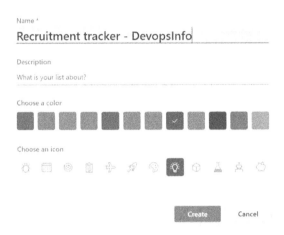

Figure 2.39 – Option to customize the default template

Now, the tab will be renamed **Recruitment tracker** based on the template that we have chosen.

Figure 2.40 – List name showing in the tab based on the template name

Moreover, there is an option to create a new item, as shown in the following screenshot. One important point to note here is if we still need to edit these column values, it is possible to do this from here. This gives us more flexibility to use the default templates and modify only the columns that we need to change.

Figure 2.41 – Create a new item

When **New item** is clicked, there is an additional page that is opened with all these default values. The default template will work pretty well for most recruitment scenarios.

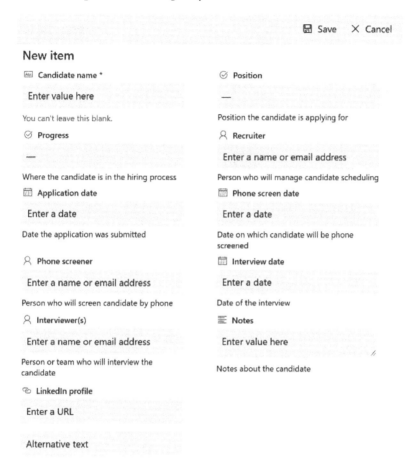

Figure 2.42 – Options in the new item

So, in our example, after populating two templates, we get a view like the following in the **Lists** tab.

Figure 2.43 – View of Lists in the team

Additionally, there is an option to choose the view or even create a new view of our own. The level of view customization is a great addition without being complicated to use.

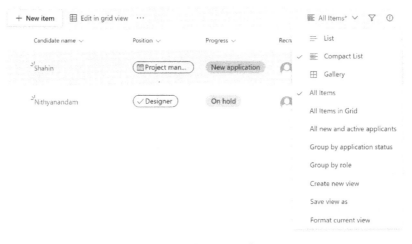

Figure 2.44 – Customize the view

For example, the following screenshot is the view when we click on **Gallery**. The **Gallery** view looks super cool. With the **Gallery** view, the entire Team tasks lists can be seen in a summary with important titles (such as in the following screenshot where it shows us the candidate's name, position, progress, application date, and the recruiter's name). The **Gallery** view provides us with an option to edit individual items, too.

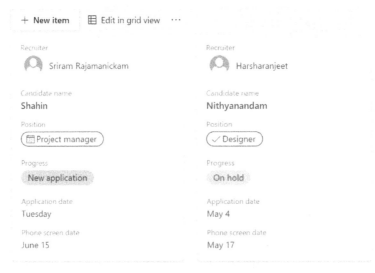

Figure 2.45 – Gallery view

When we click on **edit list**, we have an option to chat with colleagues about the progress of this task.

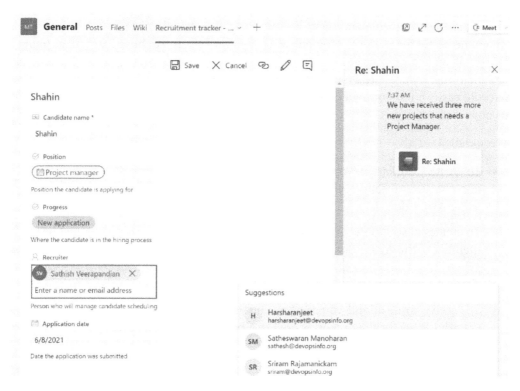

Figure 2.46 – Chat option

Microsoft Lists is a great feature with default industry-standard templates that can easily align with a business's daily project management operational tasks for most of the organization. In only a few clicks, we're able to manage tasks completely from Microsoft Teams, which provides us with a better opportunity to use this product with no additional cost (apart from an Office 365 license). The Lists app has impressed us more than we expected, and now we have the final app, Azure Boards. Let's see how it can impress us in terms of managing our projects in the final topic of this chapter.

Familiarizing yourself with Azure Boards and Utilizing them for projects

Azure Boards helps us to plan, track, discuss, and follow up on any tasks across our teams. It might be useful for us in tracking our work logs with a Kanban board, as well as being a place to tag and communicate critical ideas among the team. If your team is suited to agile work planning, then Azure Boards can be a great choice for assigning and tracking tasks. We could easily build our own board and backlog, run a daily sprint, and keep tracking our important work.

Prerequisites:

- To create a work item, you must be a contributor to the Azure Boards project. If you don't have a project yet, you can sign up and create a project. For details, see Start using Azure Boards.

- To create subscriptions in a Teams channel for work item events, you must be a member of the Azure Boards Project Administrators group or Team Administrators group. To get added, see **Set permissions** on the project- or collection-level or **Add Team Administrator**.

- To receive notifications, you must enable the **Third-party application access via OAuth** setting for the organization. See Change application access policies for your organization.

To get started with using Azure Boards, we have to add them as an app from the list of the apps that are available, just as we did for the other apps.

Figure 2.47 – Search for Azure Boards in Apps

Since we have already logged in with our Microsoft ID in Teams, we just need to add them to a team, as shown in the following screenshot. We can see this option on the left-hand side panel, the moment we click on the dropdown.

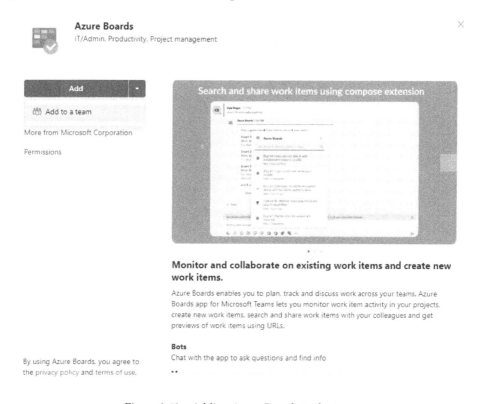

Figure 2.48 – Adding Azure Boards to the team

In our case, we have selected the team in the following screenshot, and have chosen the channel. Just clicking on **Set up a bot** will add the Azure Board to this team.

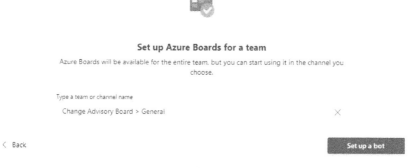

Figure 2.49 – Choose your team

After we add this to the team, when we navigate to this team channel, we will be prompted with the following pop-up screen.

Figure 2.50 – Grant authorization

Following a successful sign-in, we will be presented with the next screen, which indicates that the Azure Boards have been successfully completed.

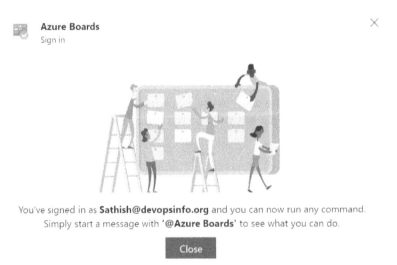

Figure 2.51 – Successful sign-in to Azure Boards

After signing in, use the following command inside the Teams channel to link your Azure projects to the Teams channel:

```
@azure boards link [project url]
```

In our example, we have an Azure board created as shown in the following screenshot:

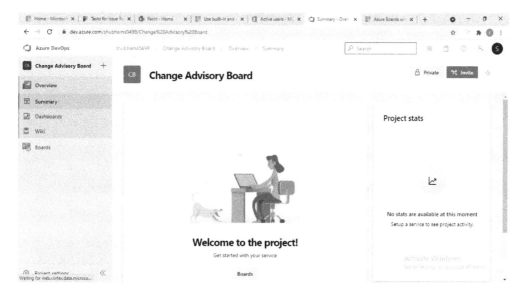

Figure 2.52 – Example Azure Boards Change Advisory Board

We need to use the next command on the Teams channel to link this Azure board to the Teams channel. You can choose the correct link based on your project that has been created in Azure Boards.

```
@azure boards link https://dev.azure.com/Sathish0131/Change%20
Advisory%20Board
```

We will then see a success message that states the person has linked this channel to a project created in Azure Boards.

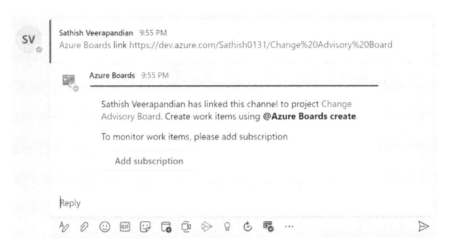

Figure 2.53 – Successful message about Azure Boards and channel integration

Once the project is linked, you can create work items using the **@Azure Boards create** command or use message actions.

Figure 2.54 – Create a work item

Here, we are prompted with the following screen. Based on the work item needed, we can choose and create the item list.

Figure 2.55 – Choosing the work item

In our example, we have given a title that describes the task to be done for the project **Area path**, which was created earlier in Azure Boards, and finally, a short description to provide an idea of the purpose of this task.

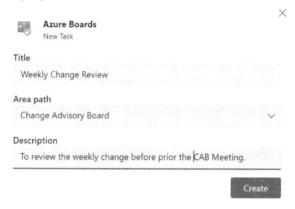

Figure 2.56 – Options while creating Azure Boards

After we click on **Create**, we can see that the task will be created and a notification message will be posted to everyone on the channel, as shown in the next screenshot.

Figure 2.57 – Azure Boards task view

In parallel, when we log in to the Azure Boards portal, we can see that the task that we created from Teams is visible over there too.

Figure 2.58 – Overview of the created task

To learn more about the commands, we can use this command:

```
@Azure Boards Help
```

If we post this to the Teams channel, it will respond to us with the available options that can be executed from the command line.

Figure 2.59 – Sample response view of Azure Boards

If you are not comfortable with utilizing the command lines, then we do have an easier option. You can click on the radio button that is present right below the channel where we have added Azure Boards.

Figure 2.60 – Azure Boards icon in the Chat taskbar

Clicking on the radio button provides us with the graphical interface to create a new work item by clicking on the + sign, as well as a nice overview of our current tasks.

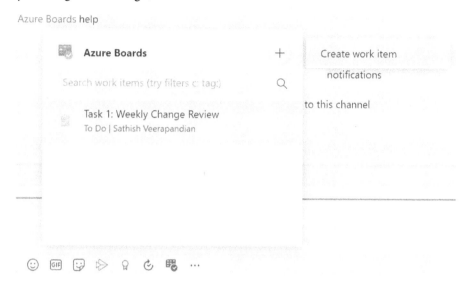

Figure 2.61 – Create work item

This has been a quick look at how you can plan, manage, and track your work via Azure Boards. If your team is accustomed to agile work planning, using Azure Boards can also be considered one of the best choices for tracking all activities from within Microsoft Teams itself.

Summary

In this chapter, we've gone over the finest solutions that are now available to enhance what Microsoft Teams can do for project management. This gives us an easier option for how we can schedule our tasks for a day, week, and month easily from one application: Microsoft Teams. If you're a project manager with numerous projects to track, all of the scenarios described in this chapter can be simply implemented using the applications that come by default with a Microsoft and an Office 365 subscription. With meetings, chat, calls, collaboration, and additional tools, Microsoft Teams is an impactful application.

We can now think of Teams as a project management application that also enables effective collaboration. We can choose the perfect application for us from the apps that come at no additional cost to create project plans, define stakeholders, monitor progress, and complete tasks with all the records stored digitally. We hope you enjoyed this chapter and were able to follow along from your own Teams client. In the next chapter, you'll learn how to use Microsoft Teams to manage your workforce.

3
Workforce Management in Teams

Managing the workforce is a key aspect of every organization because skilled employees can deliver top customer satisfaction by ensuring excellent quality of service - and this produces great businesses. **Workforce management** is a set of processes that companies use to create, manage, and measure the productivity of their employees. Currently, many organizations are looking for flexible employees who can adapt to short-term changes and availability, and of course considering the employee preferences and the work timings.

Microsoft Teams is a hub for collaboration. Microsoft has provided built-in, ready-to-use sample apps in the Microsoft Teams store that can be used for various business purposes and are divided into the categories of *productivity*, *collaboration*, *project management*, *personal apps,* and much more. A key feature of these sample apps is that they can be used as is or can be customized for your organization's needs. Sample apps can be used in a Microsoft Teams **group chat**, **channel**, or **team**. Some apps can also be used in a **conversation**.

These sample apps are developed using **Microsoft Power Apps**, which is a low-code business application development platform. Power Apps is one of the components of **Microsoft Power Platform**.

In this chapter, we will cover the following topics:

- Employee shift management using the **Shifts** app
- How approvals are now made easy using Microsoft Teams
- Collecting employee ideas through campaigns
- Balancing productivity and wellbeing
- Reporting, managing, and resolving issues using Microsoft Teams
- Sending and receiving appreciations
- Viewing leave balances, and requesting leave using the **Human Resources** app
- Building a centralized work portal using **Workhub**

At the end of this chapter, you will be familiar with using these productivity and collaboration apps. With continuous practice, you can even go the extra mile of customizing the apps based on your organization's needs.

Technical requirements

To get started with our practice, we recommend signing up for a **Microsoft Office 365** trial subscription (**Microsoft 365 E3** or **365 E5**), All Microsoft applications must be enabled by your administrator.

Employee shift management using the Shifts app

Shifts in Microsoft Teams is an effective schedule management tool that's easy to use for both managers and frontline workers. This tool helps team members to stay connected and to collaborate when needed with just a few clicks. This tool can also be used through the Microsoft Teams app on mobile devices, which is available in the **iOS** app store and **Google Play Store for Android.**

In an organization, some of the manager's responsibilities are to assign and manage the shifts of their team members, approve requests, send important communications, and more. All of these tasks can be carried out by using Shifts in Microsoft Teams.

The following sections describe tasks that can be performed by the manager (owner) of the team.

Creating a shift

1. Click on the ellipses (**…**) button (more options) on the left side of the screen, and then click on the **Shifts** button. If not found, type it into the Find an app search bar:

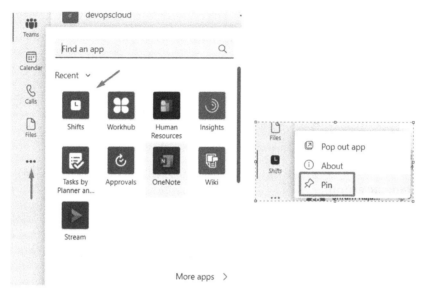

Figure 3.1 – Finding the Shifts app and using the Pin button to add it to the Teams left panel

2. In the **Create a team schedule** window, click on the **Create** button to the right of the team name for which you would like to create a schedule. This option will be enabled for the teams you own. In this example, this app is added to the **Information Technology** team:

Figure 3.2 – The Create a team schedule window

3. Select your time zone and click on **Confirm**.

Now, the window to enter the schedule is ready:

Figure 3.3 – The dashboard of the Shifts app

You can rename the group by clicking on the ellipses (...) button and then clicking on **Rename group**:

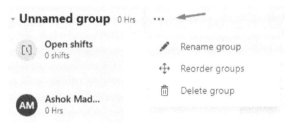

Figure 3.4 – Renaming the group

To add a shift for a member, you can click on the ellipses (...) button on the empty box next to the name of the member and click on **Add shift**:

Figure 3.5 – Adding a shift for a member

In this box, you can select the color from the dropdown, set the shift times, and add notes and custom labels:

Figure 3.6 – Shift configuration

4. Once done, click on **Save**.

   This shift has been added for one day for the member called Ashok Madhvarayan:

Figure 3.7 – Shift schedule for a day

You can copy this shift (see *Figure 3.7*) and paste it into the empty box.

5. Click on the ellipses (…) button again and select **Copy**:

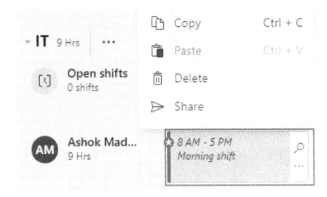

Figure 3.8 – Copying the shift

6. Click on the ellipses (…) button and select **Paste** (you can paste into all four boxes to complete the workweek):

Figure 3.9 – Pasting the shift for the workweek

7. You can schedule a shift for a day, week, or month by selecting the option from the dropdown as shown:

Figure 3.10 – Scheduling options

8. You can add more people with the **Add people** button and follow the preceding steps to create a new shift:

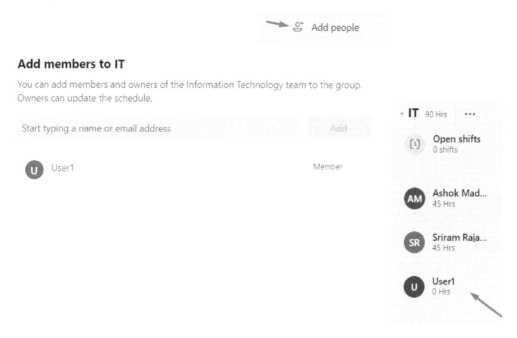

Figure 3.11 – Adding other people to schedule the shift

9. You can either add new shifts to the new members or copy shifts from the existing members:

Figure 3.12 – A shift schedule for team members

Another way of creating a shift is using a **Microsoft Excel** file. For this, you have to download the sample file, fill in the required fields, and upload it.

10. Click on the ellipses (**...**) button and select **Import schedule**:

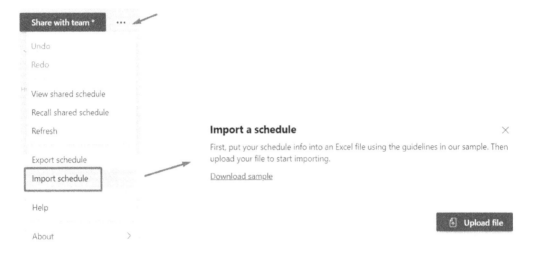

Figure 3.13 – Importing a schedule (Download sample)

The downloaded sample file looks like the following figure:

Figure 3.14 – A sample shift schedule in Microsoft Excel

Here, you can fill in the member and shift details. Please note that the **Work Email** column is important in this template as it is unique for each user.

Once ready, the file can be uploaded using the same screen (refer to *Figure 3.13*) by clicking on the **Import schedule** button followed by the **Upload file** button.

Sharing the shift with team members

Now, the shift schedule is ready to be shared with team members:

1. Click on the **Share with team** button:

Figure 3.15 – Sharing the shift

You can share the shift with the entire team or only with the members who are added to the shift:

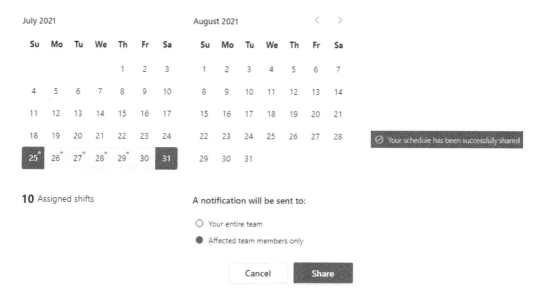

Figure 3.16 – Sharing options

Because it would be time-consuming to add a shift schedule for each member, we have an option to copy the schedule. Let's now see how that can be used to fill the shift schedule for the entire team.

2. **Copying the schedule**: You also have the option to copy the schedule, make changes if any, apply it to the date, and select the number of times to copy:

Figure 3.17 – The Copy schedule button

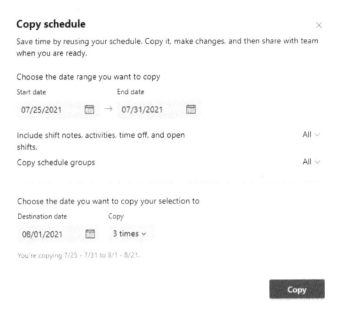

Figure 3.18 – The Copy schedule button options

3. **Updating shifts**: If you would like to make any changes to the shift for a specific team member or for the entire team, you can edit it and select **Share with team** again:

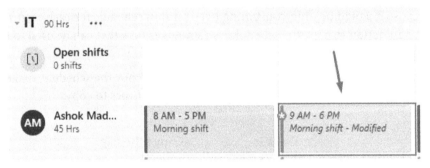

Figure 3.19 – Updating the shift and sharing it with team members

4. **Open shifts**: Members can choose this option by requesting to the manager. Open shifts are created by managers of the team that are not assigned to any member of the team. Team members can request to take an open shift if required.

Figure 3.20 – Open shift

- **Managing the settings**: Select the **Settings** tab at the top and note the following options:

  - **Time zone**: Here, the time zone for the schedule can be set.

  - **Schedule**: Here, the start of the workweek can be selected.

  - **Copying shifts**: If enabled, shift activities will be copied when copying shifts.

  - **Open shifts**: If enabled, members of this team can view and request open shifts on the schedule.

Figure 3.21 – The Settings tab in Shifts

- **Requests**: Any options enabled in this section will be available to users when requesting time off.

- **Time clock**: This option enables members to clock in and clock out. This also has an option for location detection, which requires acceptance by the members of the location request. Enabling this, we will have an option to export the time clock report:

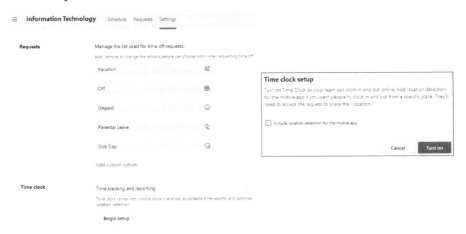

Figure 3.22 – The Settings tab in Shifts

Managing requests

To review the requests submitted by your team members for vacations or open shifts, open the **Requests** tab.

You can review the requests and take action by clicking on the **Approve** or **Deny** buttons, which will send a notification to the requester:

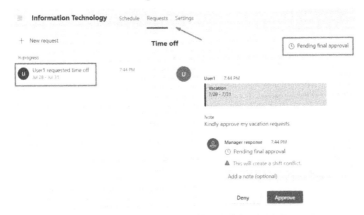

Figure 3.23 – Managing member requests

We have now seen the Shifts app options from the point of view of a manager who has created and shared a shift schedule with their team members. Now, we will see how a team member (frontline worker) can access the shift schedule and the options available to them.

Knowing your schedule

Once you log in to Microsoft Teams as a team member (frontline worker), open the Shifts app to view the schedule you have been assigned by your manager:

1. Click on the ellipses (**...**) button and open Shifts (refer to *Figure 3.1*):

Figure 3.24 – Your shift schedule

You also have an option to view your teammates' shifts as well.

2. Click on the **View** drop-down option in the right corner and select **Team shifts**:

Figure 3.25 – Your team's shift schedule

You can manage your shifts by sending requests for swapping them with your teammates, requesting time off, checking whether any open shifts are available, and more.

3.   To swap shifts with your teammates, click on any of the shifts and select **Swap**:

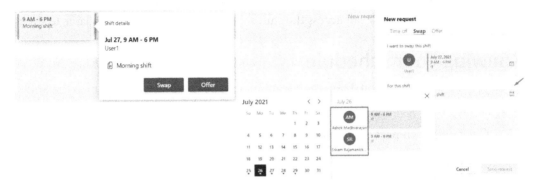

Figure 3.26 – The Swap button

4.   Fill in the details and send the request by clicking **Send request**:

Figure 3.27 – Sending a request

Once done, the request will be sent to the requester.

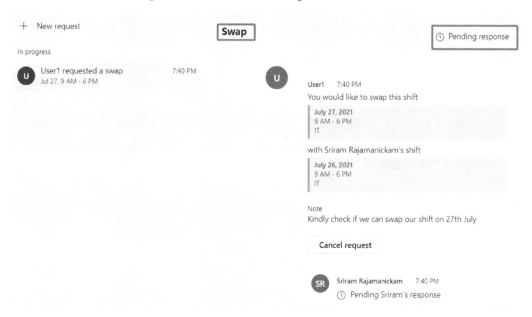

Figure 3.28 – Request details and status

Similarly, you can send requests for time off, to check for open shifts, and to offer shifts to your teammates.

Your requests can be tracked under the **Requests** tab:

Figure 3.29 – The Requests tab

5. Click on the **Open shifts** option and click on **Request**:

Figure 3.30 – Requesting an open shift

6. In the **Requests** tab, click on **New request** and click on the **Time off** tab to make requests for vacations, and so on:

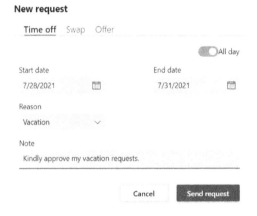

Figure 3.31 – The New request tab

7. Similarly, you can also select **Offer** in the **New request** tab and offer shifts to your teammates:

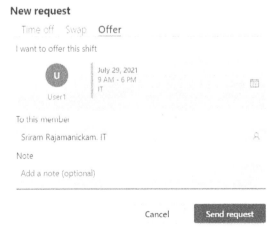

Figure 3.32 – Offering shifts to your teammates

8. **Clock in**: This option is to notify your manager of your start time for a shift:

Figure 3.33 – Clocking in to your shift

9. Once you are done with your shift, you can select the dropdown next to the time and select **Clock out**. This option is to notify your manager of your end time for a shift

Figure 3.34 – Clocking out of your shift

You can also use your Microsoft Teams app on your mobile phone when you are onsite to clock in and out of shifts to notify your manager.

We have now learned about the Shifts app in Microsoft Teams and how we can use it to manage shifts, requests, and more. In the next section, we will explore the Approvals app in Microsoft Teams.

How approvals are now made easy in Microsoft Teams

Approvals are an important process at all levels of an organization. Sending approvals by email for certain tasks is a practice that is still followed in many organizations. The Approvals app in Microsoft Teams is a great way to streamline the approval process and enables everyone to create, share, and approve requests. It also provides the flexibility to create and approve requests through chats in Microsoft Teams. Managers can create templates for frequent tasks for their employees who can easily raise requests that can then be reviewed and approved by the managers.

Let's explore the Approvals app and the options available for effective approval management:

1. Click on the ellipses (**...**) button on the left side of the screen and select **Approvals**. You can also pin this app to the **Teams** panel to avoid having to search for it every time (refer to *Figure 3.1* for adding an app).

2. This is called the **Approvals** hub, where you can view both sent and received approval requests:

Figure 3.35 – The Approvals hub

Let's suppose you have prepared a document that needs to be reviewed and approved – to do this, you can create a new request:

1. Click on **New approval request** to view the following options:

    *   **Request type**: You can select **Basic**, which would kick off the basic workflow approval process. Another option, **eSign**, is also available, and this is covered later in this section.

    *   **Name of request**: Use keywords to identify the request. This is similar to the subject of an email.

    *   **Approvers**: Type the name of the person who wishes to send the request. If you have multiple approvers, you can add them and toggle the option next to **Require a response from all recipients**. If enabled, the request needs to be approved by all approvers, and if disabled, only one of the approvers is required to approve it.

    *   **Additional details**: Here, you can provide detailed information about your request.

    *   **Attachments**: Usually, business approvals have attachments, such as Microsoft Word documents, PowerPoint presentations, Excel sheets, PDFs, and so on, which can be included for the approver/s to review.

- **Custom responses**: You can enable this to get custom responses from your approvers. If not, either **Approve or Reject** (the default options) are received.

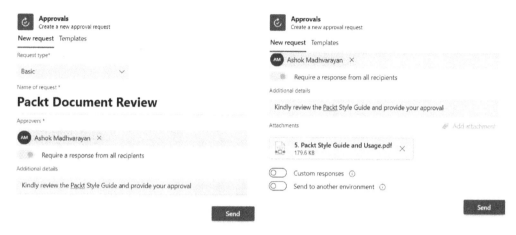

Figure 3.36 – Approval request details

2. Once you are done with filling in the details, you can click on **Send** to submit your request, and the approvers will be notified.

3. You can view the approval status by navigating to the **Sent** tab in the **Approvals** hub:

Figure 3.37 – The Approvals hub Sent tab

As an approver, you will receive a notification whenever a new request has been submitted for your approval:

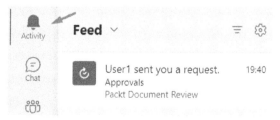

Figure 3.38 – An approver's notification

4. You can click on the request to review it and take action. Alternatively, you can also navigate to the **Approvals** hub to view the received request:

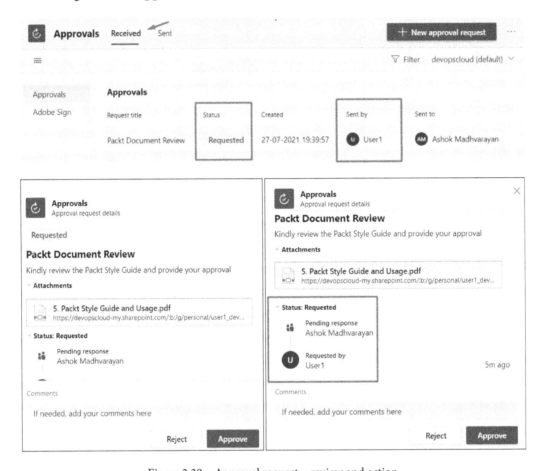

Figure 3.39 – Approval request – review and action

Here, you can add your comments, which would be sent to the requester with the approval.

The requester will be notified of the action or status change of the request.

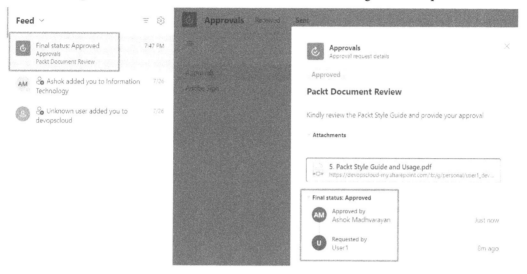

Figure 3.40 – A requester's notifications and approval request status

This basic workflow can be simplified further, as it can be achieved without the need of going to the **Approvals** hub if the requester and the approvers are in the same Teams group.

Requests can be raised, reviewed, and acted on within the chat feature in a channel within Microsoft Teams. The only criteria are that the requester and approvers should be in the same group.

5.   To achieve this, navigate to the **Teams** window and then the **channel**.

6. You can click on the **Approvals** icon, which is available just below the text field in the **chat** window:

Figure 3.41 – The Approvals icon in a Microsoft Teams channel

Once you click on the Approvals icon, this will launch the wizard for the request. You can fill in the details and submit your requests (refer to *Figure 3.36*).

As a manager of the team, you have an option to create custom templates and publish them to your team, which would be easier for the requester.

For example, request templates could be used if the sales team always required approvals for purchase orders, or the IT team required approvals for proposals, or they could be used for common requests such as working from home, time off, and so on.

Using templates

There are built-in request templates in the Approvals app that reduce the time to make and approve requests. The requester just needs to select the template and fill in the details before submitting it.

Each time, the requester doesn't need to fill in the basic template with all the details; instead custom templates are available that can be managed and published only by the manager/owner of the team:

1. As a manager of the team, navigate to the Approvals app, which launches the **Approvals** hub.

2. Click on the ellipses (**...**) button in the right corner and select **Manage templates**:

Figure 3.42 – Managing templates

3. Click on **New template**, and various templates are available for different purposes:

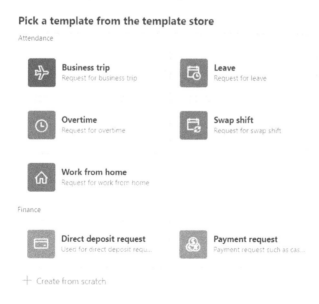

Figure 3.43 – Template selection

4. Here, we are going to publish a template in the **Work from home** tab, which will be available to the team members within that team:

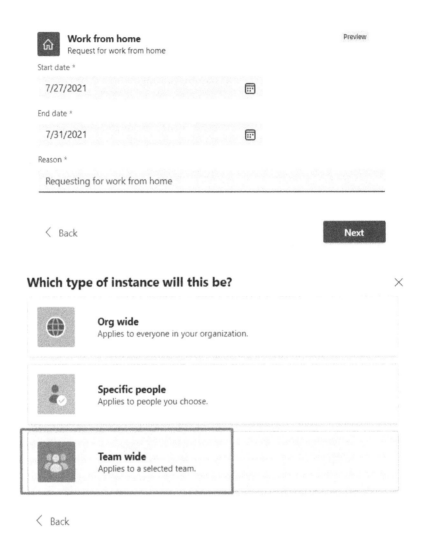

Figure 3.44 – Creating a template

5. Please note that if you are the Microsoft Teams administrator, the **Org wide** option will be available. For this illustration, as we are going to publish it to the team, we will select **Team wide**.

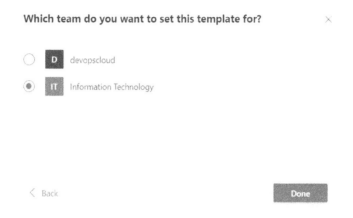

Figure 3.45 – Team selection

If you are the owner of multiple teams, all of your teams will be listed here.

6. Click on **Done**:

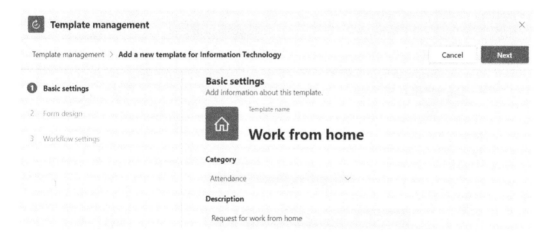

Figure 3.46 – Template details to be reviewed and modified

7. Click on **Next,** and then you will have the option to customize the form design. You can add text and dates, if required:

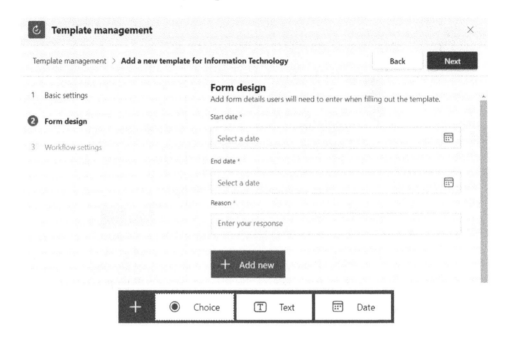

Figure 3.47 – The template form design page

After that, you can also specify the workflow settings:

- **File attachment**: This can be enabled based on the requirements of the template. For the **Work from home** template, this isn't required.

- **Approvers**: You can specify the approvers or let the requester enter the name of the approvers.

- **Responses**: You can also enable custom responses instead of the generic **Approve** or **Reject**. For instance, **Yes** or **No**.

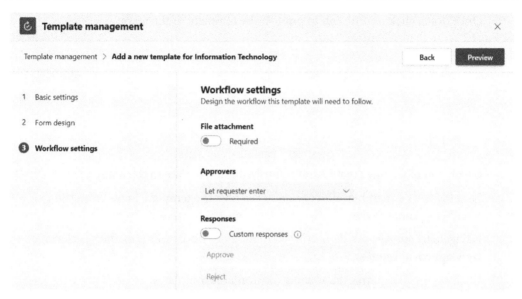

Figure 3.48 – The template workflow settings

8. Once done, click on **Preview** to preview the requests:

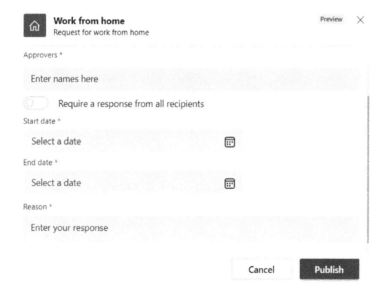

Figure 3.49 – Template preview

9. Once done, click on **Publish** to publish the template to the team:

Figure 3.50 – Published templates

Great, you have now created and published the template to the team.

10. Let's log in as a member of the team to see how the template looks from the member's point of view.

11. Navigate to the **Approvals** hub by launching the Approvals app, then click on **New approval request**.

12. Click on the **Templates** tab to view the available templates:

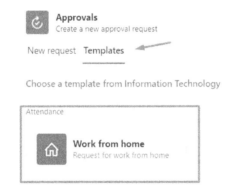

Figure 3.51 – Approvals template selection

So, now the template is available, and you can use it to submit requests.

Another interesting feature of the Approvals app is that it provides an option for electronic signatures. For now, we have an Adobe signature, which can be used by logging in with an account or with a free trial.

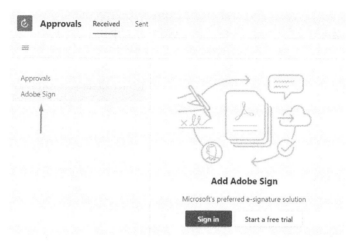

Figure 3.52 – Approvals eSign with Adobe Sign

When submitting the request, you need to select the **eSign** option and fill in the required details. You need to log in with your Adobe account details to submit/approve the requests.

Figure 3.53 – Approvals eSign request type

Thus far, you have explored the Approvals app in Microsoft Teams and the functions it offers. We hope that this information was useful, and you will be more comfortable once you start using it. In the next section, we will be looking at the Employee ideas app, which is designed to capture employee ideas through *campaigns*.

Collecting employee ideas through campaigns

The **Employee ideas** app allows organizations to create and manage *idea campaigns* to collect employees' ideas. An *idea campaign* is a category for grouping ideas around common themes. Organizations can benefit from gathering the ideas of employees and grouping them into themes. The Employee ideas app in Microsoft Teams allows organizations to add campaigns to a specific team or across the organization. The best part of this app is that campaigns, ideas, votes, and reviews can all be managed inside Teams itself, without needing to navigate to any other applications such as browsers, email services, or others.

Let's walk through the process of installing and using this app in a Teams channel:

1. Navigate to the channel of the team that you would like to add this app to and click on the + symbol:

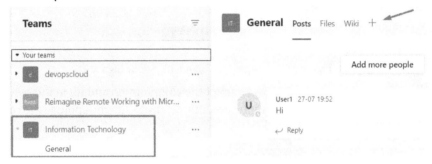

Figure 3.54 – Adding an app

2. Search for Employee Ideas in the search bar and click on the **Employee ideas** app option:

Figure 3.55 – Selecting the Employee ideas app

3. Click on **Add** to add this to the Teams channel and then click on **Save**:

Figure 3.56 – Adding the Employee ideas app

It will take few minutes to install this app and add it to the Teams channel.

You will be notified once the app is installed.

When opening for the first time, the app requires the read permissions of the user's profile, which will be used while managing the campaign.

4. In the following screen, click on **Allow**:

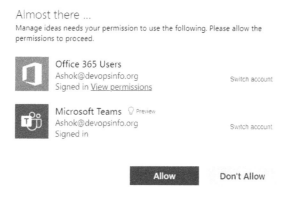

Figure 3.57 – The Employee ideas app permissions

5. Verify the team and channel name to which the app is to be added, and then click on **Let's go**:

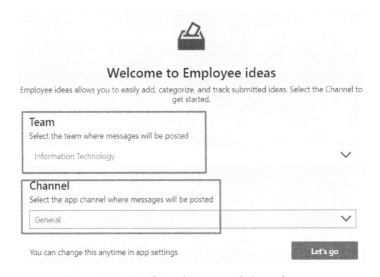

Figure 3.58 – Verifying the team and channel names

That's it. Now, the Employee ideas app has been added to the Teams channel.

This will open up the dashboard of the Employee ideas app:

Figure 3.59 – The Employee ideas app dashboard

The dashboard provides visibility of weekly top contributors, weekly top ideas, the option to add a campaign, the ability to search for active campaigns, and more.

Once the app is added to the channel, a post will be added to it for the other team members to add this app and share their ideas.

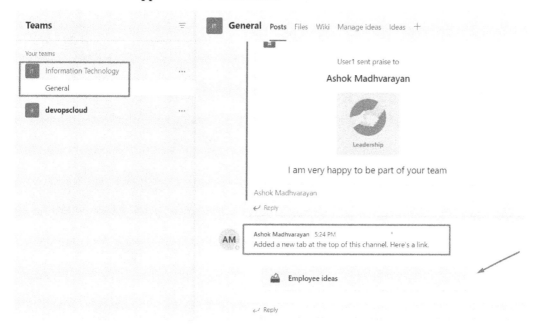

Figure 3.60 – A post in a Teams channel

The **Settings** tab in the app provides several options, such as restrictions for adding campaigns, notifications, and more:

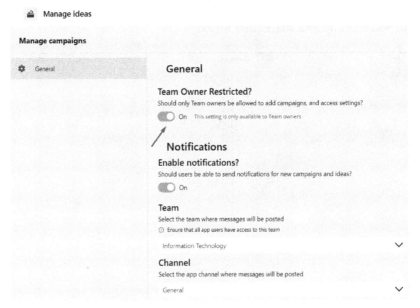

Figure 3.61 – The Employee ideas app settings

You can click on the existing active campaigns, review them, submit your ideas, and also cast your vote for any of the ideas that are interesting to you:

Figure 3.62 – Active campaigns, ideas, and votes

So far, we have explored the options available and the default campaigns. Now, let's see how a campaign is added, managed, and more:

1. To add a campaign, click on **Add campaign**:

Figure 3.63 – Adding a new campaign

2. Once you click on **Add campaign**, a new window opens where the campaign details need to be entered:

   ▪ **Campaign name**: Add a short and catchy name.

   ▪ **Description**: Provide more information on what this campaign is all about.

   ▪ **Date**: Select the date range for the campaign.

   ▪ **Idea questions**: You can edit the questions and make the response as either text or a rating. You can also add more questions by clicking on the **Add question** button.

   ▪ **Cover image**: You also have the option to add a cover image to illustrate the campaign.

   ▪ **Post to channel**: By default, this will be enabled. You can disable this to post it later in the channel, or you can enable it to post it immediately.

Figure 3.64 – New campaign details

3.   Once the details are provided, click on **Add campaign**.

Figure 3.65 – The new campaign added confirmation

You can see that the new campaign is now added to the dashboard:

Figure 3.66 – The updated dashboard with the new campaign

The post will be added to the Teams channel.

Figure 3.67 – Post in the Teams channel on adding a new campaign

4.   Team members can go into the **Manage ideas** tab in the Teams channel, view the campaign, submit ideas, and cast their votes:

Figure 3.68 – The campaign details and the Submit an idea button

5.   Click on **Submit an idea** and fill in the requested details.

You also have the option to add an image and attachments:

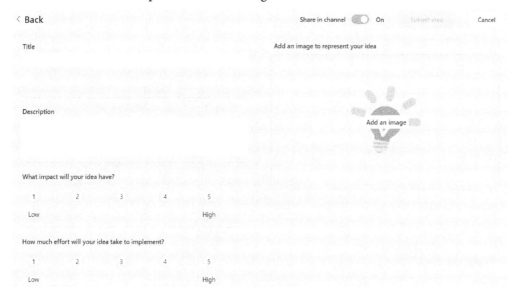

Figure 3.69 – Submitting a new idea

6. Once done, click on **Submit idea**:

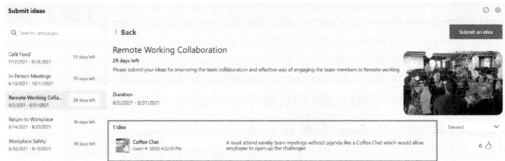

Figure 3.70 – A new idea added successfully

That's cool, you have now submitted your idea in the campaign without needing to navigate out of Microsoft Teams. In the next section, we will learn about balancing a team member's productivity and wellbeing, which can also be done in Microsoft Teams.

Balancing productivity and wellbeing

Microsoft **Viva Insights** is an app designed for balancing productivity and wellbeing. In this new style of remote working, Viva Insights can help you in scheduling one-on-one meetings, organizing your work, scheduling your breaks, and even taking **mind breaks** using **headspaces**.

Let's explore the options available in this app.

You can add this app by searching for `Viva Insights` in Microsoft Teams (refer to *Figure 3.1* for adding an app).

Once added, launch the app to explore the dashboard:

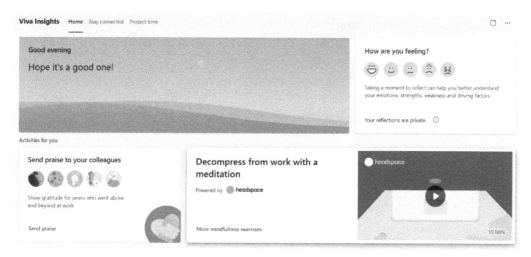

Figure 3.71 – The Viva Insights dashboard

As you can see in the preceding figure, the dashboard contains the following sections:

- **Home**: This tab provides various options for reflection, sending praise, headspace, and much more. The Up-Next card feature changes its appearance and message based on the time of day, and it also follows the schedule in your calendar.

- **Stay connected**: This tab helps you to stay connected with your colleagues by setting up one-on-one meetings, adding reminders, or pinning important contacts:

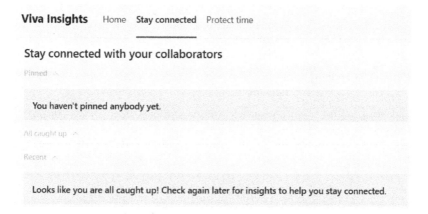

Figure 3.72 – The Stay connected tab options

- **Protect time**: This helps you to schedule focused time for yourself, which can be based on specific project tasks, learning, and more. Viva Insights will mute all Teams notifications during your focus time and help you focus on particular tasks:

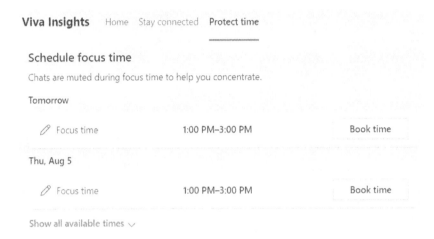

Figure 3.73 – The Protect time tab options

- **Virtual Commute**: This option allows you to mindfully close your day at work. For instance, if you would like to wrap up your work around 4 P.M. on Fridays to end your workweek mindfully, you can set a reminder for this. This option is also available in the **Protect time** tab.

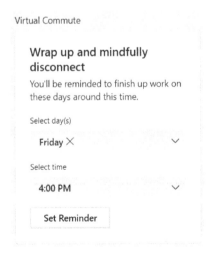

Figure 3.74 – The Virtual Commute options

- **Reflections**: This will help you to manage your emotions in your work time. You can select the emojis based on your feelings. If you do this for a while, you can view the Reflections history to know how you felt about your work at a particular time. You can also set reminders to record your reflections daily.

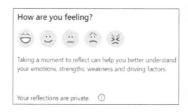

Figure 3.75 – Reflections

- **Practice mindfulness**: This is an important feature in this new era of remote working. Whenever you feel stressed or unable to focus on work, you can make use of this guided meditation to calm down and focus. Within minutes, you will be able to bounce back and start focusing on your work again.

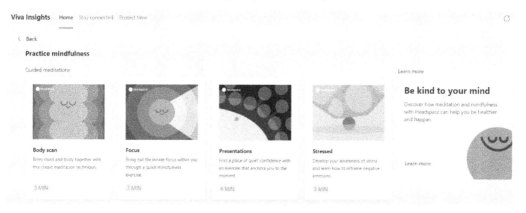

Figure 3.76 – The Practice mindfulness dashboard

That's Viva Insights for you, which is designed for individuals to improve productivity by managing their emotions, practicing mindfulness, organizing their time, and collaborating with their colleagues.

Next, we will discuss how we can manage issues in Microsoft Teams. In Microsoft Teams, we can report an issue, manage it, and get it resolved. All of this can be done in a single app called **Issue reporting**, which we will discuss in the next section.

Reporting, managing, and resolving issues using Microsoft Teams

The Issue reporting app is a sample app built into the Microsoft Power Platform. This app allows individuals to report, view, and resolve issues. The Issue reporting app is comprised of two tabs once added to the team. One tab is to report issues, and the other tab is to manage issues. The **Issue reporting** tab is used by frontline workers or end users to report issues and the **Manage issues** tab is used by managers to create templates, modify the reported issues, assign the issues to individuals for resolution, modify the SLAs, and much more. This app works along with the **Tasks by Planner and To Do** app. The tasks app is used for assigning tasks and gathers information from the "To Do" list of the individual's Outlook.

Let's walk through the process of installing and using the Issue reporting app in a Teams channel. Adding this app is similar to adding the Employee ideas app, which was discussed in the previous section (refer to *Figures 3.54, 3.55, and 3.56*):

1. Navigate to the Teams channel and click on the + symbol.

2. Type Issue reporting in the search bar, select the **Issue reporting** app, and click on **Add**.

3. Click on **Save**.

4. This might take a few minutes for the first setup.

5. Click on **Allow** to allow read permissions on Planner, Office 365 users, and Teams:

   ▪ **Planner**: This will be used for creating and managing tasks.

   ▪ **Office 365 Users**: To read the user's profile.

   ▪ **Microsoft Teams**: To add this to the Teams channel.

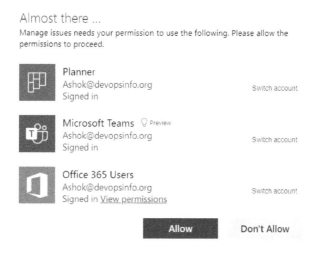

Figure 3.77 – The Issue reporting app permissions

On the initial page of the Issue reporting app, it looks for the **Tasks** tab where the tasks will be added when reporting issues:

Figure 3.78– Adding the Tasks tab

6. If you haven't created a Tasks tab yet – don't worry – just go to the Teams channel and click on the + icon. Here, we'll add the Tasks by Planner and To Do app in the same way we added the Issue reporting app.

7. Search for `Tasks` and click on **Tasks by Planner and To Do**.

8. Enter the name of the Tasks plan tab and click on **Save**:

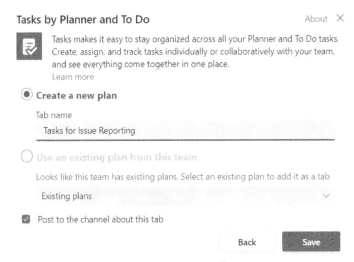

Figure 3.79 – Entering a Tasks tab name

Great, now the **Tasks** tab has been created.

Figure 3.80 – Tasks tab

9. Go back to the **Manage issues** tab for the configuration:

Figure 3.81 – Navigating to the Manage issues tab

10. Because we have created the Tasks tab in the channel, you can now click on **Continue**:

Figure 3.82 – Configuring the Issue reporting app

11. Verify the correct names are selected in the **Team** and **Tasks** drop-down menus. Then, click on **Let's go**:

Figure 3.83 – Verifying team and tasks names

12. Now, you will be taken to the dashboard of the **Manage issues** tab, where you can see the following features:

- **Insights**: This tab will provide a summary of information for the issues reported:

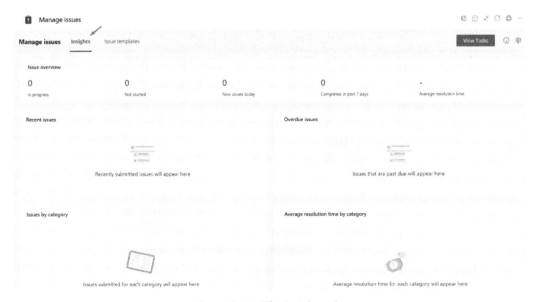

Figure 3.84 – The Insights tab

- **Issue templates**: This tab is where you can find issue templates, which will be available to users when raising issues. Default categories and templates are available:

Figure 3.85 – The Issue templates tab

These templates can be edited or duplicated, depending on the requirements of the team. New templates can also be created.

Let's create a new category and a template for the IT team:

1. Click on **Add category**. (Refer to *Figure 3.85.*)

2. Enter the name, select the icon, and click on **Save**:

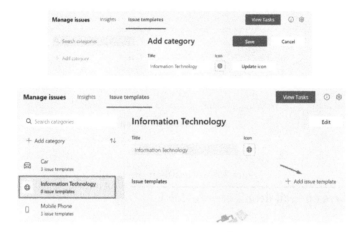

Figure 3.86 – Adding a category

3. The next step is to add templates. To do this, click on **Add issue template**.

4. Fill in the required details:

   - **Title**: Add a title for the issue template.

   - **Due within**: This is the service level agreement within which the issue needs to be resolved.

   - **Auto assign issues to**: You can add any user to automatically assign issues to when using this template.

   - **Questions 1**: You can add questions for the issue reporter to provide answers to. The responses to these questions are text-based.

- **Primary contact**: You can specify a user who will be the primary contact for issues reported specifically by this template. For instance, an expert to resolve this issue.

Figure 3.87 – New template details

5. Click on **Save** once all details are provided:

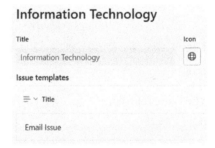

Figure 3.88 – Saving the template

6. Now, let's log in to the Issue reporting app to report an issue:

Figure 3.89 – The Issue reporting app tab

The app dashboard with the issues reported and the status of each issue will be launched:

Figure 3.90 – Issue reporting tab user dashboard

7. Click on **Report an issue** and select an issue type. You can see that the new category of **Information Technology** is available.

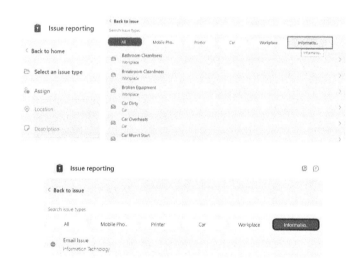

Figure 3.91 – An issue template selection when reporting an issue

8. Fill in the details and submit the issue:

Figure 3.92 – Providing details and submitting an issue

You can check the status of the issue in the dashboard, or you can view it in the **Tasks** tab:

1. To open issues in Tasks (Planner), click on **View issues**, then click on **View in Tasks**:

Figure 3.93 – Tracking an issue status

2. You can now switch back to the **Manage issues** dashboard:

Figure 3.94 – Assigning the issue

3. Let's assign the task to `user1`.

   After this, `user1` changes the status of the task to **Completed**:

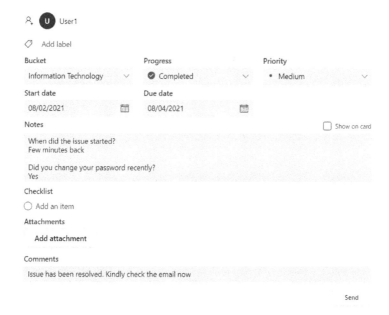

Figure 3.95 – Issue status update

4. Now, the **Manage issues** dashboard has been updated:

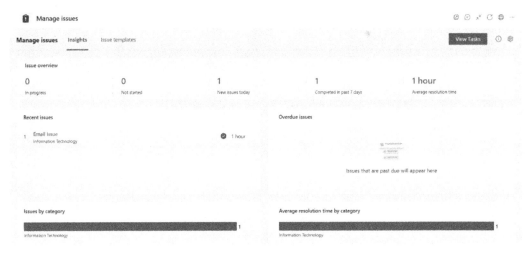

Figure 3.96 – The Manage issues dashboard has been updated

The original reporter of the issue can check the status in the **Issue reporting** tab:

Figure 3.97 – Issue reporting dashboard of the requester

Great, now reporting, tracking, and resolving issues are easy with the Issue reporting app, which can be managed within Microsoft Teams alongside the Planner app. In the next section, we will explore *appreciation*. Every employee would like to be appreciated for their work, which can be achieved easily using the **Praise** app in Microsoft Teams.

Sending and receiving appreciation

The **Praise** app in Microsoft Teams can be used to send appreciation to your teammates. Organizations believe that recognizing and appreciating the efforts of employees encourages productivity and motivates their workforce. It also improves the organization's culture. The Praise app in Microsoft Teams provides *badges* as a symbol of appreciation, which can be sent directly to your teammates through a private chat or in a Teams channel:

1. You can click on the **Praise** icon, just below the message textbox, as highlighted:

Figure 3.98 – The Praise icon in a Microsoft Teams conversation

2. This will open the Praise app with the default badges:

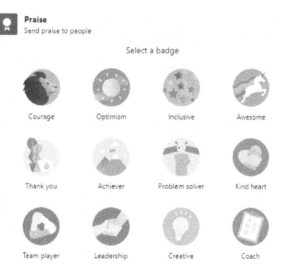

Figure 3.99 – Default Praise badges

3. Click on any of the badges that you would like to send to your teammates, and type your custom message (**Note**):

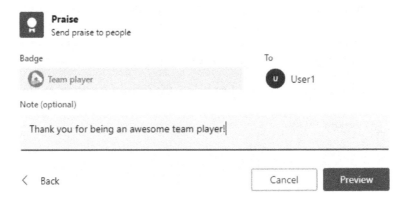

Figure 3.100 – Badge selection with a custom note

4. Select **Preview** to review:

Figure 3.101 – Badge preview

5. Once done, click **Send** to send your Praise badge to your colleague:

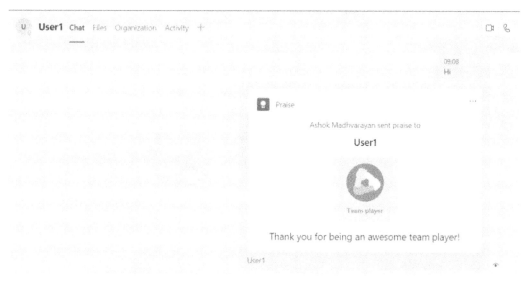

Figure 3.102 – The badge is sent to the recipient in the conversation

Now, the recipient will receive your appreciation:

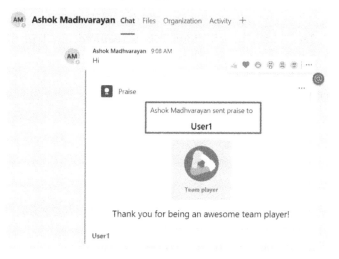

Figure 3.103 – The recipient receives the Praise badge

The same procedure can be followed to add Praise in a Teams channel.

6.   Click on a new conversation and select the **Praise** icon:

Figure 3.104 – Sending praise in a Teams channel

7.   Select the badge and add an additional note if required, and type the name of the recipient in that channel to send the praise to:

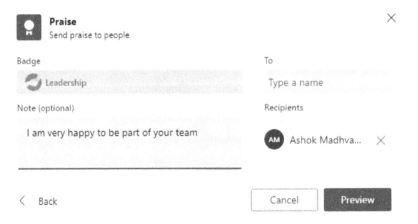

Figure 3.105 – Praise badge preview

8. Select **Preview** and click on **Send**.

Great, your praise is now posted on the channel!

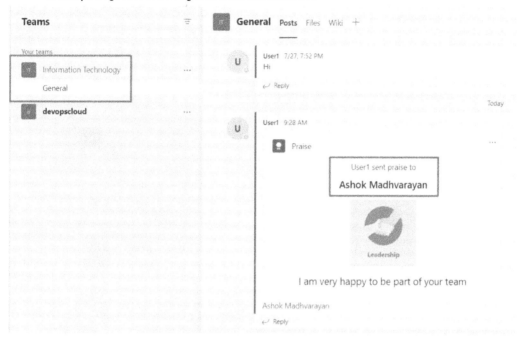

Figure 3.106 – The Praise badge is added to the Teams channel

A notification will be sent to the members of the channel.

9. Your administrator can also create custom badges and make them available to the team.

You can send an image with the following specifications to your administrator:

- File type should be .PNG

- Image file should not exceed 40 KB

- Maximum dimensions of 216 x 216 pixels

- Text and background color

  - This feature is also available in Microsoft Teams on mobile devices.

10. You can click on the + symbol and select the **Praise** icon to send praise to your teammates:

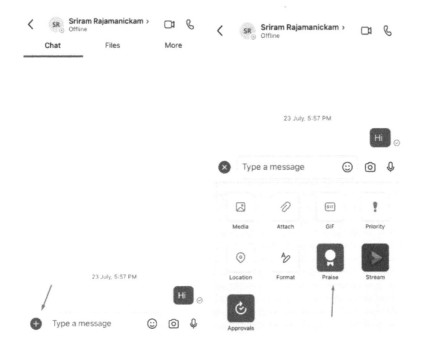

Figure 3.107 – The Praise app in the Microsoft Teams app on a mobile device

So, now we have learned about sending and receiving praise using the Praise app in Microsoft Teams. We hope that you will start using this app for encouraging your teammates. The next topic to learn about is managing leave using the Human Resources app.

Viewing leave balances and requesting leave using the Human Resources app

The Microsoft Dynamics 365 **Human Resources** app in Microsoft Teams allows users to manage their leave. This app allows users to view leave balances and request time off by submitting requests.

To add the app, you can follow the same procedure as for the other apps:

1. Click on the ellipses (...) button, then on **More apps**, search for Human Resources, and then click on the app icon.

2. Click on **Add**.

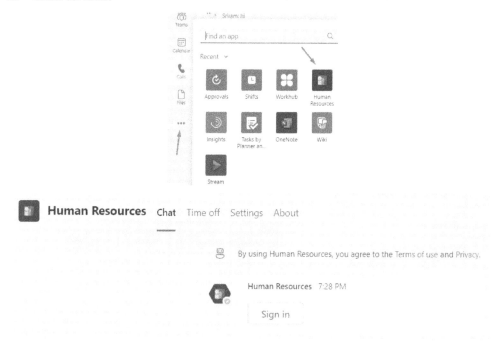

Figure 3.108 – The Human Resources app

This app has the cool feature of a chatbot from which you can view leave balances and request time off:

Figure 3.109 – Chatbot feature

Please note that this app requires a Dynamics 365 subscription, and your administrator has to set up the Human Resources app in Dynamics 365 for this to work in Microsoft Teams.

We have now explored the options of managing leave easily with the Human Resources app in Microsoft Teams. In the next section, we will learn about the Workhub app, which is a centralized work portal.

Building a centralized work portal using Workhub

Workhub in Microsoft Teams is a new app that has been added to allow the creation of a centralized work portal for an organization. Here, users can access the latest news about their organization and collaborate efficiently by integrating this with other applications.

To add this app, you can follow the same procedure as the previous apps:

1. Click on the ellipses (**...**) button, then **More apps**, search for Workhub, and click on the app icon:

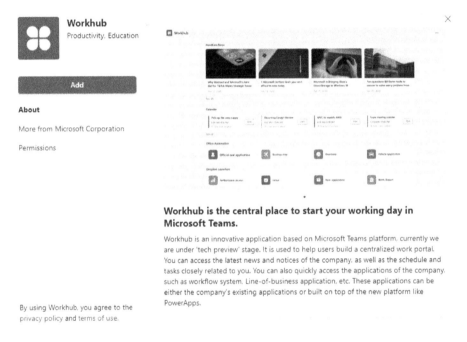

Figure 3.110 – Adding the Workhub app

Once the app is added, configurations need to be made by your administrator.

Your administrator can also make you an administrator to provide content. For instance, if you are part of the marketing team and can provide content on the latest marketing news for the company, you can be an administrator and start configuring the app so all users will be updated with the latest news.

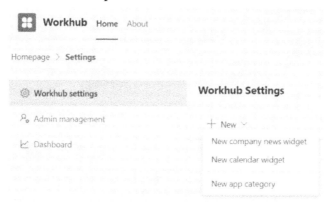

Figure 3.111 – Adding a new company news widget

2. Click on **New company news widget** and provide the required details:

- **Title**: Enter a title.

- **List Url**: This URL will be the **Microsoft SharePoint** URL. Your administrator needs to upload the image to the SharePoint document library:

Figure 3.112 – The new company news widget details

Once done, users can view the company news coverage on the **Workhub** dashboard:

Figure 3.113 – The user's view of the Workhub dashboard

In this section, we learned about using the Workhub app in Microsoft Teams to create a centralized work portal for the latest company news.

Summary

Thank you for reading this chapter. We hope that we were able to provide you with a good overview of the apps available in Microsoft Teams that can be used for workforce management.

We hope that you are now comfortable with using the sample apps available in Microsoft Teams for productivity, collaboration, and workforce management. Just keep practicing with these apps to get more comfortable with the navigation and the various options and features available, and remember that these can be customized for your organization's needs.

In the next chapter, you will be learning more about the collaboration tools available in Microsoft Teams, such as OneNote, SharePoint, OneDrive, and many more.

Section 2 – Collaboration, Events, and Communication

On completion of this part, you will have a clear understanding of collaboration, creating well-organized events, and effective communication.

In this part, we cover the following chapters:

4
Managing Collaboration in Teams

One of the main aspects required for a strong team is collaboration. There are several communication solutions that are available on the market, however, Microsoft Teams is more convenient in terms of integrating with Office software such as Microsoft Word, Excel, OneNote, and other applications. This is an important factor to consider because Microsoft Office applications have been hardwired into the work culture of a majority of people. Microsoft Teams, a communication platform built by Microsoft, aids smooth integration with these Office applications and makes end users' lives easier by utilizing these applications.

In this chapter, we will look at a few applications that can help us to improve collaboration with coworkers by using Microsoft Teams as a centered workplace environment. The intriguing aspect of this chapter is that we can be completely comfortable in using all the components that we will cover, or we can use only a portion of them and stick to the same tools.

In this chapter, we will cover the following learning objectives:

- Working together with your teammates in OneNote
- Using OneDrive in Teams to improve collaboration
- Using SharePoint to store, collaborate, and share information
- Sending emails and sending email attachments to a Teams channel
- Using Whiteboard to brainstorm ideas

After completing this chapter, you will be completely confident in using Microsoft Teams to collaborate efficiently with your colleagues and you will have gained hands-on experience with a few techniques.

Technical requirements

To begin our practice, we recommend signing up for an Office 365 trial E3 subscription via the methods outlined in our main index, and your administrator must activate OneNote, OneDrive, SharePoint, and Whiteboard, and enable the option to send emails to Teams channels.

Working together with your teammates in OneNote

Microsoft OneNote is a fundamental digital note-taking platform that is used by many people daily. OneNote helps us to store our content digitally, and access it easily as and when required. The excellent thing about OneNote is that, as the name implies, we do not need to keep saving the document every time we add lines. In addition to this, we can share our documents easily with our colleagues. There are a few methods to utilize OneNote effectively in Teams and in this section, we will go through some tips and tricks for using Microsoft Teams and OneNote together.

To get started, let's see how we can add a OneNote tab to a Teams channel:

1. So, to do that, log in to **Microsoft Teams**, navigate to your **channel**, click on the **plus sign**, and use the **Add a tab** option as shown in the following screenshot:

Figure 4.1 – Adding a tab

2. Now, in the **apps tab**, search for OneNote.

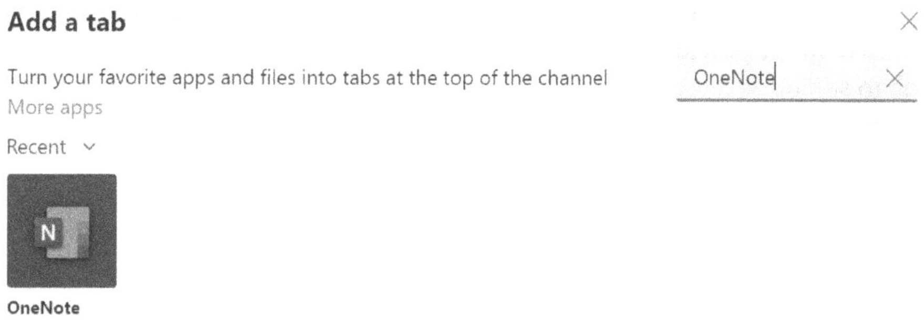

Add a tab   ✕

Turn your favorite apps and files into tabs at the top of the channel   OneNote| ✕

More apps

Recent ⌄

OneNote

Figure 4.2 – Adding the OneNote tab

We'll get the following information on the next screen. There is an option to start a new OneNote from scratch, or it will pick up and display the suggestion of an existing OneNote in this channel. It is also simple and convenient to use an already existing notebook that comes with a default team name. So, in the following example, we have selected the **Reimagine Remote Working with Microsoft Teams** channel. So, initially, when we select the existing notebook, it displays the default notebook according to the team name that we have created.

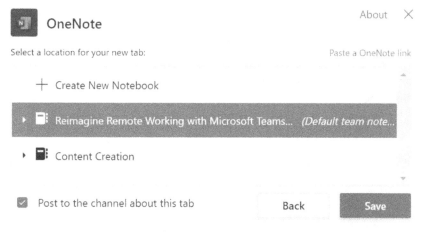

Figure 4.3 – Choose a location for your new tab

Follow these steps to successfully add the **OneNote** tab:

1. We can see that OneNote has been populated once it has been created, after we click on **Save** in the previous screen. Here, we have the option of renaming the OneNote tab to suit our needs. So, a OneNote tab in the **General** channel can contain more common information to be presented in this channel.

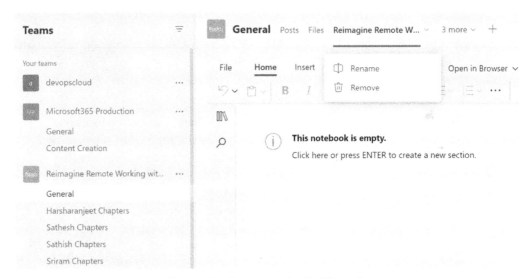

Figure 4.4 – Renaming the OneNote tab

2. In our example, we'll rename the main page of this notebook to `Authoring a book`, where we will add all the generic information and guidelines related to writing a book.

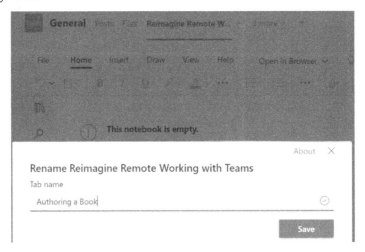

Figure 4.5 – Renaming the OneNote tab

3. After clicking on **Save**, the next screen displays a message stating that the notebook is empty. We need to add a new section with a name here. In this case, we chose `General Guidelines` as the name.

Figure 4.6 – Adding a new section

4. Once we have provided the name for the notebook, we will have a section where we can create multiple pages based on our topics that will remain in the **General** Teams channel. In our example, we have created one page called **Starter Kit** and have populated it with links that could help with how to start writing a book with *Packt* conventions.

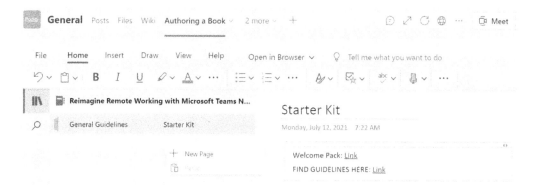

Figure 4.7 – Adding subpages

5. In the preceding example, when we right-click on the empty space, there is an option to create a new page. So, we can keep adding new sections to the individual channels. In the following example, we have moved into the next Teams channel, **Harasharanjeet Chapters**, and we need to select the **plus** icon to add a **OneNote** tab to this channel.

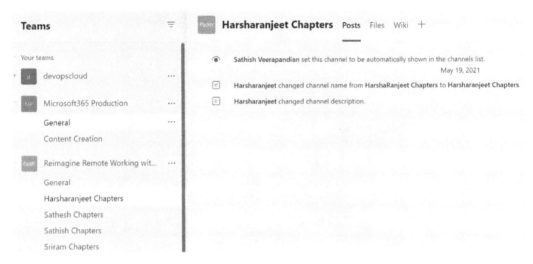

Figure 4.8 – Adding a OneNote tab to the channel

6. Follow the process of searching for OneNote again.

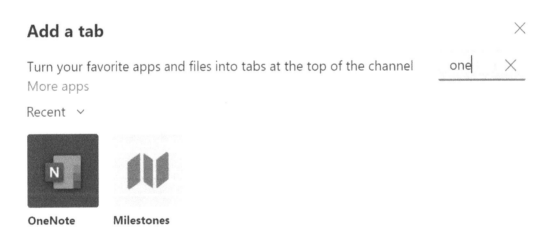

Figure 4.9 – Searching for OneNote

7. Finally, when we choose the default OneNote, we can see the next channel has its own individual section. From here, we can also start adding our individual pages.

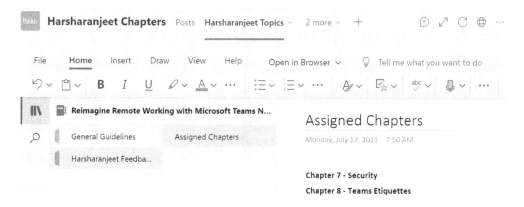

Figure 4.10 – Adding individual pages

8. If we already have a OneNote tab that was created outside of this Teams channel, we can easily add it to this channel by using the **Paste a OneNote link option**.

Figure 4.11 – Pasting a OneNote link

> **Important note**
> Only notebooks stored on SharePoint or OneDrive for Business are supported in Teams. So, we need to get the link from OneNote Online and paste it in the next window, as shown in the following example.

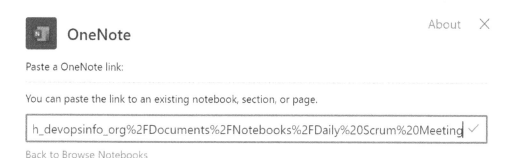

Figure 4.12 – Pasting the OneNote link

9. We can now see that the notebooks have been added successfully:

Figure 4.13 – Successful addition of OneNote

10. From here, we have the option to modify the title of the OneNote, which is more convenient to rename the title of the OneNote page.

In the following example, we have listed the roadblocks that are currently present for a team.

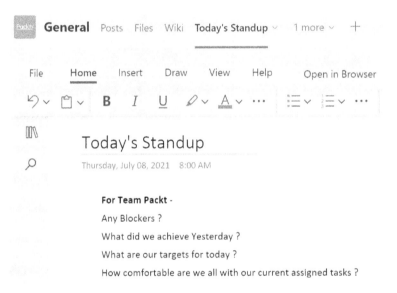

Figure 4.14 – Example 1 use case in OneNote

Another real-life scenario would be populating general information in OneNote that could be helpful to the team. With this approach, we can keep adding to the notebook so that all team members can go to this page when they need any information.

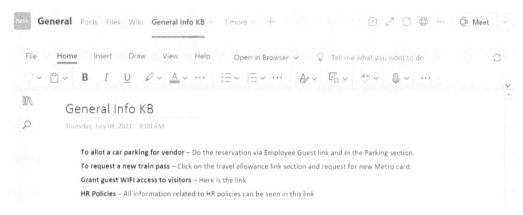

Figure 4.15 – Example 2 use case in OneNote

I believe we have covered a lot of ground on how Microsoft OneNote can help us improve our collaboration within Teams. Using this approach can assist in managing Team notes from a single location without duplicating them, and information is accessible to all members of the team. It also allows everyone on the team to update the content directly in OneNote. Let's move on to our next subject, and look at the benefits of using Microsoft OneDrive in our Teams channel.

Using OneDrive in Teams to improve collaboration

OneDrive is very efficient at storing files in the cloud, syncing files, and allowing access to files from any device at any time. Documents stored on OneDrive are completely private until we share them, and it provides a better way to collaborate on Office documents with teammates at the same time. OneDrive is also ideal for collaborating on projects and sharing them with specific individuals. In recent years, OneDrive has proven to be more useful, but people are frequently perplexed about how to use OneDrive in Teams. In this topic, we will go over all the options available for OneDrive integration with Teams.

When we create a team, we will have a corresponding **Files** tab, as shown in the following screenshot, which can be accessed by navigating to **Teams**, selecting **Posts**, and finally, we will see the **Files** tab as shown in the following screenshot.

Figure 4.16 – Files tab

When we click on the **Files** tab, we are presented with a few options that can be extremely useful in document collaboration.

Figure 4.17 – Overview of the Files tab

Sync is a very good option, which will sync your team folders in OneDrive. To sync files to your local OneDrive, click on the **Sync** icon. One major benefit is that it allows us to work on our files in offline mode. Also, you can view these files from Windows Explorer.

Figure 4.18 – Overview of the Files tab

When we click on the **Sync** icon, we may be presented with a window similar to the one in the following screenshot, asking for permission to open Microsoft OneDrive. Select the **Open Microsoft OneDrive** option after clicking in the checkmark box. There is also a notification message stating that the sync process is underway and that the files are being downloaded to your device.

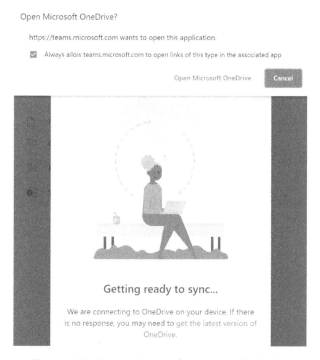

Figure 4.19 – Permission window to open OneDrive

On the next screen, we will be prompted with the following sync notification, which can be seen in the taskbar window:

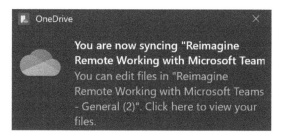

Figure 4.20 – Status of syncing

You can open the File Explorer navigation pane after a successful sync and see a small icon with a couple of buildings and your company name. When we expand this icon, we see that all of the folders and files in Microsoft Teams have been successfully synced to your local drive.

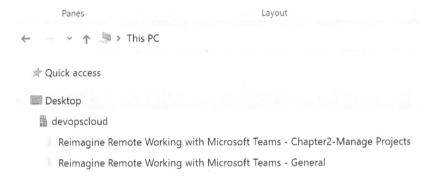

Figure 4.21 – Downloaded files view

Try not to get confused with the second option, in which we see OneDrive (a cloud icon) and the company name. That folder is for our *personal* files, and the icon with the building and company name is the location where our SharePoint sites and the Teams channel files are synced.

Figure 4.22 – Building and company name

On navigating deeper into the folder and looking at the files, we can see that the files that are present in the Teams channel are synced here locally. The **Status** column is very useful, and when we see a small cloud icon, it indicates that the file is accessible from the cloud when connected online. A status of a green checkmark means a file has been placed in this folder and is being synced to the cloud.

Name	Status	Date modified	Type
ChaptersbyAuthors.jpeg	☁	5/9/2021 6:28 PM	JPEG File
Manage Users Productivity Efficiently via Microsoft Teams	⊘	7/12/2021 7:51 AM	Microsoft
Teams book schedule.xlsx	☁	5/18/2021 9:19 PM	Microsoft

Figure 4.23 – Status of files

Files that have been recently uploaded come with a special icon – three lines on the left side of the document. It also provides us with information on when the document was last modified.

Figure 4.24 – Last modified document example

Now we have seen how to synchronize Microsoft Teams files using the OneDrive client. On the topic of Teams file locations, there are options to upload files in the Microsoft Teams channel section. We also have the option to upload a folder.

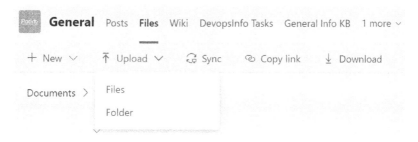

Figure 4.25 – Uploading a folder

When we select the **Folder** option, we can then select **Upload** at the bottom of the screen, which will upload the chosen folder.

Figure 4.26 – Choosing a folder to upload

Figure 4.27 – Confirmation message to upload

The interesting aspect of uploading is that it will upload the entire folder as well as the files contained within it. In the next example, there were four files, all of which were synced to the cloud.

We can see a file has been uploaded with the new file notification: three lines at the top left of the filename.

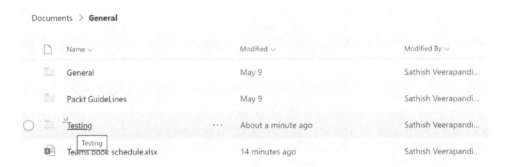

Figure 4.28 – Identifying the uploaded file

Now when we open the folder, we can see that the four files have been uploaded successfully.

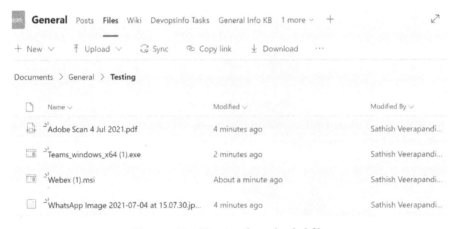

Figure 4.29 – Viewing the uploaded file

When selecting a single file, we have a number of options, so let's go through each one of them individually.

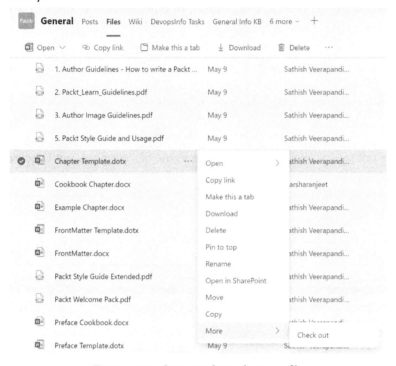

Figure 4.30 – Options when selecting a file

At the bottom, when we click on **More**, there is an option called **Check out**. When we do this, the document is *checked out* and no one else is able to edit it until it is checked back in. We'll see how this looks on the next screen.

Figure 4.31 – Check out the file

After clicking on **Check out**, the document is locked for editing by the user and they can see a red arrow next to the file, pointing toward the bottom of the page. When you have the file checked out, you can edit it online or offline, and save it multiple times, if necessary.

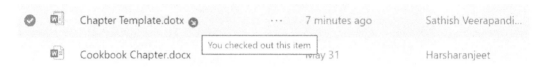

Figure 4.32 – File checked out

If you decide not to make or keep any changes to the file, simply select **Discard check out** to avoid affecting the version history.

Figure 4.33 – The Discard check out option

To release the document again, simply click on **Check in** and that will make the document available to everyone. We also get the option to **Comment** when we check in files, which is a nice feature.

Check in Chapter Template.dotx

Figure 4.34 – Check in

Copy and **Move** work in the same way, allowing users to copy/move files between teams and channels, as well as to copy them to OneDrive.

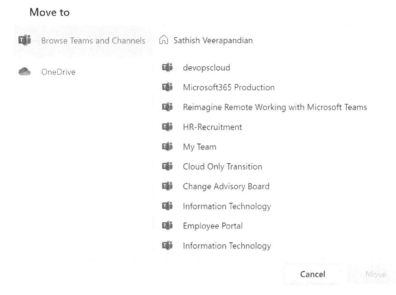

Figure 4.35 – Copy/move

Open in SharePoint opens the same files and folders that we see on the SharePoint site. We can't tell the difference between how the files appear in Teams and how they appear on the SharePoint site because Microsoft has streamlined the experience.

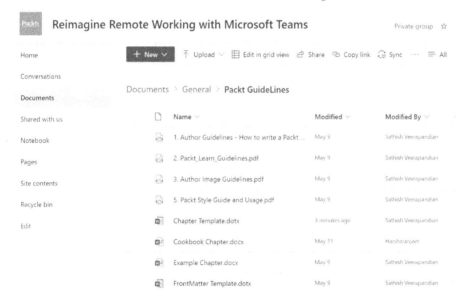

Figure 4.36 – Open in SharePoint

Pin to top is a great option that allows us to pin the files that we want to be easily locatable when navigating to the **Files** tab.

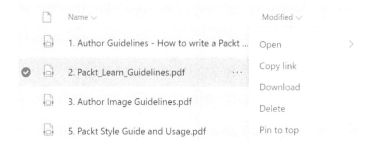

Figure 4.37 – Pin to top

In the following example, we can see that the pinned files are shown at the top of File Explorer. On selecting a file, two options are present. The first one is to move the file and the second one is to **Unpin** the file.

Figure 4.38 – Unpin

There is also the **Make this a tab** option, which can generally make any document appear as a tab. For example, we can choose a Word document and make it appear as a separate tab.

Figure 4.39 – Make this a tab

When we select the **Make this a tab** option, the Word document itself will be added as a tab at the top, along with an easy option to modify it directly from here. **Open in Desktop App** is a wonderful feature that provides the full Microsoft Word document experience from the computer.

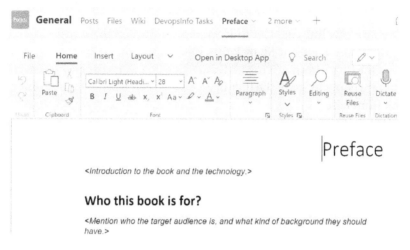

Figure 4.40 – Open in Desktop App

Don't forget to check out the view options on the right-hand side. There are currently three options available. The **Tiles** view is fantastic. There is an option to save multiple views by selecting **Save view as**, and you can also select **Edit current view**, as shown in the next screenshot.

Figure 4.41 – View options

When a file is selected, there is an option to share the file link by using the **Copy link** option.

Figure 4.42 – Copy link

After clicking on **Copy link**, the **Get link** option is shown on the screen. From here, you can choose **Microsoft Teams** or **SharePoint**. One important takeaway here is if we are going to share the link within Microsoft Teams, then we would of course select **Microsoft Teams**. If you are going to share the link in an email, then use the **SharePoint** option and copy the link from here.

Figure 4.43 – Get link

Having covered almost all of the topics in this *Using OneDrive in Teams to improve collaboration* section, we now have a final option that will be extremely beneficial to those using Microsoft Teams with OneDrive. We can see that there is a **Files** option at the bottom left of the Teams client icons. This **Files** icon is usually present by default in most cases. In the event that it is not visible, click on the three dots at the bottom and select the **Files** icon, which will pin it to the left icon pane in the Microsoft Teams client.

Figure 4.44 – Files option

Essentially, we have three choices. The first option, **Recent**, displays all files that have been opened recently. The second option is **Microsoft Teams**, which will display all the files in the Microsoft Teams channels of which you are a member. The final option is **OneDrive**, which displays the files that have been linked to Teams channels.

Connecting Microsoft Teams and OneDrive creates a powerful teamwork platform. Your documents can be uploaded to the Teams channel's OneDrive shared location. This draft copy can then be used to notify your teammates that a new file has been uploaded and is awaiting feedback. Team members can directly open the file in Teams and begin editing or commenting. When a team member saves a file to OneDrive, it is automatically added to the list. In the next topic, we will go through the options that are available in SharePoint that can boost our experience with Microsoft Teams.

Using SharePoint to store, collaborate, and share information

We have the option of working with SharePoint data through Teams. In some cases, we may have SharePoint sites with existing data, and bringing it to Teams will be extremely beneficial. In Teams, we can add a SharePoint page, list, or document library as a tab. Also, Microsoft has recently improved the file sharing experience in Teams, which is powered by SharePoint. The rich file sharing experience appears within Teams' **Files** tab, which we have seen plenty of in the previous topic because OneDrive and SharePoint share more or less the same platform.

Teams benefits from interoperability with SharePoint content services. This means that when you work in the **Files** tab across your teams and channels, you're getting the full power of SharePoint file use and management right inside of Teams – without leaving Teams. We touched a little bit on the previous part of the topic, now let's do a deep dive into what options are available from a SharePoint perspective in Microsoft Teams.

Integrating Microsoft Teams from the SharePoint portal

In the first example, let's see Microsoft Teams integration with SharePoint from the SharePoint portal.

For example, when we create a new modern SharePoint site from the SharePoint portal, we can see at the bottom left of the screen a wonderful option called **Add real-time chat**, which allows us to share IM conversations through Microsoft Teams from this SharePoint portal.

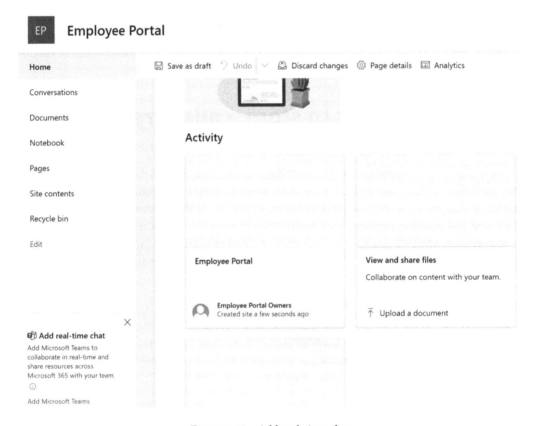

Figure 4.45 – Add real-time chat

Clicking on **Add real-time chat** pops up an additional window. So, all we need to do is to click on **Continue**.

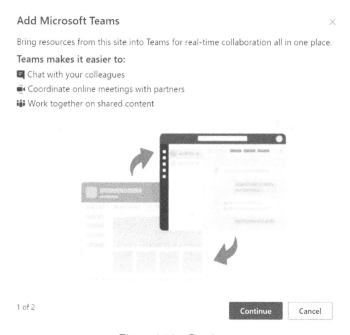

Figure 4.46 – Continue

On the next screen, we have the **Pin resources as tabs in Teams** option. Here, we can select the important documents and use the **Pin resources as tabs in Teams** option.

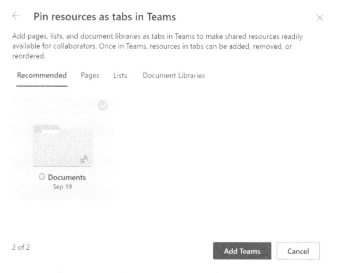

Figure 4.47 – Pin resources as tabs in Teams

Once we click **Add Teams** a **Teams** tab is populated on the left panel, as shown in the following screenshot:

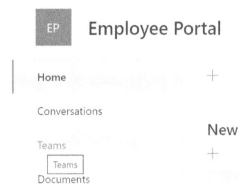

Figure 4.48 – Teams tab

Clicking on the **Teams** tab redirects us to Microsoft Teams and we can see that a separate team has been created to help people to collaborate and chat from the same location.

Figure 4.49 – Teams tab

Having seen all these options in SharePoint, let's move on to looking at the options available from the Teams client side.

Adding a SharePoint tab from the Teams client

When clicking on **Add a tab** in the Teams channel, we have three options that are available: **Document Library**, **SharePoint**, and **SharePoint Pages**. Let's go through them individually.

Figure 4.50 – Add a SharePoint tab

Firstly, the document libraries securely store files where team members can find them on any device where we have the Teams client installed, or from the Teams web app client.

Moving on to the next screen, we see there are two options that are presented to us. The first option is to display the relevant sites that are available within Teams. The second option is to use a SharePoint link, which provides us with an option to specify the SharePoint site link.

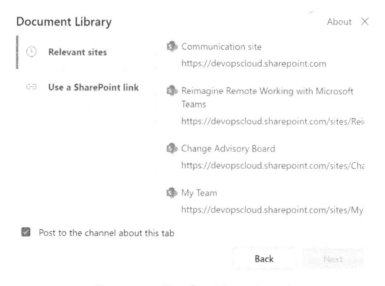

Figure 4.51 – View from Teams channel

Once the document library has been created, we can see the **Document Library** tab present in the Teams channel, and all the associated contents, as seen in the next screenshot.

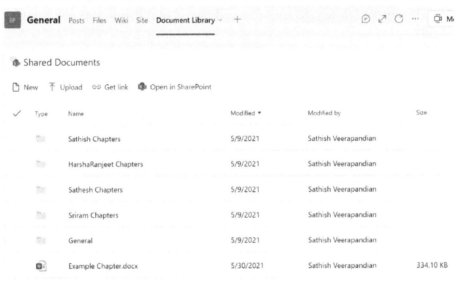

Figure 4.52 – Document Library view from Teams channel

When trying to add SharePoint, we get the following screen, showing the default SharePoint pages that were available when we created this Teams channel. We can add this as a tab.

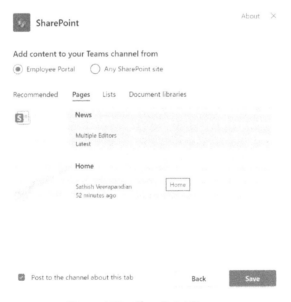

Figure 4.53 – SharePoint Pages

If we don't add it as a tab, then we have an option to add any SharePoint site, as shown in the next screenshot. In the following example, we are adding one new SharePoint site to this channel by pasting the SharePoint link.

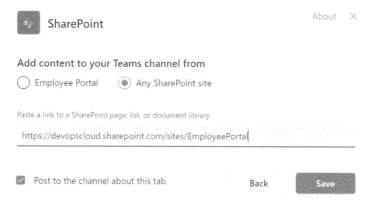

Figure 4.54 – Adding a SharePoint site

After the site has been added, we can see the SharePoint site showing in the additional tab in the Teams channel.

Figure 4.55 – SharePoint site in the Teams tab

When we search for SharePoint pages and click on them, Teams shows us the following options. Firstly, we have the default option where it picks from the preexisting SharePoint site for this team (in our case, it shows the following sites with the **Add a page from HR-Recruitment** option). Or, we can choose the **Add a page from any SharePoint site** option that we see in the following screenshot:

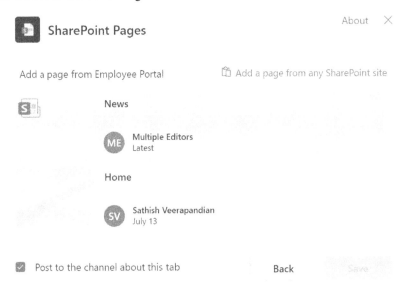

Figure 4.56 – SharePoint Pages options

The moment we click on **Save**, the Teams channel is populated with a wonderful screen as shown in the next screenshot. It shows us all the activity, has an option to add news, and has a similar look and feel to what we have seen on the SharePoint site.

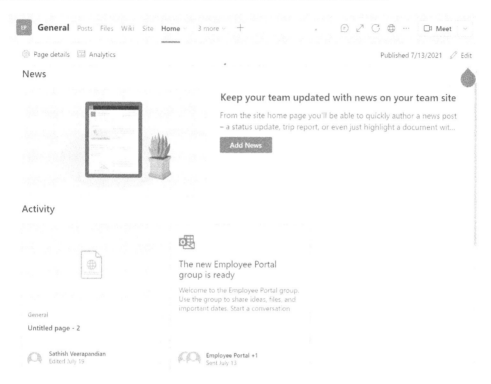

Figure 4.57 – View from the Teams channel

I believe we have covered all the points that can assist us in increasing our productivity by effectively utilizing Microsoft Teams and SharePoint together for better collaboration. This ensures a consistent sharing experience for users across all Microsoft 365 platforms. This means that no matter where you are in Microsoft 365, you will have the same control over how files are shared and accessed – with links that just work. Having said that, let's move on to our next topic, where we'll look at the features available when sending emails to a Teams channel.

Sending emails and sending email attachments to a Teams channel

There is an option in Microsoft Teams to send emails to a channel. You might want to use this feature if you receive an important email from your vendor that needs to be shared with the entire team, or in other similar use cases. No worries, there is a simple way to send this email to a Teams channel, where all recipients can see it from their side of the Teams channel.

To get started with this option, navigate to the Teams channel, hover your mouse over the three dots at the top right, and select the **Get email address** option.

Figure 4.58 – Get email address

On selecting **Get email address**, we are presented with the following screen, and there is a **Copy** button to copy the email address of this Teams channel.

Figure 4.59 – Copy email address

When we drill down to **advanced settings**, we are presented with the options listed in the next screenshot, which can be controlled from the Teams channel and by the channel owners. By default, the first option, **Anyone can send emails to this address,** is selected, allowing anyone with this email address to send emails to this channel. The second option is **Only members of this team**, making this email sending option available only to members of this team. **Only email sent from these domains** is a great option because it allows this team to only receive emails from known external partners while blocking other external domains in the channel.

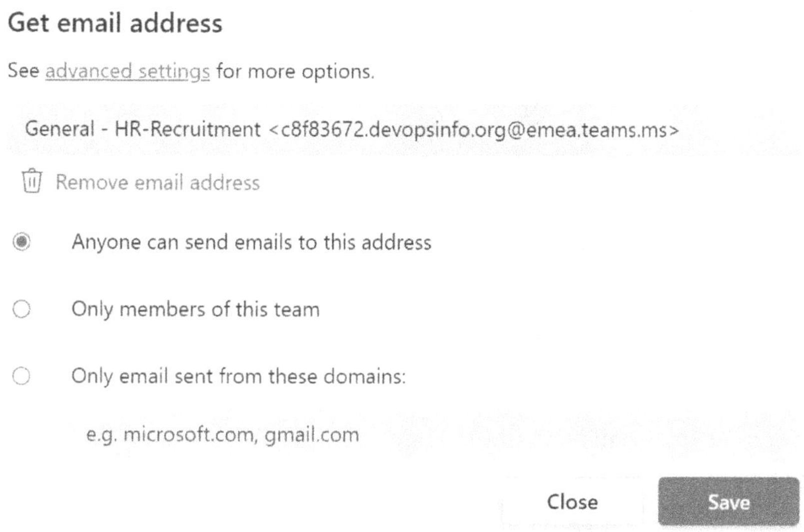

Get email address

See advanced settings for more options.

General - HR-Recruitment <c8f83672.devopsinfo.org@emea.teams.ms>

🗑 Remove email address

◉ Anyone can send emails to this address

○ Only members of this team

○ Only email sent from these domains:

   e.g. microsoft.com, gmail.com

Close   Save

Figure 4.60 – Advanced settings

So now we are sending an email to the Teams channel, as shown in the next screenshot.

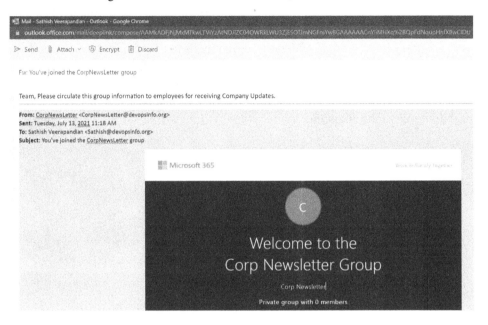

Figure 4.61 – Sending an email to the Teams channel

Finally, we can see the emails sent in the Teams channel. There is an option to **See more**, and we can also download the original email, which is a fantastic feature. We can also see the option to **Reply** to this email, but one important point to note here is that our reply will be treated as a normal post in this channel and an email will not go to the actual sender of this message.

Figure 4.62 – Viewing email from Teams channel

So, you've learned how to send a new email or forward a received email to a Teams channel. You also have a few pointers on how to control an email flow in a Microsoft Teams channel. The final topic in the chapter is Whiteboard, which can help us collaborate better within a team.

Using Whiteboard to brainstorm ideas

Microsoft Whiteboard is a free-form digital canvas whiteboard that allows people to brainstorm, discuss their ideas, and collaborate in the same meeting. It provides us with a real-life collaborating experience, complete with digital pens, erasers, and sticky notes, which will undoubtedly aid in collaborating and bringing great ideas to the team. From October 2021, any new whiteboards that are created in Microsoft 365 applications will be stored in OneDrive for Business. This is mainly to provide a rich content management experience for Whiteboard as well.

In our example, we will go through the options that are available in Microsoft Teams for Whiteboard. As a prerequisite, Whiteboard is enabled by default for all Office 365 tenants, however, it's good practice to check with your IT admin to see if Whiteboard is enabled in your Office 365 tenant.

To utilize Whiteboard in Teams when you are in a meeting as a presenter, click on the upward arrow, which opens the share tray.

Figure 4.63 – Open share tray

On the next screen, when we hover the mouse towards the bottom right of the screen, we can see **Microsoft Whiteboard** as a screen sharing option.

Figure 4.64 – Choose Microsoft WhiteBoard

Once Whiteboard has been opened, we see the screen in the next screenshot, which is a whiteboard, with pens, sticky notes, erasers, textboxes, and even a few shapes. Furthermore, we see there is an option for us to open Whiteboard in the app, which will open this whiteboard presentation in the Whiteboard app that is locally installed on your laptop. Here, we have the option to name our whiteboard according to our topic. In our example, we have just named it **Testing Whiteboard**.

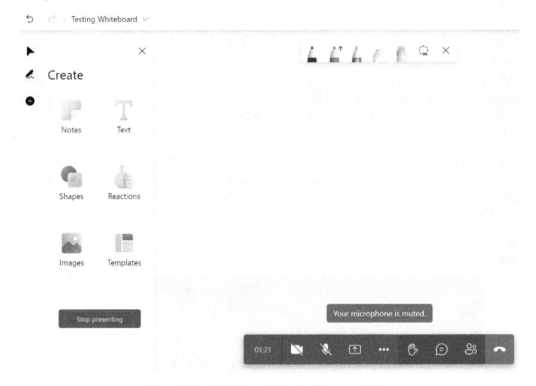

Figure 4.65 – Whiteboard view in the presentation

When clicking on the settings gear icon, we have the option to share the ideas discussed on this whiteboard, by exporting it as a PNG image. We also have the option to share the permissions of this whiteboard. When the blue toggle switch is turned off, it's only the presenter who has shared the screen who can edit and use the whiteboard. This can be useful, especially in scenarios where a teacher is training students.

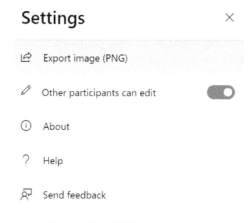

Figure 4.66 – Whiteboard Settings

The next screenshot is an example of how we can collaborate live in a Teams meeting. The best part is when we set the **Other participants can edit** option because it allows for better collaboration with the team.

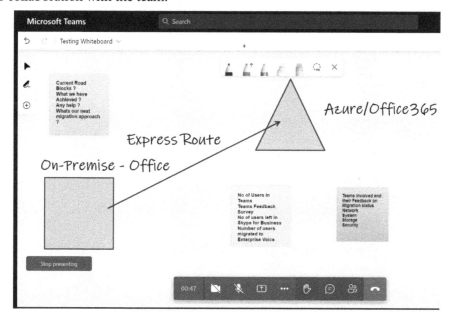

Figure 4.67 – Sample utilization of Whiteboard

We've gone over all of the possibilities for using Whiteboard as an app in Microsoft Teams. Whiteboard allows team meeting participants to draw, sketch, and write together on a shared digital canvas, which can spark incredible ideas within a team.

Summary

So, in this chapter, we've gone over the best solutions for what Microsoft Teams can do right now to help you efficiently collaborate with your teammates. Microsoft 365 apps have become the default way for most people to work and save files for daily tasks. It provides a fantastic experience when we can use these apps for recurring tasks, projects, or collaboration with our colleagues. With the consistent experience across these apps, we can provide a seamless, uncluttered experience to all end users while also keeping Microsoft Teams as a single platform from which we can easily do all of our work.

It is unquestionably beneficial to effectively use Microsoft Teams with all these various file sharing and collaborating experiences. We hope you enjoyed this chapter and were able to follow along by practicing these methods from your own Teams client. Keep an eye out for the next chapter, which will go into greater detail about effectively managing your communication via Teams.

5
Managing Communication in Teams

Microsoft Teams helps customers to seamlessly and securely collaborate in a workplace. Teams also integrates with other products in the Office 365 suite to facilitate effective communication, which in turn helps your employees or customers stay on top of information. These collaboration tools are built with the idea that any communication is a two-way process where employees or customers can effectively communicate back and forth about information and voice their thoughts to the organization. Organizations can take feedback to help them understand the needs of their employees or customers and design their strategy accordingly.

In this chapter, we will cover the following applications that can help you to communicate effectively:

- Group chats in Teams
- Enterprise streaming for your corporate training or delivering a CEO message to employees via Stream
- Corporate social media platform with Yammer
- Federation from Teams to external parties
- Creating interactive reports with Sway

Upon successful completion of these topics and after getting hands-on with a few practice scenarios, you will be fully comfortable with managing your meetings effectively with these tools.

Group chats in Teams

Microsoft Teams group chats allow you to create a personalized group and add multiple members at once for effective collaboration. As you are already aware, you can have a channel created with members who are part of a particular project; however, it gives some comfort to users to create a group chat and add members of their choice for a quick chat, to make an audio or video call, or to share files. It is sometimes required to have a small group of members in one place to discuss ideas and group chats can be used as an option for this.

Creating a group chat

Please follow these steps to create a group chat for collaboration:

1. Select **Chat** from the menu on the left navigation bar on the Teams client or the web and start a new conversation.

Figure 5.1 – Starting a new chat conversation

2. Start searching for users by typing in their names; Teams should help you to pick people when you start typing the first letter of the user.

Figure 5.2 – Searching for users

You can keep adding multiple users by selecting the users shown in the people picker or pressing the *Tab* key on the keyboard.

Figure 5.3 – Adding multiple users

Microsoft Teams even allows you to add external recipients if your organization allows you to communicate with external domains. Group chats allow you to add up to 200 participants.

3. Once users are added, you can click the *Enter* key to start a new conversation with all the people added.

4. Always check the participants and their titles again before starting a conversation to avoid data being leaked to an unauthorized user. This can be done by clicking on the participants icon in the top-right corner.

Figure 5.4 – Viewing participants

5. A group chat has been successfully created and you can start a conversation in the group.

Renaming and pinning a group

Naming conventions play a vital role when you use any collaboration tool. This helps you to quickly identify the group and the members that are part of it to meaningfully communicate the purpose. Naming is very important when you work with multiple projects, which is usually the case for any user, as it helps you to locate the right group. Hence, when a group is created, it is highly recommended that you give a name to the group that gives a logical understanding to the owner and the group members of what it's for. Groups can be renamed by clicking on the edit icon.

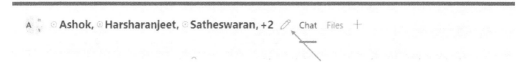

Figure 5.5 – Editing a group

You can give any logical name for the group and click on **Save**.

Figure 5.6 – Renaming a group

Group chats can be pinned so that you can quickly access the group under the pinned option on the Teams client or Teams on the web. To pin a group chat, select **...** next to the group name and click on the **Pin** option.

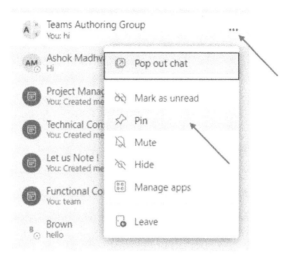

Figure 5.7 – Pinning a group

Adding and removing members to and from group chats

The following steps can be used to add or remove members to and from group chats:

1. Click on the participants icon in the top-right corner to view all the members. You can click on the **X** icon next to the username to remove a user.

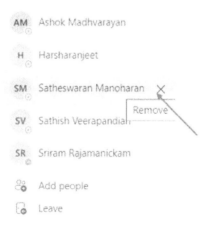

Figure 5.8 – Removing participants

2. Teams will ask for confirmation to remove any users. To confirm, click on **Remove**.

Figure 5.9 – Removing a user

3. To add a new user to the participants in a group chat, you can click on **Add people**. When you add a new user, Teams allows you to make the entire chat history of the group chat viewable to that user, allow them to view the chat history for a certain number of days, or exclude the chat history.

Chat history is a key feature to note when you add participants. For example, in a technical group chat, you might need to add an accounts team member to discuss commercials and they don't need to know any of the information from previous conversations, so you can add the user without including any chat history. On the other hand, you may need a technical employee who was onboarded recently to go through the chat and so they can be added with the ability to view all chat history.

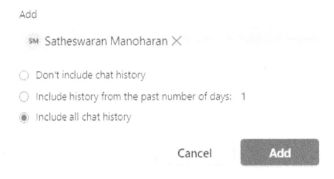

Figure 5.10 – Adding a new user with or without chat history

Collaboration options in group chats

Group chats allow you to make an audio/video call on an ad hoc basis to all the group members. You can make a video or audio call by clicking on the calling options in the top-right corner of the Teams client or web browser.

Figure 5.11 – Calling options in Teams

Group chats also allow you to share content. You can choose from the various sharing options available when you click on the **Share Content** icon in the top-right corner of the screen. You can share the complete desktop, specific windows, or any open applications with all members of the group.

Figure 5.12 – Sharing content in group chats

Microsoft Teams automatically creates a group when you have a meeting and all the meeting members are added to the group. The group is named the same as the meeting name. Users can continue using the group to collaborate on any topic related to the meeting once it has ended. They will have all the options mentioned previously that they can continue using in the group chat.

> **Note**
>
> Teams administrators can disable settings on the tenant so participants do not
> have access to the group chat once the meeting is over.

Group chats also allow you to use the standard chat and file-sharing options, such as setting
the importance for a message, sharing files, sharing emojis and GIFs, and creating meetings.

Figure 5.13 – Chat options in group chats

The **Files** tab in a group chat can be used to see all the files shared in the group for
quicker access.

Figure 5.14 – Using the Files tab to access shared files

In the preceding section, we covered the group chat options available in Teams to allow
group communication for easy collaboration. In the upcoming section, you will learn
about Microsoft Stream, which is an enterprise video service that can be used in your
organization. In this book, we will cover Microsoft Stream Classic features to provide
custom video rendering services for your organization that are more secure and within
your Office 365 tenant boundary, not in the public cloud.

Microsoft Stream Classic

Microsoft Stream is an enterprise video storage platform built on top of the Office 365 suite of products that empowers you to create your videos, including corporate training videos and CEO messages, in a secured way. Microsoft Stream helps you to secure your content as the content stays within your Office 365 boundary and you can apply strict permissions on who has access to the content itself.

Microsoft Stream helps you to organize content via channels and groups, so it is convenient for users to find content easily. Microsoft Stream is seamlessly integrated with Teams, SharePoint, and Yammer, which again helps users to get quick access to Stream videos. There are a lot of use cases where Stream can help your organization, for example, to conduct corporate training or to deliver a message from the CEO to all staff; all individual users even have some storage quota as part of their Office 365 license to add their own videos. Stream has apps for your computers, tablets, and mobile devices so you have access to your videos anywhere, anytime.

Stream licensing requirements

Microsoft Stream follows the per-user license mode like any other product in the Office 365 suite. Please review the following table, which gives you insights into the Stream license requirements. It is important to verify with your organization administrator before you start consuming Stream:

	Firstline F1 GCC, GCC High, DoD F1 '1'	Education A1	Microsoft 365 Business Premium/ Essentials	Enterprise E1/E3 Education A3 GCC, GCC High, DoD E1/ E3/M365 G3 '1'	Enterprise E5 Education A5 GCC, GCC High, DoD E5 '1'	Microsoft 365 Stream feature add-on
View videos or live events	•	•	•	•	•	•
Upload/modify videos	•	•	•	•	•	
Create live events in Microsoft Stream				•	•	
Search automatically generated transcripts	•	•	•	•	•	•

Stream data locations

Microsoft Stream is available in all regions; however, the data may not be stored in your geographical region as Stream currently hosts data in the following regions only:

- United States
- Europe
- Asia Pacific
- Australia
- India
- United Kingdom
- Canada
- United States **Government Community Cloud (GCC)**

Microsoft Stream will host data in the following, as well as other, regions in the future:

- China
- Germany
- GCC-High/GCC-DoD

There are compliance requirements for many countries that cloud data should be within their region, so if you have an Office 365 tenant in a region where Stream is not available and you start using Stream, then the data will be saved in the nearest data location. It is important to take advice from the compliance team or the IT team to host the data outside the region if Stream is still not available in your data center region.

Stream quota

Microsoft Stream tenants start with a fixed allocation of 500 GB of storage for the complete organization. On top of the organization limit, every licensed user will get 0.5 GB of storage, which is illustrated in the following figure:

Figure 5.15 – Stream quota structure

The organization is allowed to take **Stream Storage Add-On** directly from the purchasing services on the tenant. The add-on can be bought for an additional $100 for 500 GB of data.

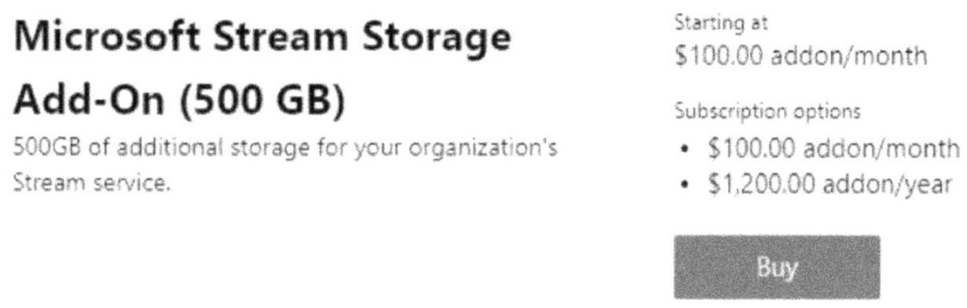

Microsoft Stream Storage Add-On (500 GB)

500GB of additional storage for your organization's Stream service.

Starting at
$100.00 addon/month

Subscription options
- $100.00 addon/month
- $1,200.00 addon/year

Buy

Figure 5.16 – Storage add-on for Stream

Accessing Microsoft Stream

Microsoft Stream can be accessed directly by going to `https://web.microsoftstream.com/` and signing in using your corporate credentials. A valid Stream license user will be taken to the home page, where they can start configuring Stream, upload videos, and a lot more.

1. Stream can also be accessed via the app launcher in the top-left corner of your Office 365 default home page by clicking on **Stream**.

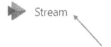

Stream

Figure 5.17 – Accessing Stream from Office 365

2. Users can add Stream to their Teams client and directly access the services.

Figure 5.18 – Adding Stream to Office 365

Configuring Microsoft Stream

On successful login to Microsoft Stream, you can start to discover the available videos for your organization, follow a channel, and upload your videos. The following subsections will give you deep insights into the various options available in Stream.

Trending videos

Once you log in to Stream, on the welcome home page, you can see the trending videos of your organization. The Microsoft engine analyzes videos from your organization where users are liking and commenting and stores and pops them up in the trending section for users to see the videos directly.

Figure 5.19 – Trending videos

Navigation bar

You have a simplified navigation bar at the top of the home page, where you can do most of the actions available in Stream.

Figure 5.20 – Stream navigation bar

Creating content

On the welcome home page, you can directly start uploading videos by clicking on the **Create** drop-down menu and clicking on **Upload video**.

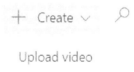

Figure 5.21 – Uploading a video

Once the video is uploaded onto Stream, you can do the following so users can find more details on the video that is uploaded. There are a lot more options available to add more details to videos, which helps users to search for them easily:

- **Name**: You can provide a name for the video relevant to the content.

- **Description**: A detailed description of the complete video content can be added here. You can add time codes (H:MM:SS) for interesting points in the video. You can also use **#hashtags** so that users can click and see related videos. Also, links can be used so users can click on and read about the content before they watch the video.

- **Language**: Once the video language field is set to a supported language, Stream can automatically generate captions using **speech recognition** technology. Automatic captions take approximately twice the amount of time as the video duration to be generated. For example, if you have a 10-minute video, you need to wait at least 20 minutes for the captions to be generated. Stream also allows you to upload a caption file manually if you don't want the system to autogenerate them. Automatic captions have some limitations, which are mentioned in the following information box.

> **Note**
>
> English, Chinese, French, German, Italian, Japanese, Portuguese, and Spanish are the languages currently supported for autogenerated captions. Note: For USGOV, Stream only supports English and Spanish.
>
> Only MP4 and WMV files are currently supported for automatic transcripts.
>
> You have a choice: either autogenerate captions or upload a caption file. You can't autogenerate captions if you have already uploaded a caption file. You can't upload a caption file if you have selected the **Autogenerate a caption file** option.

Figure 5.22 – Captions for videos

- **Thumbnail**: Once the video is uploaded onto Stream, the engine allows you to choose from a variety of thumbnail images. It also allows you to upload a relevant thumbnail for the image.

Permissions and privacy

It is important to configure the permissions and privacy of the video that is being uploaded. The permissions allow users to view the content or own the video and edit and change the content. Stream allows everyone in the organization to view the video if the organization wants to float an open video to all employees. On the **Permissions** tab, you have the option to allow all organization employees to watch the video. Any person or group added to the share list will automatically get viewer access to the video.

Shared with

The **Shared with** option allows you to define who can own/view the video and the groups/channels that the video is part of:

- **My groups**: Add your video to a group that you can contribute to.

- **Channels**: Add your video to a channel directly, including company-wide channels.

- **People**: Grant permission to individual people, AD security groups, and/or Office 365 groups that you don't have contribute rights to.

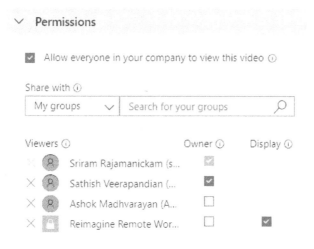

Figure 5.23 – Mapping permissions for Stream

Finally, you can turn on/off the comments section where users can comment on the video. Stream also allows you to enable noise suppression. Noise suppression can be enabled in the following scenarios:

- Videos longer than 2 hours

- Videos larger than 3 GB

- Videos without an audio track

- Videos with more than one audio track, such as two embedded language tracks that you can switch between

Finally, you can publish the video and make it available on Stream for end users.

Editing a video

At times, we need to edit an uploaded video due to some errors or changes to the content. Stream allows you to do a lot of editing even for an uploaded video. Click on **My Videos** on the Stream home page, which displays all videos uploaded by you, then click on the dots (…) icon next to the video.

Figure 5.24 – Editing an uploaded video

Stream allows you to trim a video if you feel the content is too long once published.

You can also replace it with a new video, delete the video, share it via email or Yammer, and make the video available to the entire organization.

You can also modify the entire configuration that is done while uploading the video if you feel the content is not apt or you'd like to add a new caption, or if you want to share it with another Teams channel, group, and so on, by simply clicking on the edit option next to the video.

> **Note**
> If a video is deleted, it is available in the Recycle bin for 30 days if you'd like to recover it.

Adding polls to videos

Another nice-to-have option with Stream is that you can create surveys and polls using Microsoft Forms and link to the video that is uploaded. Click on the video that is uploaded and select the **Interactivity** tab. You have an option to add a form that redirects you to Microsoft Forms, where you can create a form for surveys and polls.

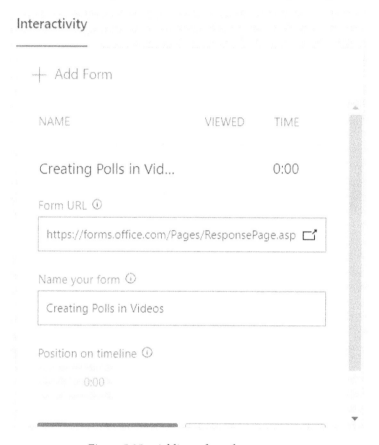

Figure 5.25 – Adding a form for a survey

Important to note is the placement of the form when the video is rendering. You can use the slider on the video to position the time to pop up the survey.

Figure 5.26 – Positioning on the timeline

Recording your screen

Stream allows you to record your screen for up to 15 minutes, which can be useful to show a demo in a video format. Screenshots help people to understand an idea; however, video can be even easier for users to follow:

1. Click on **Create** then **Record screen** on the Stream home page.
2. The browser will prompt you to allow Stream access to your microphone and camera.
3. Select the microphone and camera and click on **Start Recording**.

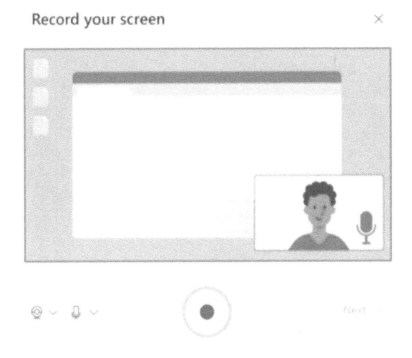

Figure 5.27 – Starting a video recording

4. Stream allows you to choose whether you wish to share the entire screen or an application or browser window. You can choose only the required screen to record.

Entire Screen   Window   Chrome Tab

Figure 5.28 – Record screen selection

5. Wait for the timer to begin recording. Once you see the timer showing the 15-minute time limit, you can switch on the application to record.

6. Once the recording is completed, you will have the option to upload the recording and configure permissions for the video. All the previously mentioned permission and edit options are also available for screen recordings.

7. There are a few limitations with screen recordings:

    -   The following browsers support screen recording: Microsoft Edge for Windows 10, and Microsoft Edge, version 79 and above on Windows 10 and macOS.

    -   Google Chrome, version 74 and above on Windows 10 and macOS.

    -   Safari on macOS is not supported.

    -   Microsoft Stream mobile on iOS and Android is not supported in mobile browsers.

    -   Recording system audio is available only on Windows, not macOS.

    -   Including the camera in the recording is available only when recording the entire screen, not when recording an application window or browser tab.

    -   Screen recordings are limited to a maximum length of 15 minutes. For longer content, break up your video into shorter segments.

Creating groups/channels

Stream allows you to create groups/channels from this console. Groups are similar to Office 365 groups where a video can be linked to. Similarly, you can create channels, which are not the same as the default Teams channels, however; these channels are used in Stream to have segregation. You can use the **Create** button on the home screen to create groups and channels.

The Discover dropdown

The **Discover** dropdown is used to discover the videos available on Stream for the whole organization. There are a lot of **Filtering** options available where you can search based on groups, channels, content, and keywords:

1. Click on **Search** at the top of Microsoft Stream and type in a keyword to search for a video across the Stream tenant.

2. Click on the **Discover** option on the home page, where you have a lot of sorting options to get to your video quickly.

3. You can search for videos in channels, people, and groups and you can sort by categories such as **Trending**, **Name**, **Publish date**, and **Likes**, which drill down your search to the exact match.

Figure 5.29 – Discovering video search options

Stream also allows you to do a deep search where you can narrow down your search for a word that is used in a video. For example, on a training video, if you would like to search for a configuration related to Microsoft Teams, you can click on the video and type the keyword. The caption window will show all occurrences where that word appears in the text. This will allow you to move the slider to get to the exact information.

The adoption of Stream helps organizations to effectively communicate with employees via video. In a world where employees still adopt working from home, Stream will help you to connect with people to deliver content consistently. Security plays a vital role when you want to deliver a video rendering solution to share messages within an organization, hence a public cloud may not be a suitable option, and this was one important reason why Microsoft built such a powerful tool for collaboration. The above section gives insights into Stream.

In the upcoming section, we will cover Yammer, which is almost the equivalent of an enterprise social network platform to promote effective communication and collaboration.

Microsoft Yammer

Yammer connects people across the organization, builds communities, helps share knowledge, and engages employees. Communities help people to break barriers irrespective of their physical location and support each other. Yammer is built on the Office 365 suite of products and hence enterprise security can be achieved while collaborating. Yammer can be used to ask questions and find experts across your organization. The following are the key features of Yammer:

- Yammer is available on the web, mobile, and Microsoft 365 apps.

- Yammer is integrated with SharePoint Online, Stream, and Teams.

- The platform can be secured using Microsoft enterprise security.

- It connects people across the organization, which helps employees to stay on top of information.

- Yammer allows you to share files, photos, GIFs, and even videos to deliver content that helps others in the organization.

- Users can ask questions and create polls/surveys to get employees' feedback.

- Yammer notifies users via their inbox to manage important messages and responses to feeds.

- Yammer allows you to join communities and connect with colleagues to gather and share ideas.

Yammer bridges the gap between users and top management where everyone has an opportunity to voice their thoughts and others can listen and take feedback. Employee suggestions are vital in an organization, which helps management to define or change their strategies.

Organization administrators have the option to turn off Yammer based on their compliance requirements. Before getting started, please check with the administrator whether Yammer is turned on in your Office 365 tenant.

Configuring Yammer

In this section, we will cover the various options available in Yammer:

1. Yammer can be accessed via the App launcher in the top-left corner of your Office 365 default home page by clicking on **Yammer**.

2. Yammer takes the user details from Office 365. If you edit your Office 365 profile, it will automatically be populated to Yammer.

3. Click on **Edit** in the top-right corner of the screen and configure the notification settings for your profile. This is very important as notifications help you to know if you have responses to any questions or if there is an update on a feed that you follow. It is self-explanatory to enable/disable the required notifications. Enabling all notifications sometimes floods your inbox, so Yammer gives you the option to pick and choose which you want to see.

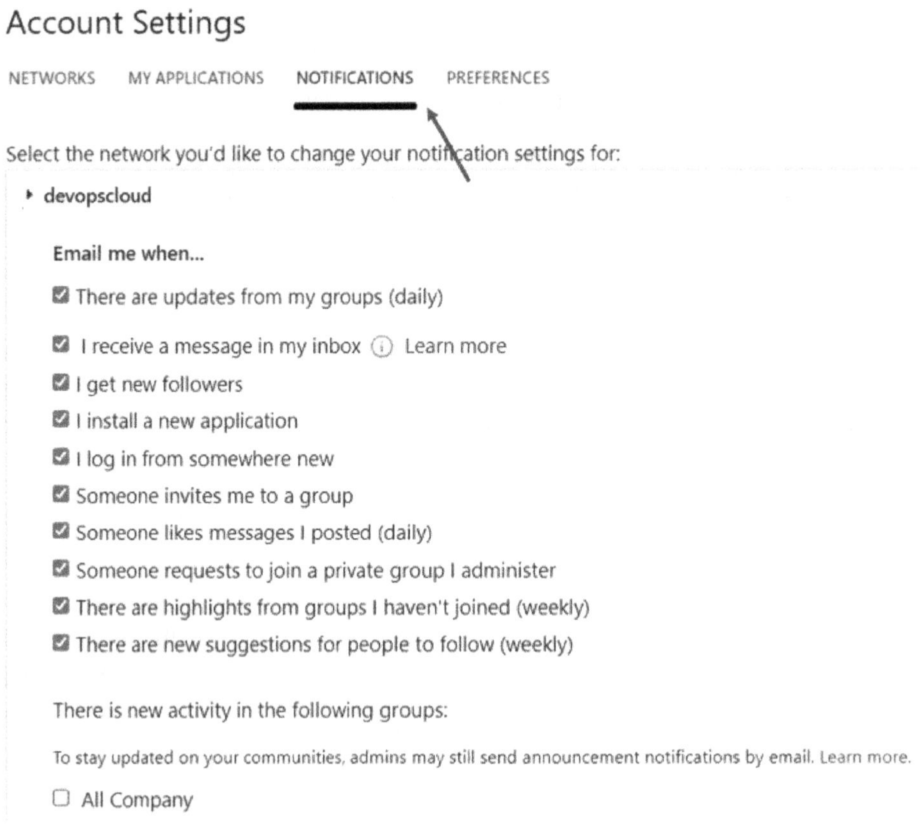

Account Settings

NETWORKS   MY APPLICATIONS   **NOTIFICATIONS**   PREFERENCES

Select the network you'd like to change your notification settings for:

▸ **devopscloud**

   Email me when...

   ☑ There are updates from my groups (daily)

   ☑ I receive a message in my inbox ⓘ Learn more

   ☑ I get new followers

   ☑ I install a new application

   ☑ I log in from somewhere new

   ☑ Someone invites me to a group

   ☑ Someone likes messages I posted (daily)

   ☑ Someone requests to join a private group I administer

   ☑ There are highlights from groups I haven't joined (weekly)

   ☑ There are new suggestions for people to follow (weekly)

   There is new activity in the following groups:

   To stay updated on your communities, admins may still send announcement notifications by email. Learn more.

   ☐ All Company

Figure 5.30 – Configuring notifications for Yammer

4. Once notifications are configured, you can create communities by clicking on **Create a Community**. Communities are logical groups that people can follow and get notified on the posts and feeds in that community. Users can set the privacy setting of the community to make it available as a public or private community.

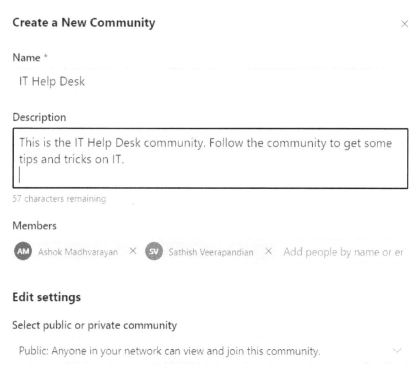

Create a New Community   ✕

Name *

IT Help Desk

Description

This is the IT Help Desk community. Follow the community to get some
tips and tricks on IT.

57 characters remaining

Members

(AM) Ashok Madhvarayan ✕ (SV) Sathish Veerapandian ✕ Add people by name or er

Edit settings

Select public or private community

Public: Anyone in your network can view and join this community.   ⌄

Figure 5.31 – Creating a new community

5. Users can also search for and join new communities that are open to everyone.
    Click on **Communities** on the left navigation pane and you can see all the
    communities in your organization. Click and join to get instant updates and
    notifications.

Figure 5.32 – Searching for and joining a community

6. Users can also search for answers by directly typing any keywords into the search bar available on the home page. This helps users to get to the information that they need and start collaborating. Based on the search result, users can follow the community or the user who has already posted about the search keyword. This helps you find experts in your organization and follow their feeds.

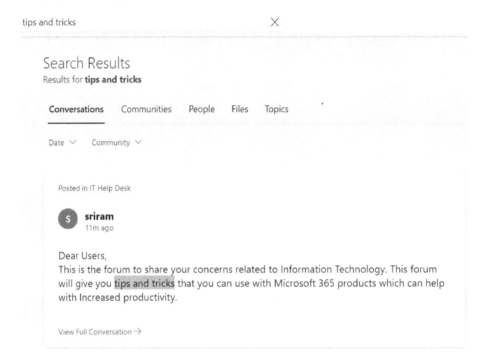

Figure 5.33 – Keyword-based search

7. Users can join in conversations, reply to any posts, like posts, and mention others in any conversation. Emoji responses help to gain more insights from users.

Figure 5.34 – Replying, mentioning, and liking comments

8. When any users like a comment or reply to a feed, the author of the post will be notified via their inbox in Yammer and also via Outlook.

Figure 5.35 – Notifications in the Yammer inbox

9. Yammer also allows you to create polls and post questions and answers to get votes from other users.

10. Users can praise a collaborator for the contribution they have made to any work. To do this, at the top of the home page, select **Praise**, type in a comment, and tag people so that others in the organization know about the work done by the employee. Appreciation motivates users to achieve more in their day-to-day work.

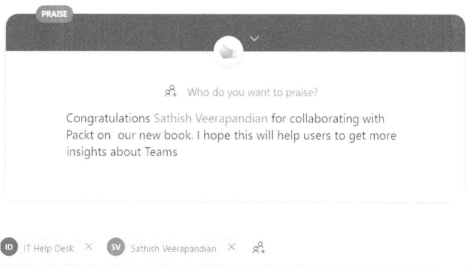

Figure 5.36 – Sending praise to a colleague

Yammer helps you to stay connected with your organization and bridge the gap between employees who may be physically separated by thousands of miles to exchange ideas, which brings innovation to the person or the organization. In an enterprise, data is key, so the organization needs to protect their company data. Yammer as a social engagement platform is built on top of Azure and enterprise-grade security is still applicable. Once Yammer is successfully deployed in your organization, this automatically improves the communication between employees.

In the next section, we will discuss the Teams federation options available in Microsoft Teams and the interoperability with Skype for Business. This helps internal users in your organization to collaborate with external users from other organizations. This may be highly useful in projects where there is vendor engagement, and they would need to access your internal resources.

External access and guest access to Microsoft Teams

External access in Microsoft Teams can be achieved in two ways. If the scope is limited only to chats and calls, then external access should be okay to allow. However, if users want to have complete collaboration capabilities to give access to channels and files in channels, then Azure AD guest access is the right choice. The following table helps you to better understand how to choose between guest and external access.

> **Note**
> It is highly recommended to go through the following table as when we are elevating privileges to a third-party member outside the organization, wrong access would cause data leakage, which can cause disaster for an organization.

Privileges for internal users:

Users can	External access users	Guests
Chat with someone in another organization	Yes	Yes
Call someone in another organization	Yes	Yes
See whether someone from another organization is available for a call or chat	Yes	Yes (1)
Search for people in other organizations	Yes (2)	No
Share files	No	Yes
See the out-of-office message of someone in another organization	No	Yes
Block someone in another organization	No	Yes
Use @mentions	Yes (3)	Yes

Privileges for external users:

People outside your organization can	External access users	Guests
Access Teams resources	No	Yes
Be added to a group chat	Yes	Yes
Be invited to a meeting	Yes	Yes
Make private calls	Yes	Yes (5)
View the phone number for dial-in meeting participants	No (4)	Yes
Use IP video	Yes	Yes (5)
Use screen sharing	Yes (3)	Yes (5)
Use meet now	No	Yes (5)
Edit sent messages	Yes (3)	Yes (5)
Delete sent messages	Yes (3)	Yes (5)
Use GIPHY in conversations	Yes (3)	Yes (5)
Use memes in conversations	Yes (3)	Yes (5)
Use stickers in conversations	Yes (3)	Yes (5)
Presence is displayed	Yes	Yes
Use @mentions	Yes (3)	Yes

The following are the **limitations** for the previously mentioned features of guest and external access:

1. The user must have been been added as a guest and is signed in with the guest account.
2. Only by email or **Session Initiation Protocol** (**SIP**) address.
3. Supported for 1:1 chat for Teams-only to Teams-only users from two different organizations.
4. By default, external participants can't see the phone numbers of dialed-in participants.
5. Allowed by default, but can be turned off by the Teams admin.

External access is enabled by default in Microsoft Teams, which means users can search for external users outside the organization and if the other organization has allowed external access, they can collaborate directly. Teams administrators can control the settings via the Teams admin center to decide whether they would like to allow or block all domains or allow or block certain domains. Users can verify with the Teams administrator their external access configuration before they collaborate with a user from another organization:

1. Log in to the Teams admin center as a global administrator or Teams administrator.

2. Click on **Users** on the left pane and select **External access**, then select the appropriate option for your organization from the dropdown.

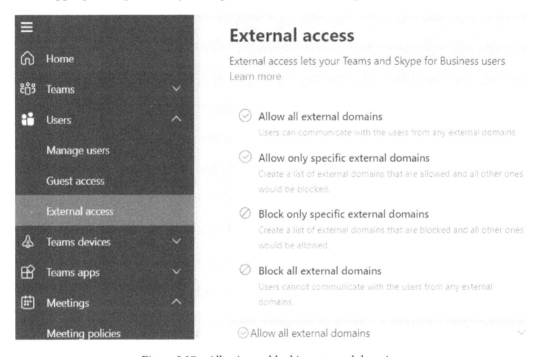

Figure 5.37 – Allowing or blocking external domains

Guest access

As you can see from the preceding table, guest access elevates more privileges to your organization for external users. Guest access allows users to gain access to your internal teams, documents inside channels, resources, chats, and organization applications. There are more settings to be turned on for users to be able to invite guests. Users should be cautious before providing guest access to external users. Users should reach out to IT admins and verify whether guest access is allowed or blocked.

One added benefit of guest access over external access is that guest accounts are available in your Azure AD as a guest, hence the Conditional Access policies that are being applied to secure your infrastructure apply to the guest user, which prevents potential data leakage.

The following steps will help you to set up guest access in Azure AD:

1. Configure the Azure AD external collaboration settings by logging in to Azure AD as a global administrator. Click on **Azure Active Directory** on the left pane, then select **External Identities | External Collaboration**. Ensure the settings on this page are set so guest access is not being blocked. Microsoft provides feedback on the privileges obtained by selecting each option.

2. **Under Guest invite settings, select Member users and users assigned to specific admin roles can invite guest users including guests with member permissions.**

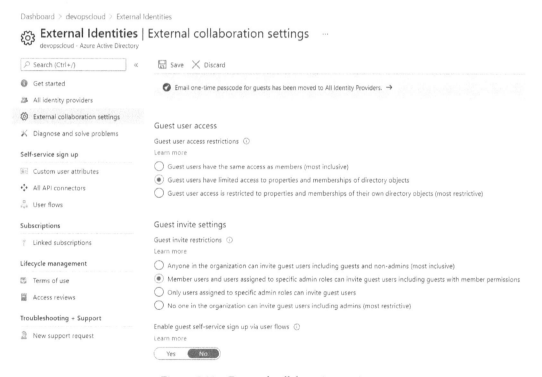

Figure 5.38 – External collaboration settings

3. Once the external sharing is configured, allow guest access in Teams. Guest access in Teams can be allowed by logging in to the Teams admin center as a global or Teams administrator and clicking on **Users | Guest access** on the left pane.

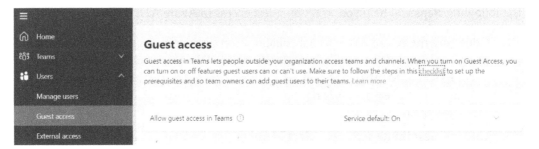

Figure 5.39 – Allowing guest access in Microsoft Teams

4. Teams uses Microsoft 365 groups for team membership; Microsoft 365 groups should be allowed to accept group members outside your organization.

5. Log in to the Office 365 admin center, click **Settings | Org Settings | Microsoft 365 Groups**, and ensure the **Let group owners add people outside your organization to Microsoft 365 Groups as guests** and **Let guest group members access group content** checkboxes are both checked.

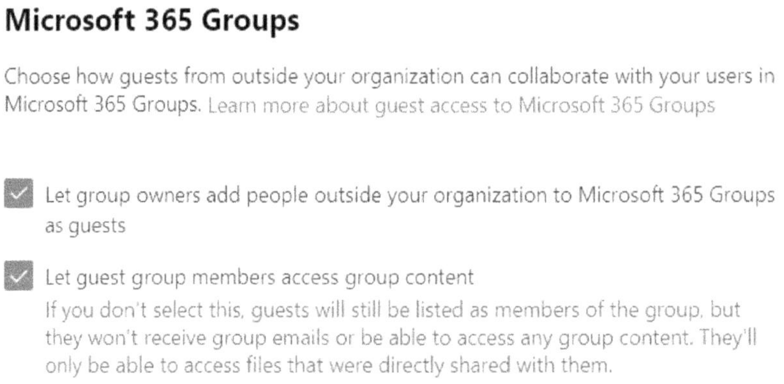

Microsoft 365 Groups

Choose how guests from outside your organization can collaborate with your users in Microsoft 365 Groups. Learn more about guest access to Microsoft 365 Groups

☑ Let group owners add people outside your organization to Microsoft 365 Groups as guests

☑ Let guest group members access group content
If you don't select this, guests will still be listed as members of the group, but they won't receive group emails or be able to access any group content. They'll only be able to access files that were directly shared with them.

Figure 5.40 – Allowing guest access in Microsoft 365 groups

6. Finally, enable SharePoint organization-level sharing settings that allow guests to have access to Teams channels as Teams uses SharePoint sites at the backend. This setting is applicable for the complete SharePoint configuration and is not limited to Teams.

7. To configure SharePoint settings, please log in to the Office 365 admin center as a global administrator or SharePoint administrator and click on **Policies | Sharing**. Ensure **Anyone** and **Guest** are selected.

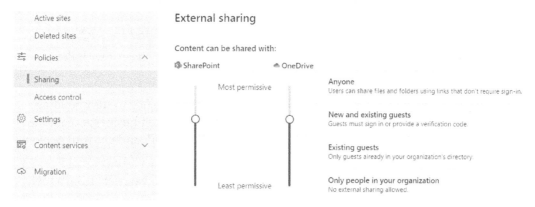

Figure 5.41 – Allowing guest access in Microsoft 365 groups

Once the preceding configuration is done, users will be able to invite guests to collaborate in their company workspace.

Note

Guest access can be reviewed by setting up a guest review in Azure AD. Admins must do access reviews for guest accounts as per the standards they follow for other user access reviews.

In the next section, we will discuss Microsoft Sway. Sway helps you to build modern, customized, and interactive reports, personal stories, and presentations. In this section, we will set up Sway.

Microsoft Sway

Sway helps users to create reports, presentations, and newsletters in a modern way. Sway helps users to check for sources online related to the content they are working on and import them into Sway. Sway also allows users to create Sways directly on the web where there is no requirement to have a licensed product. Once a Sway has been created, the recipients just need a web browser to see the Sways; no licensed product is required. Sway has built-in layouts, which save a lot of time for users as they can select a template that matches their requirements. Sway also allows you to completely customize your layout if you are not satisfied with the predefined one. You can import images, video, and Office documents to merge them into one Sway.

> **Note**
>
> Sway is free to use for anyone and does not require an Office 365 license. Sway can also be used with your personal Microsoft account (Hotmail and Outlook accounts) and does not require your business accounts to be used while logging in.

Please follow these steps to log in and create your first Sway and share it with the intended people:

1. To get started, please visit `https://sway.office.com/my` to start building Sways. As mentioned, you can use your personal or Microsoft business account to log in. It is better to use the business account for official work and use your personal account for personal Sways.

2. On the welcome page, you have the option to create a new Sway, start from a topic, or start from a document:

    I. **Create New** allows users to create a new Sway, add content manually, and define personalized layouts.

    II. **Start from a topic** allows users to search for a topic on the internet and import content directly from the web sources, and then customize content based on the needs, use advanced Sway features on the content, and use a customized layout.

    III. **Start from a document** allows users to upload a document into Sway that reads the content from the document and imports it into Sway. Once imported, you can modify the content using advanced Sway features.

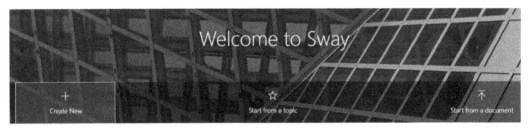

Figure 5.42 – Sway options

3. On the welcome page, you also have the option to select predefined templates. If you don't have prior experience with designing, you can select a template and start customizing the content. For example, if you would like to build a business presentation, you can click on a suitable template and Sway will prepare the template in the background for you to add your content.

Start from a template

Get inspired by a featured Sway

Figure 5.43 – Predefined templates in Sway

4. For demo purposes, I have imported a Word document with content into Sway and started designing with the options available. Once the document is imported into Sway, you can design the layout and modify the content.

Figure 5.44 – Importing a Word document into Sway

5. Start Sway by importing an image as a logo for the Sway. The beauty here is that Microsoft understands the content on your document with their powerful algorithms and suggests content from the internet. Click on **Drag an image here** and on the right side, you will see the suggestions.

Figure 5.45 – Importing image into Sway

6. If you already have a customized image, Sway allows you to import it from your computer, OneDrive, Flickr, or YouTube. Click on the suggested dropdown in the top-right corner and it will show you various sources you can import an image from.

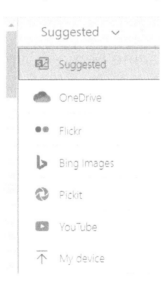

Figure 5.46 – Importing images manually

7. Once the image is imported, you can configure focus points to be visible on the thumbnail of the Sway. To do so, click on **Focus Points** in the top-right corner, which will allow you to open the image and mark the key areas on the image so that it will be well accommodated into the thumbnail. You can even select the entire image if required.

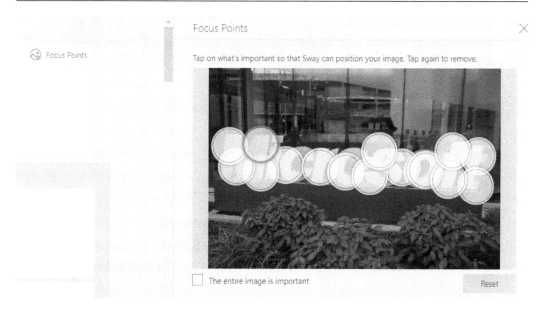

Figure 5.47 – Configuring focus points

8. Users can use the **Emphasize, Accent, Bullets, Numbers,** and **Link** options or even modify the fonts options to enhance the content.

Microsoft   Teams   is a hub for teamwork in Office 365. A key part of being successful in collaborative work is to stay on top of all the meeting schedules and *manage* them promptly without any overlap. Microsoft   *Teams helps you to meet smarter and to have focused meetings which can eventually increase users' productivity*.

1. Microsoft Teams delivers a unique end-to-end meeting experience that features the human element of face-to-face   Interaction, while helping people stay focused before, during, and after meetings to accomplish more together. Meetings in an enterprise have changed drastically, with the majority of the workforce connecting remotely, and, in this topic, we will cover the key features that are available in Microsoft Teams.

This chapter will cover the following main topics:

*   The various meeting options available in Microsoft Teams to schedule or join meetings
*   Creating survey, polls, Customer Feedback, Employee Satisfaction via Microsoft Forms
*   Seamless document meeting notes via Microsoft One   Note
*   Channel Calendar to stay up to date on a particular Teams channel
*   How Microsoft Bookings helps in organizing meetings and appointments with stakeholders

Upon successful completion of these topics and getting hands on with a few practice scenarios, you will be fully comfortable in managing your meetings effectively with Microsoft Teams.

Figure 5.48 – Content modification

9. Users can click on the + icon under every slide and upload various file formats, such as **Image**, **Video**, and **Audio**, and upload a slide show to make their Sways more interactive.

Figure 5.49 – Other file types supported in Sway

10. Once the Sway is created, you can click on the **Play** button in the top-right corner of the Sway home page to go through the full preview and edit it if there are any modifications.

11. Post finalizing the Sway, we can click on **Share** in the top-right corner and share the Sway with selected groups or the whole organization, so anyone using the same organization account can see the Sway or share it anonymously. If shared anonymously, anyone with the link can open the Sway. We can also control whether viewers can edit or view the file.

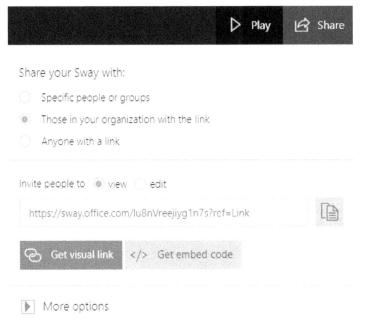

Figure 5.50 – Sharing the Sway

In this section, we have built a model Sway and covered all the options available in Sway to build an interactive report or stories. Sway is a completely on-the-web platform, so anyone can see Sways on the go if they have valid permissions.

Summary

In this chapter, we discussed group chats, which allow you to message multiple recipients in Teams without creating a channel. Stream allows you to create enterprise-class video content for your organization. Yammer is an enterprise social media platform and provides external federation options with Teams. Sway helps you to build interactive Sways, which is the new, modern way of building presentations. These tools are highly effective once you start using them as these products are tightly integrated to enable effective user communication.

In the next chapter, you will learn more about organizing virtual events via Teams, where you can explore webinar options available in Teams, live events, and lobby configuration, which are relatively new services added to the Microsoft Teams feature list.

6
Organize Virtual Events

Virtual events are events that involve people interacting in a virtual environment rather than at a physical location such as an office or a meeting room. The Virtual Events is otherwise termed as an **online event**. Virtual events are extremely popular now, in this new era of remote working. These events are not limited to the geographical location of the attendees as they happen over the internet. Virtual events could include webinars, training, conferences, live events, and much more.

Organizing these events takes great skill as it involves many factors, such as promoting the event, knowing the target audience, setting the goal, providing a clear agenda, engaging attendees, and many others.

By now, you know that MS Teams is a great tool for collaboration. MS Teams also provides an option for organizing live events, which can be internal to the organization, or even with external participants.

We will have the following objectives in this chapter:

- Teams live events
- Webinars
- The new Teams view-only experience
- Advanced Communication license (customize the lobby and meeting limit)
- Custom image branding experience

By the end of this chapter, you will be able to organize virtual events for your organization.

Technical requirements

To get started with our practice, we recommend signing up for an Office 365 trial subscription, following the steps that are mentioned in our main index. All Microsoft applications and configurations must be enabled by your administrator.

Teams live events

Live events in MS Teams are a feature for setting up a broadcast meeting. Live events are used for one-to-many communication. Unlike regular meetings, these live events aren't meant for collaboration. Instead, they are used for broadcasting information to large audiences. With that said, live events can accommodate 10,000 participants. During this pandemic time, the limit has been increased to 20,000 until the end of January 2022. In live events, attendees wouldn't be able to interact except for Q&A (if enabled). An example of when MS Teams live events would be useful in an organization is when an executive would like to share important announcements with all their employees.

There are certain roles to be understood for the effective usage of MS Teams live events. Let's learn about the roles involved in live events:

- **Organizers**: Organizers are the ones who schedule the live events, configure the live event settings, invite attendees, and assign roles such as producers or presenters.
- **Producers**: A user who is assigned this role is a host of the meeting who can share videos, desktops, and control attendee settings such as muting all participants. They can start and end the live event, and much more.

- **Presenters**: Users assigned this role can present audio, video, screen sharing, and can moderate Q&A in the live event.

- **Attendees**: Attendees are the users who receive the live event meeting and join it from their MS Teams app. External users can also be an attendee of the live event if the live event has been configured to allow external participants.

The following table provides information on the supported platform for joining MS Teams live events.

Role	Desktop	Web	iPad	Mobile
Producer	Yes	No	No	No
Presenter	Yes	No	Yes	No
Attendee	Yes	Yes	Yes	Yes

Table 6.1 – Supported platforms

So, now let's look at the types of live events available in MS Teams:

- **MS Teams app**: The first one is using the MS Teams app for audio and video, which uses the laptop/desktop webcam and audio devices. This is like the regular team meeting option, which is also available for live events. Producers and presenters of the live event can use the MS Teams app available on their desktop/laptop to get the full features of the live event, and attendees can join from any of their devices, such as desktop, mobile, and more, as stated in *Table 6.1*.

- **An external app or device**: This option is used when the content of the live event needs to be produced from various sources. This method uses an encoder that compresses the audio and video and sends that to **MS Stream**. MS Stream is an enterprise video service that can be used to upload, view, and share videos. Your MS Teams administrator needs to assign an MS Stream license and configure the supported encoder for this option to be used for live events. For instance, an encoder such as Wirecast can be used for the live streaming of the event using MS Stream.

We now have an idea of what exactly an MS Teams live event is, its usage, roles, and the types available. Let's now walk through the steps involved in setting up a live event.

Scheduling

The first step is to schedule the live event. This needs to be done by the organizer of the event:

1. Navigate to the **Calendar** option on the left pane of MS Teams, click on the drop-down option next to **New Meeting** and select **Live event**.

Figure 6.2 – Live event navigation

2. Once you click on **Live event**, a window opens with options that look similar to when you're setting up regular meetings.

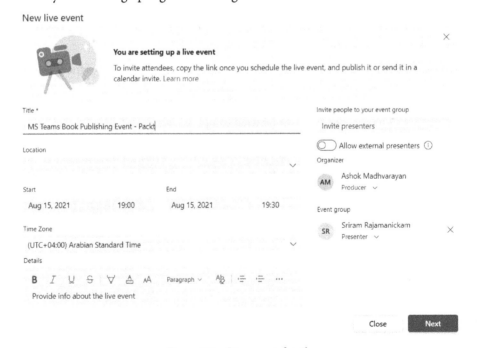

Figure 6.3 – Live event details

This is the first page of the live event scheduling, and the following details can be configured:

- **Title**: Name of the event.

- **Location**: Event location details.

- **Start** and **End** date and time of the live event.

- **Time Zone**: You can select your time zone for this meeting.

- **Details**: Additional details to be provided or an agenda for this live event.

- **Invite people to your event group**: You can add additional producers or presenters for the live event. Make sure to add people here for hosting, presenting, and moderating the Q&A in the event.

- **Allow external presenters**: You can turn this on if your MS Teams administrator has configured it.

3. Once the details are added, click on **Next** to look at the options available.

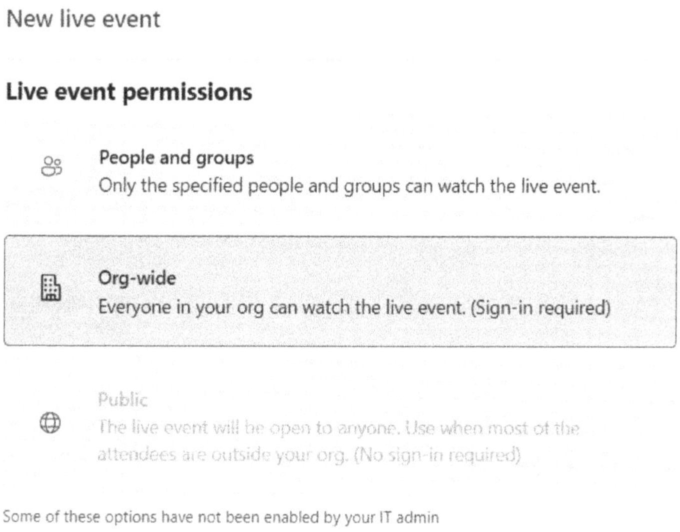

Figure 6.4 – Live event permissions

4. Live event permissions decide the attendees:

    •   **People and groups**: Select this option if the live event is restricted to a specific group of people.

    •   **Org-wide**: Choose this option if this event is to be available to everyone in your organization.

    •   **Public**: If there is a requirement to invite attendees from outside the organization, select this option. Your MS Teams administrator must enable this option.

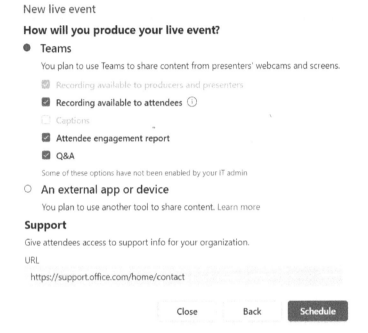

Figure 6.5 – Live event settings – Teams option

Here, you can choose options such as making the meeting recording available to all attendees, enabling Q&A in the event to address any queries raised by the attendees, reports for the Microsoft Teams administrator to review about the live event, and adding support information.

5. If you choose **An external app or device**, the following options will be available:

How will you produce your live event?

○   Teams

   You plan to use Teams to share content from presenters' webcams and screens.

●   An external app or device

   You plan to use another tool to share content. Learn more

   ✓ Recording available to attendees ⓘ

   ☑ Captions (available after the event)

   Spoken language English (United States) ∨

   ☑ Q&A

Some of these options have not been enabled by your IT admin

Figure 6.6 – External app or device option

6. Once you have selected your option, click on **Schedule**. Here, I will be choosing the **Teams** option. You will be prompted with the live event details as shown in the next screenshot:

MS Teams Book Publishing Event - Packt

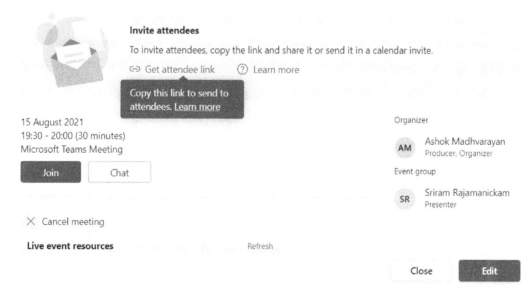

Invite attendees

To invite attendees, copy the link and share it or send it in a calendar invite.

⊖ Get attendee link   ⑦ Learn more

Copy this link to send to
attendees. Learn more

15 August 2021
19:30 - 20:00 (30 minutes)
Microsoft Teams Meeting

| Join | Chat |

✕ Cancel meeting

Live event resources   Refresh

Organizer

AM   Ashok Madhvarayan
     Producer, Organizer

Event group

SR   Sriram Rajamanickam
     Presenter

| Close | Edit |

Figure 6.7 – Live event details

7. You can click on the **Get attendee link** option to copy the live event link, which can then be sent to the attendees.

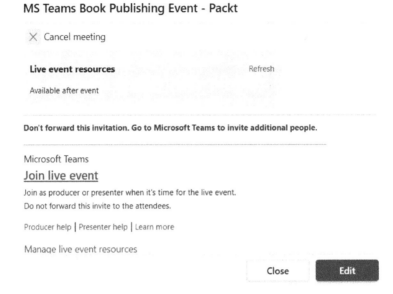

Figure 6.8 – Live event join link

You can click on **Edit** and modify any of the listed settings if required.

Inviting attendees

As the organizer of the live event, you have now created the live event with the required producer and presenter. It's time now to send this invite to all the attendees. We must use MS Teams or Outlook (email application) to send this information to the attendees.

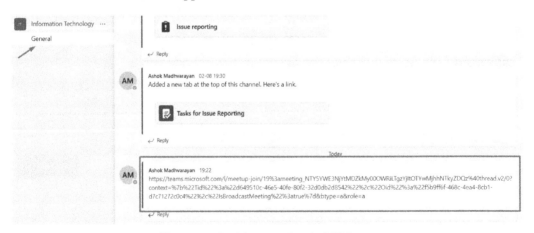

Figure 6.9 – Inviting attendees in MS Teams

If you have an org-wide MS Teams app, you can paste the link copied from the live event and send it in the conversation in the Teams channel or use an email application such as Outlook to send invites.

Producing or presenting the live event

Click on the live event link and select **Join now**. At the top of the invite, it should say **Join as a producer**.

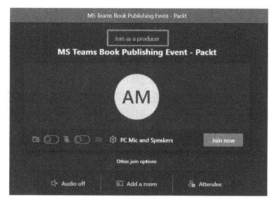

Figure 6.10 – Join live event as a producer

The next screenshot is the producer view of the live event in which the majority of the options are controlled. In this, the producer can turn on video/audio options, share content, mute all attendees, and review the Q&A.

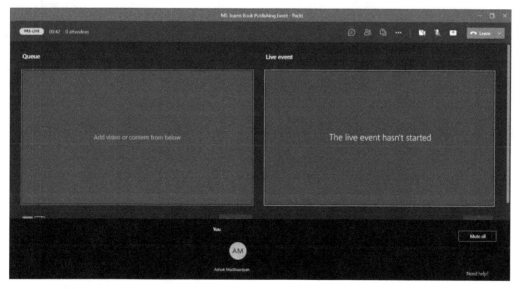

Figure 6.11 – Producer view of the live event

Let's start the event by sharing the content. Once you have selected the content, it will be available on the left side and once you are ready, click on **Send live**. Content will now be available on the right side with the option to **Start**. Once you click on it, the live event will be started.

Figure 6.12 – Sharing content in the live event

It's important to note that once you click on **Start**, you can't restart it. Options available are **Leave** and **End**. So, please make sure everything is ready before you click on **Start**.

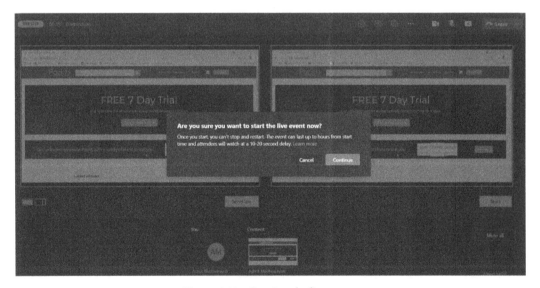

Figure 6.13 – Starting the live event

At the top, you will notice that the status has changed from **PRE-LIVE** to **LIVE** with the number of attendees.

Figure 6.14 – Live event – confirmation

Attendees view of the live event

So far, we have seen the producer's view of the live event and the options available. Let's now look at the attendees' view of the event. As an attendee of the live event, you can watch the live event, participate in the Q&A, and configure your device settings for better audio and video quality (audio and video are only to hear and watch the live event). You can also join the live event using the Microsoft Teams desktop application, web browser, or even using the Microsoft Teams app on mobile devices.

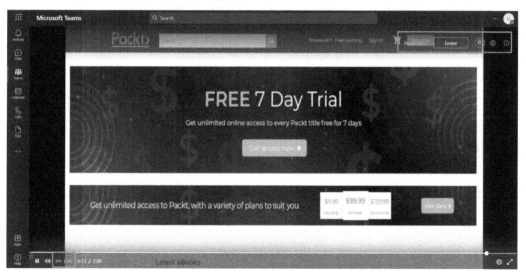

Figure 6.15 – Attendees view of the live event

Ending the live event

Stop sharing any content before you end the event. Once done, click on **End** in the event. You will notice that the status will change from **LIVE** to **ENDED** at the top left of the event.

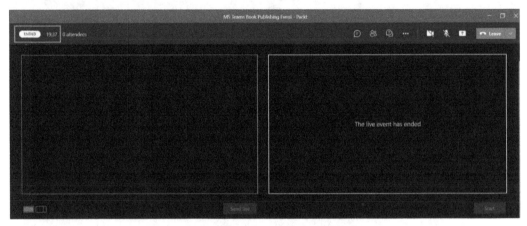

Figure 6.16 – Ending the live event

As a producer, you have the option to download the Q&A reports and recordings. Navigate to the live event meeting invite in the Teams calendar and open the event.

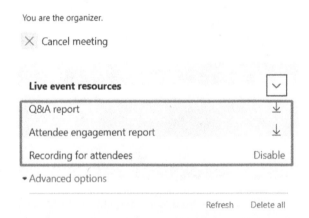

Figure 6.17 – Live event resources

Great, you have now learned about the life cycle of an MS Teams live event right from scheduling till ending the event. You are also aware of the different roles and types of live events. Let's move on to the next topic, in which you will learn about webinars.

Webinars

Webinars are a recent feature that has been added to MS Teams. Unlike live events, webinars can be used for collaboration with an audience, however, this can be controlled as well. Webinars have a great feature: **registration forms**, where attendees must fill in their details before attending. An example of when it could be used is for training, where the trainer would like to get details of the students enrolled in the webinar and to allow the students to interact when required during the webinar.

Let's explore the roles involved in the webinar:

- **Organizer**: The organizer is the one who plans, schedules, configures, and adds more presenters to the webinar, and sends invites to the attendees. Also, the organizer can view the registration report.

- **Attendees**: These are the participants who register themselves using the registration link and get an email invitation to join the webinar.

Scheduling a webinar

Now, let's explore the steps involved in the successful creation of the webinar:

1. To schedule the webinar, navigate to the Teams calendar, click on the **New meeting** dropdown and select **Webinar**.

Figure 6.18 – Navigating to the Webinar option

2. A new window opens with the options to schedule the webinar.

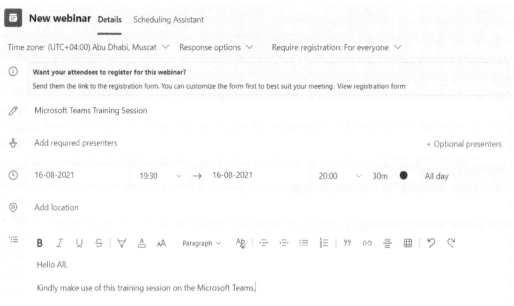

Figure 6.19 – New webinar Details

3. Most of the options are similar to scheduling a Teams meeting:

-   **Title**: Webinar title.

-   **Optional presenters**: You can add optional presenters who can organize/present in the webinar.

-   **Time**: The time and date of the webinar.

-   **Location**: A location can be added, if there is one.

-   **More Information**: Additional notes to the attendees can be added here.

4. You may wonder whether this is the same as a regular Teams meeting, and if not, then what's the difference? Here is the key feature of webinars, which is the **Registration** option.

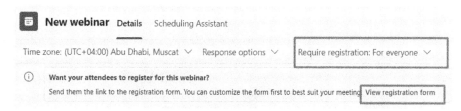

Figure 6.20 – Registration settings

5. Once you have filled in all the meeting details, you can click on **View registration form**, which will open a new window like the following screenshot:

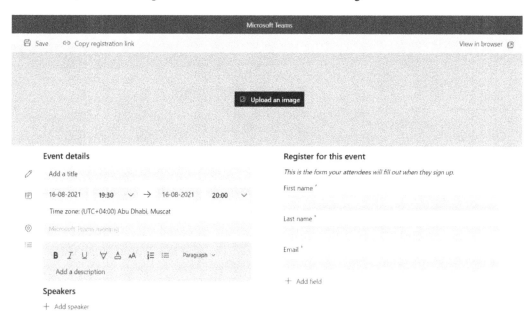

Figure 6.21 – Registration form

6. You can fill in the details, add an image, provide details about the speaker, and even customize the field for the registration on the right side, which the attendees will use to fill in their details. By default, attendees need to fill in **First name**, **Last name**, and **Email**, but you also have an option to add more fields.

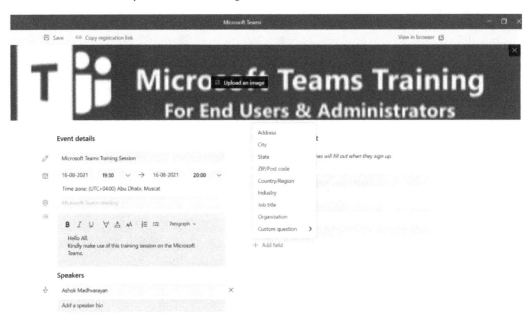

Figure 6.22 – Registration form information

7. Once you have provided all the information, click on **Save** at the top left. You can preview using the **View in browser option**.

8. Great, now you have scheduled the webinar. You can copy the link using **Copy registration link** and share it with the attendees using MS Teams, email using Outlook, or through company portals.

Figure 6.23 – Copying the registration link

Once the link has been shared, attendees will click on the link and land on the following page.

Figure 6.24 – Attendees registration page

9. Attendees must provide **First name**, **Last name**, and **Email** to register now. Once done, they will receive an email notification for the webinar.

Figure 6.25 – Attendee registration confirmation

10. The next screenshot is the email confirmation that will be received by the attendees upon registration.

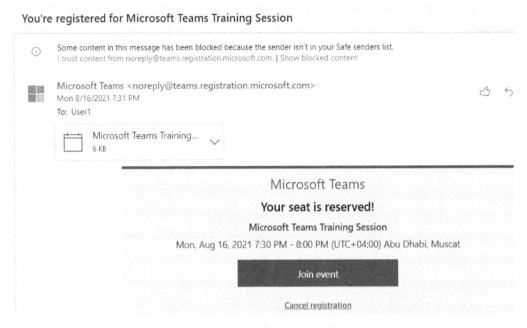

Figure 6.26 – Email confirmation to the attendee

That's perfect.

Hosting the webinar

So, now we have learned about scheduling and registering for the webinar. Let's explore the options available in the webinar:

1. Once you join the webinar as an attendee, you will be waiting in the lobby until the organizer approves.

Figure 6.27 – Attendee joining the webinar

2. As an organizer of the webinar, you need to approve the attendees waiting in the lobby before starting the event. So, for this, the organizer can join a bit early in the webinar and can also wait for 2-3 minutes before everyone joins the webinar.

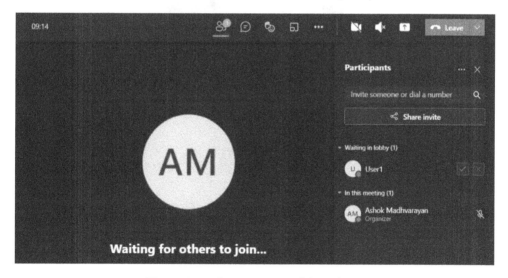

Figure 6.28 – Organizer view of the webinar

3. As an organizer, you can control the attendee's options in the meeting. You can click on **More options** next to the attendee's name and options are available as shown in the next figure.

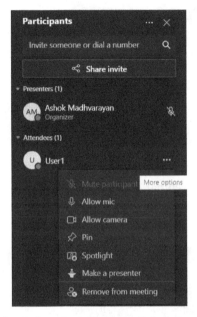

Figure 6.29 – Controlling the attendee's collaboration in the webinar

4. Organizers can customize webinars with options such as enabling full screen, turning on background images, recording, and much more, as shown in the following figure:

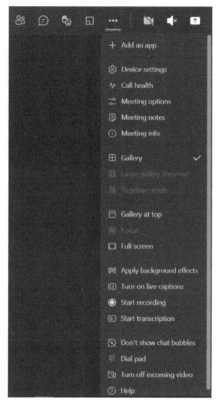

Figure 6.30 – Webinar settings

5. Once you are at the end of the session and would like to get feedback from the attendees on the event, you can create a poll and send this to the Teams channel. To do so, navigate to your Teams calendar, click on the webinar event, and select **Chat with participants**.

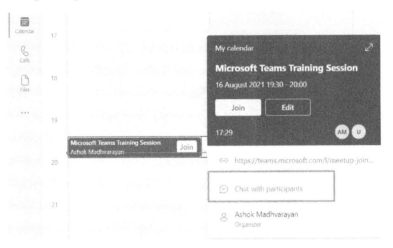

Figure 6.31 – Chat with participants

6. This will open a new chat in Teams with the title of the webinar. Click on the + symbol.

Figure 6.32 – Adding a new form to the webinar chat

7. Search for **Forms** and click on **Add**.

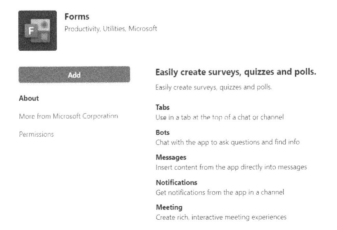

Figure 6.33 – Adding a form

8. This will add a new tab to the Teams webinar chat called **Polls**. Click on **Create New Poll**.

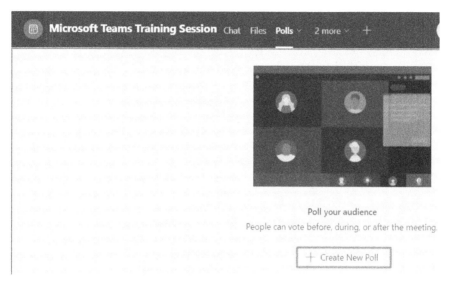

Figure 6.34 – Create New Poll

9. You can choose from the default poll templates or create a new one.

Figure 6.35 – Poll options

You can also select multiple answers if you like, or you can add additional options as well.

Figure 6.36 – Poll settings

10. Once done, click on **Save**. Once done, you will see that a new option, **Polls**, has been added to the webinar. Once reviewed, click on **Launch** to add the poll to the webinar chat.

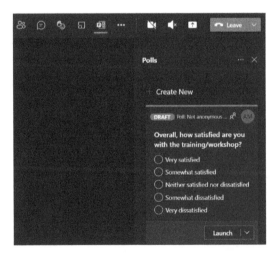

Figure 6.37 – Launching a poll in a webinar

11. Attendees will receive a notification in the participant's chat with the poll question. You can select an option and click on **Submit Vote**.

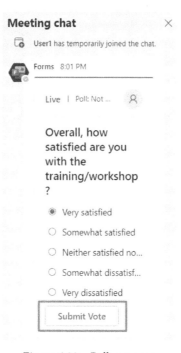

Figure 6.38 – Poll response

The organizer can view the results in the webinar chat.

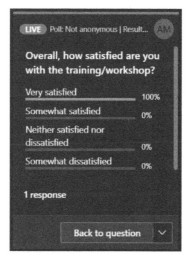

Figure 6.39 – Poll results

12. Once done, you can click on **End meeting** to end this webinar.

Figure 6.40 – Ending the webinar

13. After you end the meeting, you can go back to your Teams calendar and open the webinar meeting event. You can see the registered attendees, attendance, polls, and much more.

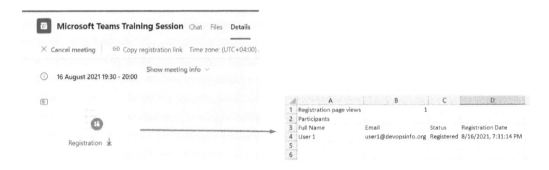

Figure 6.41 – Registered attendee's details

14. Click on the **Attendance** tab to check how many attendees there were and how long they were in the webinar by checking the duration.

Figure 6.42 – Attendees' attendance

That's great. Now you have learned about the webinar feature in MS Teams. You can use this based on your organization's needs. Just remember, this webinar can support up to 1,000 collaborative attendees. In the next section, we will learn about the Teams **view-only experience**.

The new Teams view-only experience

MS Teams meetings have a limit of 1,000 interactive users, which means that attendees can experience all features of the meetings such as audio, video, shared content, and more, once enabled in that meeting. This may lead to the following questions for MS Teams users, specifically in the new work culture of remote working:

- What happens if there are more than 1,000 attendees?

- Is it a hardcoded limit of 1,000?

Microsoft has addressed these questions by adding a feature called the view-only experience. With this new view-only experience, a Teams meeting can have up to 10,000 attendees. Wow, that's great news!

Please note that your MS Teams administrator needs to enable this option.

Let's explore what exactly this view-only experience means from an attendee's point of view:

- If the meeting capacity has been reached, meaning there are 1,000 attendees in a meeting, a participant who joins after this will get a popup reading **The meeting has reached capacity. You are joining in view-only mode**. Additionally, you will see **Your audio and video have been disabled because the meeting has reached capacity**.

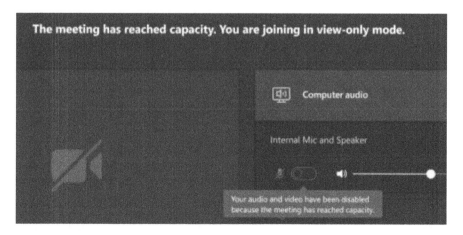

Figure 6.43 – Notification of view-only mode

Once you click on **Join now**, you will get the following experience:

- Your audio and video will be disabled.

- You will be able to listen to the presenter or speaker of the meeting.

- You will be able to see the video of the presenter.

- You will be able to see the content being shared in the meeting.

Although it is a great feature to accommodate more participants, there are some limitations that attendees cannot experience when joining in view-only mode. Some of them are as follows:

- Like audio and video, attendees cannot see or participate in chat.

- Attendees cannot join the meeting and will be waiting in the lobby until the organizer approves.

- Attendees will see one screen at a time, which means viewing either the video or content that is being shared.

- Different meeting view experiences will not be available, such as in a gallery view, the large gallery view will not be available in the meeting.

So, we have seen the experience from an attendee's standpoint. Let's explore the experiences of a presenter or an organizer.

Both the organizer and the presenter of the meeting will get the following notification:

This meeting has reached capacity. Participants who will join now will have view-only access.

One of the great pieces of news is that, as an organizer of the meeting, you always have the full interactive experience even if you leave and re-join the meeting later. This means that an organizer will have a guaranteed place in the meeting.

However, this does not apply to the presenter. The presenter should join the meeting before it reaches capacity because a presenter who joins the meeting after it reaches capacity will also have a view-only experience.

Some of the limitations for the presenters and organizers are as follows:

- They cannot see or get the attendance report of the attendees who joined in view-only mode.

- They cannot promote any view-only attendee to the main meeting to get the full experience.
- Similarly, they cannot remove view-only attendees.

Though there are some limitations for attendees, presenters, and organizers of the meeting, this is a great feature that organizations can use to conduct Teams meetings. In the next section, we will explore the newly added Advanced Communications license.

Advanced Communications license

Advanced Communications is an add-on that has been added to provide more features to enhance meetings and communication using MS Teams.

Let's explore the features provided by this add-on:

- We can add 20,000 attendees to meetings or events using this add-on.
- This add-on can also help in organizing concurrent events (up to 50).
- Another great feature is that event duration can now be 16 hours using this add-on.

Wow, that's great. This can be used by organizations when there is a need for running long events, covering a greater number of attendees, and concurrent events.

This add-on also provides more features to your MS Teams administrator, which are listed here:

- The company's logo can be added to the Teams meeting, which provides attendees with a custom branded meeting lobby experience.
- Custom policy packages can be created and assigned to the users.
- It can help in monitoring, tracking, and analyzing data on the users' devices.
- There is a compliance recording option through APIs.

Policy packages are created by your Teams administrator to control the Teams features in your organization. This could be a calling policy, event policy, and more.

Please note that at the time of writing this book, this add-on is not yet available to our organization's tenant. Kindly contact your Teams administrator to purchase this add-on if your business needs features provided by this add-on. Now we know that an Advanced Communications license is an add-on that provides enhanced meeting features and customizations. Let's explore one of the customizations provided by this add-on, which is called the custom image branding experience, in the next topic.

The custom image branding experience

As the name states, this is a feature to provide a custom feel to your meeting attendees. This feature is part of the aforementioned **Advanced Communications add-on**. Using this feature, you can provide different meeting experiences to your attendees.

You might be wondering what exactly this feature does. It provides an option to upload your company logo to your MS Teams admin portal, which appears on the meeting pre-join and lobby screens of meetings.

Great, but how is this done? You can share your company logo with your MS Teams administrator and the administrator uploads it using the following option and assigns it to you:

1. As a Teams administrator, log in to the MS Teams admin portal, navigate to **Meetings** in the left pane, and select **Customization policies**.

2. Click on **Add**, upload the company logo, and click on **Save**.

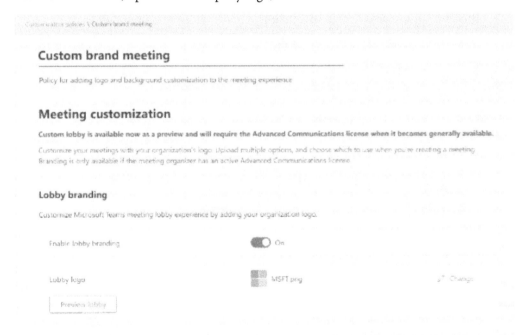

Figure 6.44 – Lobby branding option

3. You also have an option to preview the lobby. Once done, you can assign this policy to your users.

Great, now you know how to provide a different experience for your Teams meetings using the custom image branding experience and with the help of your MS Teams administrator.

Summary

We have now reached the end of this chapter on organizing virtual events in MS Teams. As stated earlier, we hope that you are now comfortable with organizing live events and conducting webinars with different roles involved in them. Based on your organization's business needs, you can plan for organizing virtual events that provide a better experience to all your users.

In the next chapter, you will be learning about an important aspect of MS Teams, which is security. You will learn about sharing documents securely, handling different types of access, and much more.

Section 3 – All about Security, Client Automation, Teams Etiquette, and Tips and Tricks

Security plays a major role in avoiding any data breaches and leaking any important confidential company data, so we will cover some tips on the topic. Apart from that, we will effectively see a few easy client automation steps, Teams etiquette, and tips and tricks that are going to be beneficial.

In this part, we will cover the following chapters:

7
User and Data Security

Security becomes essential when business data or information is shared among users. Keeping track of basic data operations, such as reading or modifying, is vital for compliance auditing. Having said this, we long for a miracle to save us from the manual effort of recording each and every operation in a Teams collaboration.

Through the Microsoft Teams admin center, we can control how Teams works in our organization, from deciding who joins chats and the apps they're allowed to run, to monitoring the content of messages to prevent the sharing of sensitive information. We can also keep track of who performed any file operations. While many of these features and services are enabled by default, others are enabled on a case-by-case basis.

Microsoft Teams is a collaboration tool for users and in this chapter, we will discuss the users of Teams and the data security of data shared among these teams or via third-party tools. In addition to this, we will discuss Teams' security model and best practices for keeping data secure on common channels.

In this chapter, we will discover best practices for providing security to users and shared data. We will discover advanced security features for preventing both malicious attacks and accidental data loss.

The chapter will cover the following main topics:

- Understanding the Microsoft Teams security model
- Identifying common security weaknesses
- Discussing the Microsoft Teams security framework
- Security roadmap insights
- Exploring security, privacy, and compliance
- Recommendations for Microsoft Teams security

Technical requirements

To understand security and compliance, a basic understanding of a user directory is required. Hands-on knowledge of Azure AD is encouraged, as well as admin knowledge of Microsoft Teams. Basic knowledge of PowerShell is recommended.

Microsoft Teams and security

When we hear about collaboration, the first thing that springs to mind is security, be it data or user security. Collaboration is synonymous with sharing, and sharing may lead to business information leaks.

The solution we seek must be a secure collaboration tool and the good news is that Microsoft Teams provides enterprise-level security to meet business needs. As part of the Microsoft 365 suite, Microsoft Teams uses best practices and procedures to implement security.

Figure 7.1 – Microsoft Teams security

Teams is an enterprise-class collaboration tool, so you should be aware of some of the common security attacks that could compromise its infrastructure and communications. Let's identify the common threats and how Microsoft handles each threat:

- A **distributed denial-of-service attack (DDOS)** is an attack where the attacker floods the network resource with superfluous requests, resulting in its breakdown and unavailability to valid users.

  Mitigation: Teams uses Azure DDOS network protection against this form of attack, and additionally it throttles client requests from the same source, such as endpoints, subnets, and federated entities.

- A **compromised key attack** is when a private key is compromised and the attacker can leverage this compromised key to decrypt the business data without the sender knowing about it.

  Mitigation: Teams uses a **Transport Layer Security (TLS)** connection to share the media encryption keys. Additionally, it leverages the **Public Key Infrastructure (PKI)** features to secure the key data used for encrypting the connection itself.

- **Eavesdropping** occurs when an attacker has access to the private data transmitted over the network and is able to modify or delete that data.

  Mitigation: **Mutual TLS (MTLS)** is used for server communications, and TLS is used while connecting clients to the service for authenticating all parties and encrypting all traffic.

- **Identity spoofing** is when the attacker successfully compromises someone's identity, and hence, their security credentials without authorization. It enables the attacker to impersonate and operate as the victim.

  Mitigation: TLS is used for authenticating all parties and encrypting data in transit. With an impersonated identity, an attacker could easily obtain the **Distributed Name Service (DNS)** server address but, as Teams uses authentication certificates, this would prevent an attack without a valid certificate.

- A **man-in-the-middle attack (MITM)** occurs when an attacker intercepts communications between two parties, either to secretly eavesdrop or modify traffic traveling between the two.

  Mitigation: Teams uses the **Secure Real-time Transport Protocol (SRTP)** to encrypt the media traffic, and the cryptographic keys used for connecting two endpoints are negotiated over proprietary signaling protocols, namely, TLS and ACM.

These attacks are quite common, and Teams has a secure way to safeguard against such attacks. Since Teams is built in consideration of the Microsoft Trustworthy Computing **Security Development Lifecycle (SDL)**, Teams architecture is infused with industry-standard security measures.

Microsoft Teams security framework

The Microsoft Teams security framework helps to ensure that information and identities within Teams are protected. It has three core components, namely, Azure AD, TLS, and industry-standard protocols. The following diagram demonstrates these components:

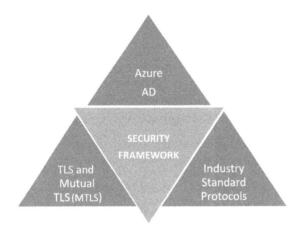

Figure 7.2 – Teams security framework

The core components can be defined as follows:

- **Azure Active Directory (Azure AD)** is a user directory service. It stores all information about the objects and policy assignments.

- **TLS and Mutual TLS (MTLS)**: These protocols ensure that all the communication is encrypted and that the network is only comprises trusted servers. MTLS is used for communication between servers, while TLS handles client-to-server communication.

- **Industry-standard protocols** are used in Teams for user authentication.

Microsoft Teams privacy commitment

Microsoft ensures an organization's privacy via contractual agreements and by being transparent and providing user control. The following diagram shows Microsoft's commitment to privacy:

Figure 7.3 – Microsoft Teams privacy

Let's describe the privacy commitments for a better understanding:

- **Controlled by You**: Microsoft provides user control and transparency.

- **No Data Profiling**: Microsoft will not share your personal data in any way for commercial gain.

- **Strong Legal Protection**: Microsoft does not allow any backdoors, or make encryption keys available, or assist in decrypting your personal data.

- **GDPR for all Customers**: Microsoft extends the **General Data Protection Regulation (GDPR)** to customers across the globe, and not just in Europe.

- **Listening to Customers**: Microsoft actively engages in compliance regulations for customers.

Microsoft takes user consent before using personal data. Microsoft has no access to uploaded content. Teams follows the Microsoft Trust Center for privacy guidelines. Refer to the **Online Services Terms** to understand the policies Microsoft has to apply in relation to the use of personal data, and whether this is required for legal/legitimate requirements, and Microsoft remains the sole controller for such processing. For more information regarding Microsoft's trust and security guidelines, please visit the **Microsoft Trust Center** (https://www.microsoft.com/en-us/trust-center).

> **Note**
>
> Microsoft only processes personal data for its own legitimate business purposes and remains the sole controller for such processing.
>
> Source: https://www.microsoft.com

Security, privacy, and compliance in Microsoft Teams

Microsoft Teams is built on the M365 enterprise-grade, scalable cloud, providing cutting-edge security and compliance competences to its customers. When planning for security in Microsoft products, the security roadmap is a good recommendation. The security roadmap includes top recommendations for implementing security capabilities to protect the business environment.

Planning for security and compliance can be summarized in the following six steps:

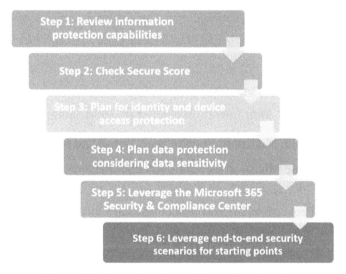

Figure 7.4 – Security and compliance planning steps

> **Note**
>
> Licensing is key to what capabilities are available. For example, Teams DLP, Customer Key, and other advanced features will require an E5 license.

While administrators are in charge of protecting identities, information, and devices, Microsoft is responsible for protecting **M365** services. **M365** and **Enterprise Mobility + Security (EMS)** can be combined to provide best-fit protection for businesses. To proceed with the ideal implementation, we can follow a detailed approach described in a Microsoft Ignite session called *Secure Microsoft 365 like a cybersecurity pro: Top priorities for the first 30 days, 90 days, and Beyond* (`https://www.youtube.com/ watch?v=luignzNyR-o`). The session was presented by Mark Simos and Matt Kemelhar, Enterprise cybersecurity architects.

This roadmap is staged across the following three phases in a logical order:

Figure 7.5 – Security roadmap

The following table summarizes the tasks defined and followed in the three-stage security roadmap:

Area	Tasks		
	30 Days	**90 Days**	**Beyond**
Security management	Secure Score is checked (https://securescore.office.com) Auditing is enabled. Reports are reviewed.	Follow the recommendations as suggested in Secure Score. The reports and compliance manager is reviewed for sharing risks. Software updates are implemented. The attack simulator is leveraged for testing.	Reports are reviewed for sharing risks. Continue using Secure Score. Check and continue implementing software updates. Include eDiscovery for legal processes.

Threat protection	For monitoring anomalous behaviors, **connect M365 to Microsoft Cloud App Security.** Implement protection for admin accounts: • Use dedicated admin accounts for admin activity. • Enforce multi-factor authentication (MFA) for admin accounts.	Advanced protections implemented for admins: Configure Privileged Access Workstations (PAWs) for admin activity. Implement Azure AD PIM. • Implement the SIEM tool to collect logging data. As the audit log only keeps data for 90 days, leverage SIEM for longer storage.	Configure secure access for identity objects. Initiate monitoring threats via Cloud App Security.
Identity and access management	**Initiate AADIP**	Configure multi-factor authentication. Configure conditional access policies.	Refine policies. Leverage identity protection to assess threats.
Information protection	Start with: O365 General Data Protection Regulation **Implement Teams with three tiers of protection.**	Adapt and implement information protection policies selected in 30 days. Implement DLP policies in M365 for data.	Revisit the protection policies.
Note	These are quick tasks and do not have a significant impact on users.	These tasks are somewhat time-consuming but enhance the business security posture.	These are important security measures that build on previous work.

When the aforementioned roadmap phases are completed with all the suggested recommendations, the planning phase for security and compliance is complete. On the roadmap, we will achieve the following outcomes for the respective phase:

Time frame	Outcomes
30 days	Quick configuration: • Protect Administrator • Logs and Analytical information • Protect Identity Configuring tenants.
90 days	Enhanced options: • Protect administrator • Protect user and data principles Evaluate risk, compliance and user requirements Implementation of existing policies
Beyond	Adjusting & refining policies Extending the protections to all dependencies Integrating with business needs

Hence, we have a plan for data and user security while using Teams. User collaboration and data sharing require a very granular security policy to avoid any data or user information leakage.

Now that we understand Microsoft's enterprise-grade security for its business tools, we will discuss the Teams architecture in more detail and see how we can achieve an attack-proof infrastructure.

> **Note**
> For more details on the security roadmap, you can refer to this link:
> ```
> https://docs.microsoft.com/en-us/microsoft-365/
> security/office-365-security/security-
> roadmap?view=o365-worldwide
> ```

Security in Microsoft Teams

Teams ensures team and organization-wide security via SSO and two-factor authentication through Active Directory and secures the data via encryption. Security is a key concern for administrators of any modern business system, including Microsoft Teams. Security threats include malicious attacks, disgruntled users, poor procedures, and human error. Microsoft Teams' security, privacy, and compliance introduce a set of features and tools that can be used to secure business data in Teams and prevent both malicious attacks and accidental data loss.

To access the security features, please visit `https://security.microsoft.com`.

The M365 portal provides a range of threat management options as follows:

Figure 7.6 – Security and Compliance dashboard

Teams handles secure communication via the following security features:

Figure 7.7 – Security features

Let's have a closer look at each security option provided by Teams:

1. **Safe Links**: When a protected user clicks the link in Teams, the URL is checked against a database of known malicious links. A safe policy can be created as shown in the following screenshot:

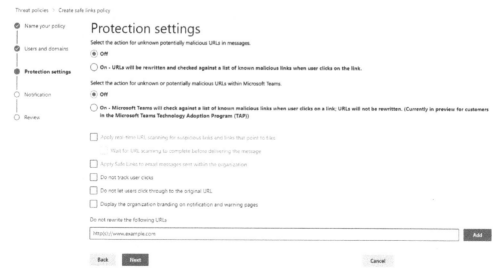

Figure 7.8 – Safe Link policy creation

2. **Conditional Access policies**: This enables the admins to set risk-based policies to allow access based on device health, user setting, user location, and more.

3. **Secure Score**: This is a means of assessing the security posture of a business, where a higher score indicates additional room for improvement, while a lower score affirms a secure setup with further recommendations. Secure Score recommendations can assist a business in building a protective environment shielded from threats. Secure Score can be checked from the dashboard for improvement actions, as shown in the following screenshot:

Figure 7.9 – Microsoft Secure Score

4. **Safe Attachments**: This feature enables user security by inspecting and detecting malicious attachments sent over Teams channels/chats. A new policy can be created from **Create Safe Attachments policy**, as shown in the following screenshot:

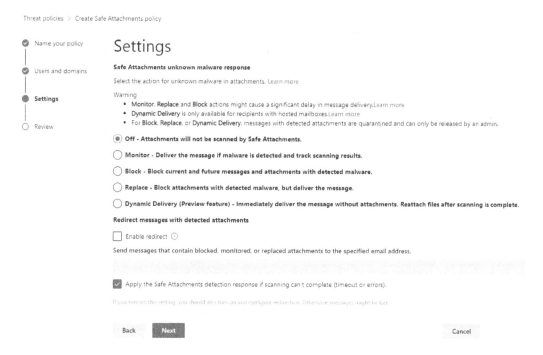

Figure 7.10 – Safe Attachments policy creation

5. **Microsoft Defender for Endpoint**: Defender is used for detecting and blocking files identified as malicious. It guards endpoints against any cyber attacks, automates the management of security events, and also detects advanced threats and data breaches. The Defender dashboard has an option for incidents and alerts, as shown here:

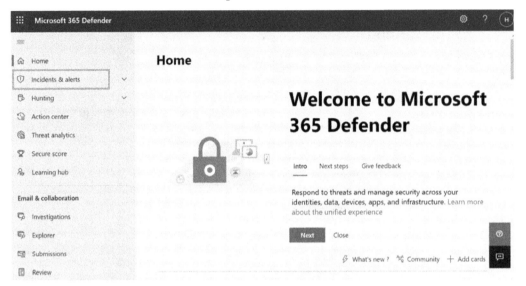

Figure 7.11 – Microsoft 365 Defender dashboard

Security is one of the three pillars in the Teams security framework, although it leaves an important footprint on user and data security. However, compliance is also required to mark the remaining areas.

Let's discuss compliance in the next section.

Compliance in Microsoft Teams

Compliance provides the opportunity to protect data and comply with standards and regulations across your Microsoft 365 services, including Teams. Microsoft provides **Compliance Manager** for managing compliance needs using integrated solutions for data protection, data governance, risk assessment, discovery, and so on.

Compliance Manager supports the organization in simplifying compliance and reducing risks around data protection and regulatory standards. A compliance score reflects the current compliance status and helps to see what requires attention. Microsoft Teams admins can quickly set up policies to monitor user communications across channels for inappropriate and sensitive content so that they can be examined by designated reviewers.

Note

To access the advanced features, a Microsoft 365 E5 license or Advanced Compliance add-on to the E3 license will be required. Compliance Manager offers a number of solutions for maintaining business regulations. For more information, visit `https://compliance.microsoft.com/homepage`.

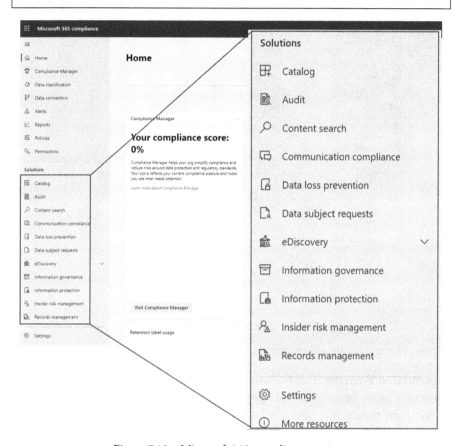

Figure 7.12 – Microsoft 365 compliance options

Teams provides the following options regarding compliance regulation:

Figure 7.13 – Microsoft compliance regulations

The compliance regulations are discussed in the following points:

- **Information Barriers**: This feature sets policies in place to block the communication between people or groups, as this could be a business requirement or company policy. It is now available in the public cloud and was rolled out for the GCC cloud in January 2021.

- **Communication Compliance**: This feature ensures clean communication among the people or groups in both public and private Teams channels. It functions by scanning for sensitive information, offensive language, and information related to the organization's regulatory policies.

- **Retention Policies:** This feature ensures that important chats and channel messages are retained, also periodically getting rid of the unwanted data. In case of a conflict between deletion and retention of the same content, retention precedes.

- **Sensitivity Labels**: This feature protects and regulates access to sensitive business data shared/created while users are collaborating within Teams. Once the sensitivity labels are configured in the Microsoft compliance center, these labels are ready to be applied to existing or new teams. It is currently (at the time of writing this content) unsupported in class teams for customers using Teams Education SKUs.

> **Note**
>
> Check out the following link for the latest updates on Microsoft services:
>
> ```
> https://docs.microsoft.com/en-us/office365/
> servicedescriptions/teams-service-description.
> ```

The **Sensitivity Labels** option can be accessed under **Information Protection** in the Microsoft 365 Compliance Center, as shown in the following screenshot:

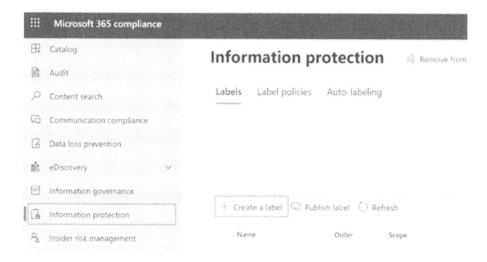

Figure 7.14 – Sensitivity Labels creation

Let's discuss the privacy options one by one:

- **Data Loss Prevention (DLP)**: This feature defines policies that stop users from sharing any sensitive information while connecting over the Teams channel or in a chat session. Content is analyzed for primary data matches to keywords through the evaluation of regular expressions, by internal function validation, and by secondary data matches that are in proximity to the primary data match. A DLP policy can be created from an existing template or a custom setup, as shown in the following screenshot:

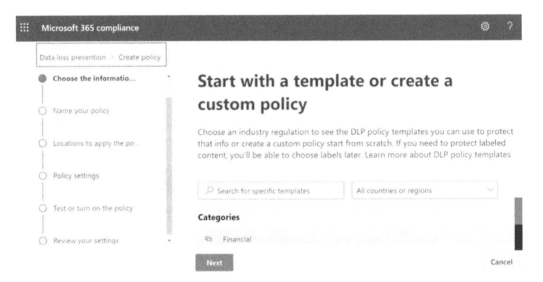

Figure 7.15 – Data Loss Prevention (DLP) policy creation

> **Note**
> The DLP feature will require a Microsoft 365 E5 license or Advanced Compliance add-on.

- **eDiscovery**: This feature assists in locating, identifying, and retrieving relevant information when a legal or regulatory request is made. Additionally, eDiscovery's search and analytical tools can cut expenses and streamline the responses. It can even preserve the retrieved information in place, thereby dispensing with the need to create an additional archive.

> **Note**
> The Advanced eDiscovery feature will require a Microsoft 365 E5 license or Advanced Compliance add-on.

- **Legal Hold**: This feature can be used to place a legal hold on either a user (user mailbox) or a team. This hold could be an **In-Place Hold** (holding the subset of a mailbox) or **Litigation Hold** (holding the entire user mailbox). This hold guarantees the availability of mailbox content even if the user tries to modify or edit the existing messages.

- **Compliance Content Search**: This is one of eDiscovery's tools for searching for in-place content such as emails, documents, and instant messaging conversations in your organization. After the search is run, the number of search results and the number of content locations become available on the search flyout page, and summary statistics can be viewed by exporting them to a local computer if required.

We can use PowerShell commands/scripts to locate a private channel's files and messages and add them to the content search.

> **Note**
>
> Prerequisite:
>
> To run these commands, first, we need to install the SharePoint Online Management Shell and connect it to SharePoint Online. Please follow the given link for the installation guide:
>
> `https://docs.microsoft.com/en-us/powershell/ sharepoint/sharepoint-online/connect-sharepoint- online?view=sharepoint-ps`

I. The first step is to list all SharePoint site collections that a private channel in the team has:

```
Get-SPOSite
```

II. Now, collect a list of all SharePoint site collection URLs that a private channel in the team has and also get the parent team group ID:

```
$sitelist = get-sposite -template <Template>
foreach ($site in $sitelist)
 {
$y= get-sposite -identity $site.url -detail;
$y.relatedgroupID;
$y.url
 }
```

III. Now, to identify all private channel sites for each team or group ID, we run the following command:

```
$sitelist = get-sposite -template <Template>
$groupID = <GroupID>
foreach ($site in $sitelist)
{
$y= Get-SpoSite -Identity $site.url -Detail;
if ($y.RelatedGroupId -eq $groupID)
{
$y.RelatedGroupId;
$y.url
}
}
```

IV. Run the command to obtain a list of all the private channels in a team so as to include private channel messages in a content search:

```
Get-TeamChannel -GroupId<GroupID> -MembershipType
Private
```

- Now, obtain a list of private channel members from the Sales channel:

```
Get-TeamChannelUser -GroupId<GroupID> -DisplayName "Sales"
-Role Member
```

V. Include mailboxes of all members from the private channel.

- **Auditing and Reporting**: The audit log can assist in investigating various activities, including team creation, team deletion, modifying settings, and the channels added.

Turn on auditing in the Security & Compliance center to access the audit data:

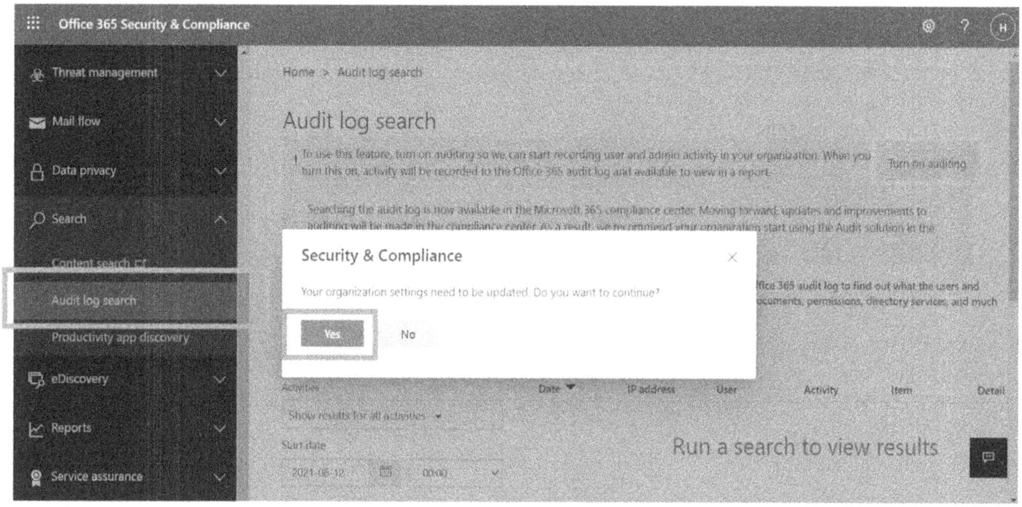

Figure 7.16 – Enabling audit logs

- **Customer Key**: At the application level, a customer key is used to encrypt Teams files saved in SharePoint Online. It serves as an additional layer of security for extra protection against data access by unauthorized users or systems and complements BitLocker disk encryption.

> **Note**
> The customer key feature will require a Microsoft 365 E5 license.

- **Policy-based recording for calls & meetings**: Policy-based recording empowers businesses to regulate the meeting and call recordings, also setting up the retention setting for the recordings as required by the organization-wide regulatory policy.

Interaction recording use cases can be assigned to four primary categories of recording functionality, as shown in *Figure 7.17*.

> **Note**
> The meeting recorder must be able to handle your interactions (voice, video chat, and screens).

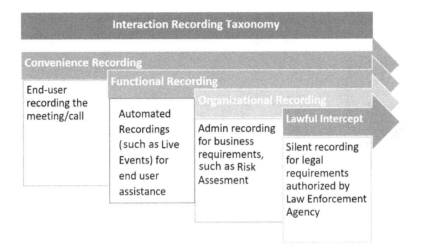

Figure 7.17 – Enabling an audit

> **Note**
>
> Teams has integrated compliance recording solutions. The core component of this solution is the recorder, and it provides direct interaction with the calls or meetings communication platform APIs and provides the endpoint for media ingestion.

The Teams solution follows industry-standard compliance and guidelines, while also considering the privacy of user information and data. Next, we will discuss privacy in Microsoft Teams.

Privacy in Microsoft Teams

Teams is a cloud-based service that has to process numerous types of personal data in order to provide the service. Privacy is to be addressed at each and every level of a shared working environment. The collaboration facilitates the group tasks to be achieved in time, although there is always a potential risk of personal data leaks.

This personal data includes the following:

- **Content**: The data generated by recordings, meetings and chats, shared files, transcriptions, and so on.
- **Profile Data**: User information shared with the organization.
- **Call History**: A record of the calls to be reviewed later.

- **Call Quality Data**: System admins can review the details of user meetings and call data.

- **Support/Feedback Data**: Record of the troubleshooting tickets or feedback submitted to Microsoft.

- **Diagnostic and Service Data**: Service usage reports sent to Microsoft for performance analysis and improved service delivery.

Microsoft processes users' personal data for its own legitimate business requirements, as mentioned in the **Online Services Terms** (`https://www.microsoft.com/en-us/licensing/product-licensing/products`), and Microsoft remains the sole controller for such processing.

Teams provides the following privacy and security controls for video meetings:

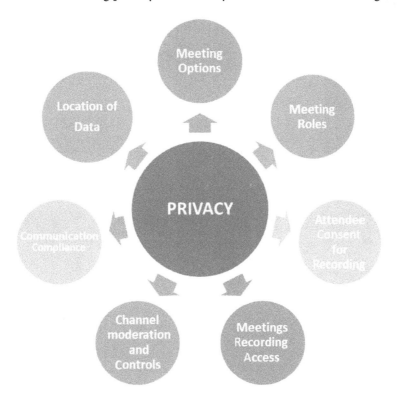

Figure 7.18 – Microsoft privacy options

Let's discuss the privacy options one by one:

- **Meeting options:** With meeting options, the organizer can allow guest users to join the meeting, or include a wait lobby to admit people later. Participants can also be removed even when the meeting is in progress.

  The meeting options can be accessed from the Microsoft Teams admin center by going to **Meetings > Meeting policies > Manage policies**. Click the existing policy or create a new one, and then scroll down to **Participants & guests** and select your desired option.

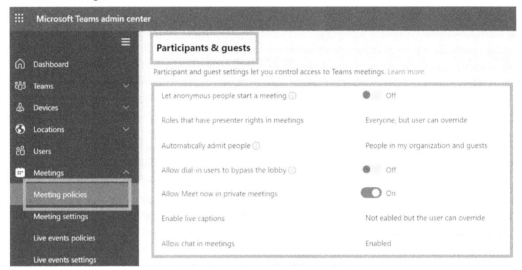

Figure 7.19 – Teams admin center

During a live meeting, if an admin wants to change the meeting options, they can click on the ellipsis (...) to access the options.

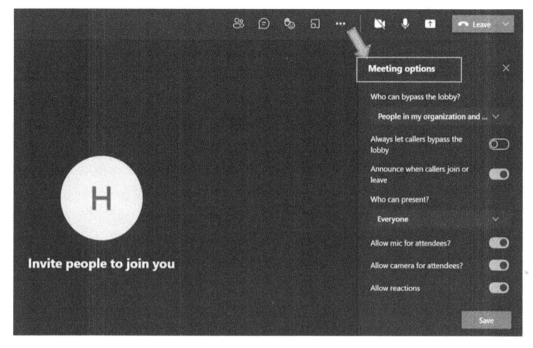

Figure 7.20 – Meeting options

- **Meeting roles:** A meeting organizer has the option to define roles as "presenters" and "attendees," and can also control which meeting participant has the right to present content.

The meeting roles can be accessed from the Microsoft Teams admin center by going to **Meetings** > **Meeting policies** > **Manage policies**. Click the desired policy or create a new one, scroll down to **Participants & guests**, and click on the drop-down menu alongside **Roles that have presenter rights in meetings** to select the role.

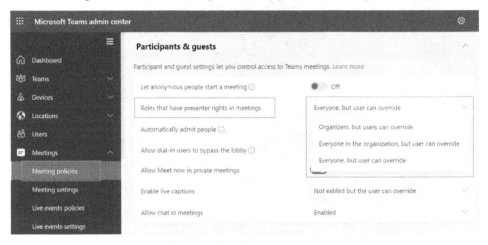

Figure 7.21 – Meeting policies

- **Attendee consent for recording:** Recording is initiated with a message to all the attendees that the recording is going to start. Before implementing the recording feature in the organization, it is recommended to ensure user consent on the privacy policy.

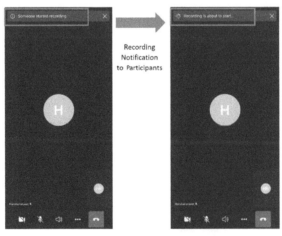

Figure 7.22 – Meeting Recording Notification

- **Meetings recording access:** The meeting recording can be accessed by limited users and the meeting organizers can set the authorization. The recordings are stored in Microsoft Stream and can be shared/downloaded by authorized users.

Microsoft Teams has an option to disable the recording center > **Meetings** > **Meeting Policies** > **Manage Policies**. Click the desired policy or create a new one, then scroll down to **Recording and transcription** and toggle on **Cloud recording**:

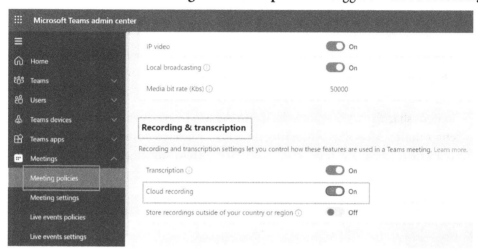

Figure 7.23 – Cloud recording

Meeting recordings can be accessed in Teams channels.

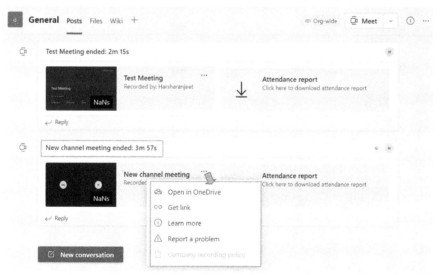

Figure 7.24 – Meeting recording access

> **Note**
>
> Microsoft Teams now uses the new stream for the meeting recordings and has adopted a new method to save the meeting recordings. To initiate the transition from classic Microsoft Stream to the new stream, it now stores recordings on Microsoft OneDrive for Business and SharePoint in Microsoft 365.
>
> For more information, refer to the following link: `https://docs.microsoft.com/en-us/microsoftteams/tmr-meeting-recording-change`.

- Channel moderation and controls: Channel owners can control the shared content in a channel and moderate the conversations to ensure that only suitable content is viewed and shared.

  Content sharing can be controlled from the Microsoft Teams admin center under **Meetings** > **Meeting policies** > **Manage policies**. Click the desired policy or create a new one, scroll down to **Content sharing**, and then manage the options.

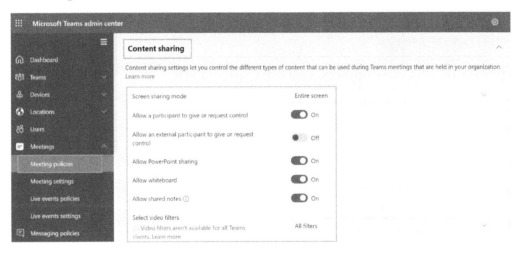

Figure 7.25 – Content sharing settings

- Communication compliance: This option enables organizations to build policies to prevent bullying or harassment, monitor conflicts of interest, and so on.

Select **Communication compliance** > **Policies** > **Create policy** to configure a template-based policy or create your own custom policy.

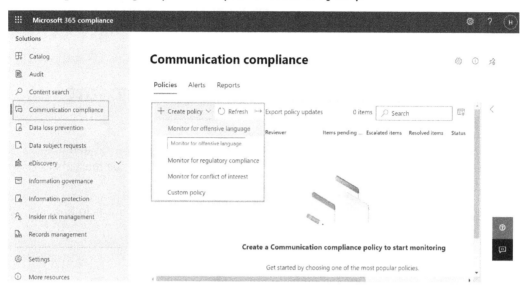

Figure 7.26 – Communication compliance policy

- Location of data: In Teams, the data is stored in the geographic region associated with the M365 or O365 account.

To see the location of the data, go to the Microsoft 365 admin center under **Settings** > **Org settings** > **Organization profile**. Then, click on **Data location**.

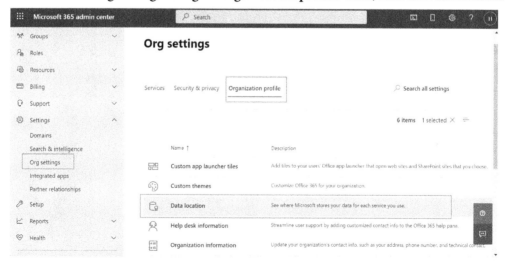

Figure 7.27 – Data location in Teams

Microsoft takes user and data privacy very seriously and follows strict policies to prevent any data leakage. To use Microsoft products or services, organizations have to demonstrate regulatory compliance. There are a few recommendations when it comes to further securing and aligning Teams for secure collaboration. We will discuss these recommendations in the next section.

Recommendations for securing Microsoft Teams

While Microsoft ensures that the security, compliance, and privacy of users and data remain intact during collaboration via Microsoft Teams, as an admin, we must also follow the layered security approach. Here are a few recommendations.

The top 12 recommendations for a secure collaboration environment are as follows:

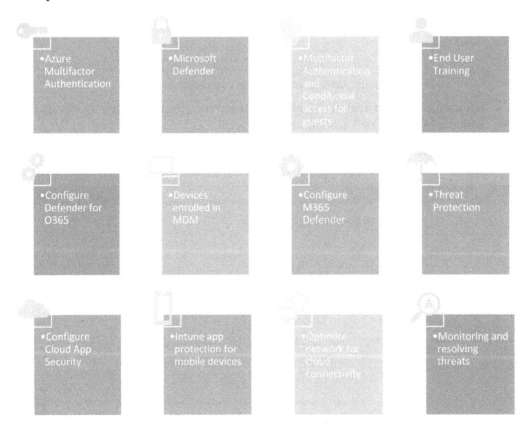

Figure 7.28 – Recommendations for a secure collaboration environment

To achieve the afore mentioned tasks, an appropriate license is required. Please check the following table to make sure that an appropriate license is selected to successfully implement the desired functionality:

	Task	All Office 365 Enterprise plans	Microsoft 365 E3	Microsoft 365 E5
1	Enable Azure AD Multi-Factor Authentication (MFA).	Y	Y	Y
2	Protect against threats.	Y	Y	Y
3	Configure Microsoft Defender for O365.			Y
4	Configure Microsoft Defender for Identity.			Y
5	Turn on Microsoft 365 Defender.			Y
6	Configure Intune mobile app protection for phones and tablets.		Y	Y
7	Configure MFA and conditional access for guests, including Intune app protection.		Y	Y
8	Enroll PCs into device management and require compliant PCs.		Y	Y
9	Optimize your network for cloud connectivity.	Y	Y	Y
10	Train users.	Y	Y	Y
11	Get started with Microsoft Cloud App Security.			Y
12	Monitor for threats and take action.	Y	Y	Y

More than 90 regulatory and industry standards are met by Microsoft:

- Compliance and regulatory standards: To comply with global, national, regional, and industry-specific regulations, Teams supports more than 90 regulatory standards and laws, including HIPAA, GDPR, FedRAMP, SOC, and the **Family Educational Rights and Privacy Act (FERPA)** for the security of students and children.

- Information barriers: Information barriers allow you to control communication between users and groups in Teams to protect business information in cases of conflict of interest or policy.

- eDiscovery, legal hold, audit log, and content search: eDiscovery and its related features allow you to easily identify, hold, and manage information that may be relevant in legal cases.

- Retention policies: Retention policies allow you to manage content in the organization by deleting or preserving information to meet organizational policies, industry regulations, and legal requirements.

Location of Teams data at rest

Microsoft Teams data is stored based on the type of content generated.

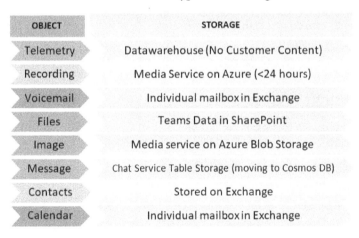

OBJECT	STORAGE
Telemetry	Datawarehouse (No Customer Content)
Recording	Media Service on Azure (<24 hours)
Voicemail	Individual mailbox in Exchange
Files	Teams Data in SharePoint
Image	Media service on Azure Blob Storage
Message	Chat Service Table Storage (moving to Cosmos DB)
Contacts	Stored on Exchange
Calendar	Individual mailbox in Exchange

Figure 7.29 – Data location

Security for Microsoft Teams meeting attendees

Admission to a Teams meeting can be controlled via a setting in the lobby. Through structured meetings, you can also control access to the information presented in the meetings.

Amend the settings in the Microsoft Teams admin center via **Meeting policies >
Participants & guests > Automatically admit people**.

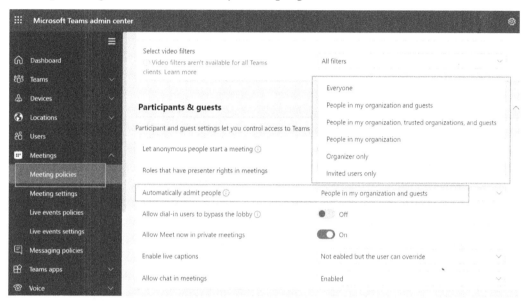

Figure 7.30 – Meeting policies for attendees

Managing guest users in Microsoft Teams

Teams allows outside people to join the meetings and access the allowed content. This is required when employees are required to connect with clients, stakeholders, contractors, and suchlike. The **Guest access** option is available and can be configured and enabled via the Teams admin center.

To enable guest access, sign in to the Teams admin center and select **Org-Wide settings > Guest access**. Toggle the **Allow guest access in Teams** switch to **On**.

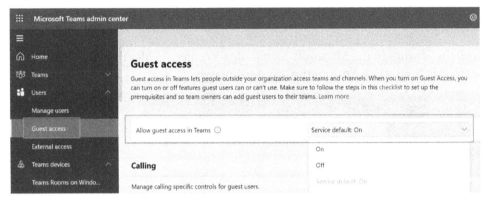

Figure 7.31 – Guest access in the organization

You can also enable or disable guests or turn off the **Calling**, **Meeting**, and **Messaging** settings for guests from the same page.

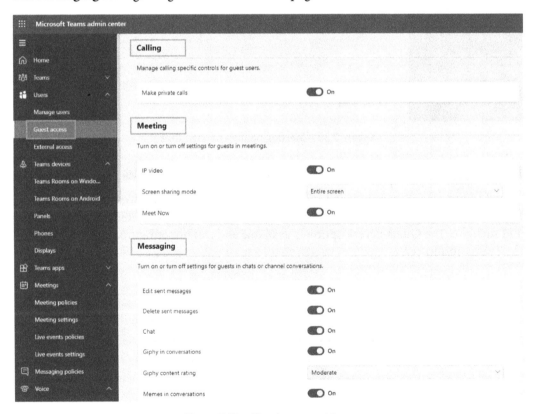

Figure 7.32 – Guest access settings

Once guest access is enabled, we now need to ensure that access is secure. There are a few steps to be followed:

1. Configure **Azure AD** to allow guests in Teams.

2. Configure **Microsoft 365 groups**.

3. Configure **Sharing in Microsoft 365**.

4. Verify **Sharing settings in SharePoint**.

5. Set up **Guest permissions in Teams**.

6. Turn on **Anonymous users can join a meeting** if necessary.

Summary

Microsoft defines Teams as a single place to meet, chat, call, and collaborate. The product is designed for everyone to keep their documents, photos, videos, chat history, and meeting notes in one place. Teams also has a free version that requires no commitments.

In this chapter, you've explored some of the ways to scale Microsoft Teams to meet your business compliance and security requirements. You've seen the breadth of security capabilities available to safeguard the data, how it's shared, and how Teams can flag, identify, and prevent data breaches. Taking all the information from this chapter into consideration, it becomes important to secure the communication channel with the latest security practices, as it is not just the data that is shared via the channels/collaboration, but also user information, the leakage of which may lead to breaches of privacy. User and data privacy, security, and compliance is ensured by Microsoft via a number of security solutions and policies discussed in this chapter. Although security counts as the first choice for protecting the data, it is equally important to follow the best practices and recommendations from Microsoft. We will discuss Teams etiquette and best practices in the next chapter.

8
Teams Etiquette and Best Practices

In a world of remote working and working from home, inevitably, we will occasionally deviate from professional courtesy – so much so that at times, we might overlook the presence of individuals that we interact with every single day. Yes, we see them online, but they are more than just a video image. Each of them deserves the same respect that we would give to a co-located colleague. While working online, it becomes essential to follow the same etiquette as working in offices. Also, online collaboration tools need to be used similar to when we use them in offices.

Best practices are recommendations on how to achieve a balanced and ideal workplace. Remote working has become a popular work style, and with that comes the need for high-speed internet, collaboration tools, and security. Collaboration tools have emerged as one of the important dependencies that need to be configured while considering the best practices set out by Microsoft. In this chapter, we will learn about online meeting etiquette, as well as the best practice recommendations for using Teams.

This chapter will cover the following main topics:

- Microsoft Teams everyday etiquette
- Microsoft Teams best practices
- Teams limits and specifications

Technical requirements

A basic understanding of using Teams for meetings and collaboration is required to complete this chapter.

Microsoft Teams everyday etiquette

Basic etiquette is a necessity for a healthy work environment. All collaborators are entitled to basic courtesy and should follow the meeting guidelines. No matter what your role is, knowing your company's chat and online meeting etiquette is a must. Efficiently managing channels, meetings, and instant messaging at work can help minimize distractions and overstimulation, while increasing efficiency. Maintaining a respectful chat etiquette can also help foster accessibility, inclusivity, and equity. Let's discuss the recommended practices to adhere to while attending group meetings or calls on Teams.

First things first

There are some initial steps to consider before joining a meeting, and setting up your app on a desktop and/or mobile is one of these steps. Let's discuss some more measures that are recommended when you start working with Teams:

- **Get the Teams app on your computer and phone**: For a better experience, download the Teams app on your computer and a mobile device to unlock additional features.

- **Teams is your internal collaboration tool; email is for more formal, external communication**: This depends on the organization and how they want to isolate internal and external communication if needed.

- **Use the required features**: Apart from conversations, you also get a Stream channel, a SharePoint site, Approvals, Shifts, and many more functionalities, so use what is needed.

- **Manage app notifications**: Set up notifications in the Teams app so that you get alerts when someone is trying to reach you via chat or add you to a meeting. You will find the **Notifications** option under **Teams settings**:

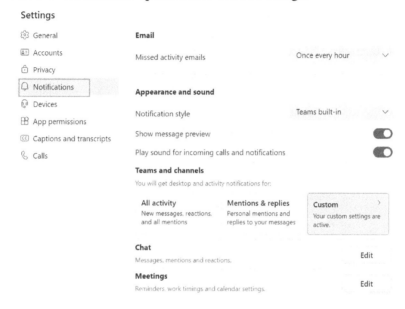

Figure 8.1 – Notifications

- **Use Reactions**: The thumbs-up icon is for acknowledging a message, which can help keep the sender notified. The icons for love, applause, wow, sad, and anger should perhaps be kept for informal messages and jokes:

Figure 8.2 – Reactions in Microsoft Teams

- **Don't over-invite people to your meetings**: If the Team is not working on dedicated deliverables and the meeting is more informational, allow optional joins for invitees.

- **Do not create a team unless required**: Microsoft Teams has a collection of tools, users, and content for different projects within an organization, so when a new project starts, it is recommended to create a new team.

- **Make your out-of-office response Teams-friendly**: Your out-of-office (OOO) response should be displayed in Teams as well. This lets your colleagues know that you are currently unavailable. You can set an OOO message by going to your profile picture at the top of Teams and selecting **Set status message | Schedule out of office** at the bottom of the options.

Figure 8.3 – Out of Office setting

- **Share links to documents rather than sending them as attachments**: One of the advantages of Microsoft 365 is its ability to co-edit documents—take advantage of it. Stick to a single source rather than multiple versions of the same document:

Figure 8.4 – File links in Teams

- **Track Team tasks with Planner**: Utilize the built-in **Planner** tab and keep track of the project deliverables and tasks. We can plan tasks like so:

Figure 8.5 – Planner in MS Teams

- **If you are an owner of a team, you have etiquette rules as well**: Collaboration etiquette should apply to the owners of teams as well. They need to be up to date about new invitees, as well as maintaining the teams.

Video, audio, and environment setup

When working with Teams, it is crucial to set up your audio, mic, and video for a seamless meeting experience. The virtual backgrounds are a boon when attending a meeting from home. Let's discuss some additional measures for an ideal meeting environment:

- **Use microphone headsets**: The microphones on headsets cut down on noise and ensure your voice is clear and audible for the other attendees. You can also use a phone for an optimal voice experience.

- **Do not sit with a bright light source in the background**: The bright light from a window or bulb can affect your video, so choose a background with an appropriate amount of light for clear visibility.

- **Set an appropriate meeting background**: Be more considerate while choosing the meeting background as moving people or objects can distract others. Consider leveraging the blur background feature in MS Teams, as shown in the following screenshot:

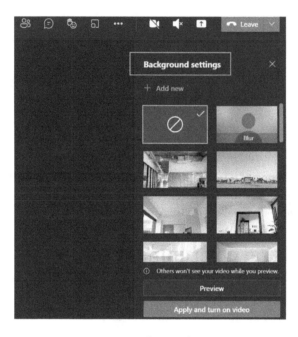

Figure 8.6 – Background settings

- **Join meetings in isolated rooms**: Many of us are working from home, where others may unintentionally interrupt the meetings.

Joining a meeting

Teams is widely used for collaboration, and when joining a meeting, there is etiquette that should be followed. Let's understand the basic recommendations:

- **Try to arrive early**: This gives you enough time to cross-check the audio/video and ensure that everything is working fine.

- **Keep other apps and devices silent**: Always keep your cell phone on silent mode and avoid other distractions while connected on Teams.

- **Enter muted**: At times, your microphone can send a distracting voice or jittering sound, so make it a habit to join muted with your camera off, and then unmute yourself and enable video.

- **A moderator is recommended**: For large meetings, it is recommended to assign a moderator. This person can assist in managing the chat questions and meeting guidelines for the attendees. You can find **Channel settings** by clicking the ellipsis (…) and then **Manage Channel**:

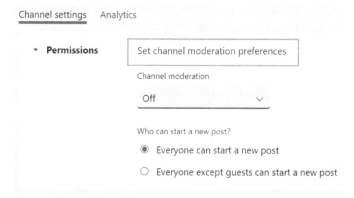

Figure 8.7 – Channel moderation

Attending and participating in a meeting/call

While in a call, you must remain muted unless you are required to speak. We have seen a ton of online videos where the host or participants have forgotten to mute and accidentally exposed something personal. To work formally, we need to abide by a few guidelines, as shown here:

- **Keep muted**: Unless you are speaking or leading the discussion, you should keep your microphone muted. Any unwanted sounds or voices can be a distraction for others. Unmute yourself to begin speaking when needed. People who have joined via a call-in will need to press *6 on the dial pad to unmute themselves. The microphone icon should be clicked to mute and unmute, as shown in the following screenshot:

Figure 8.8 – The microphone button to mute and unmute

- **Avoid talking to people in your environment while unmuted**: It becomes frustrating when people start talking to others in their surroundings rather than those present in the meeting. This can lead to confusion for the participants.

- **Be clear while addressing**: Speak clearly so that the attendees can hear you properly. Occasional pauses are recommended to assure that the attendees have enough time to ask questions or offer their input.

- **Camera usage**: It's good practice to use your camera when other participants have their video on. Turn off your camera if it is disrupting others or if you're on low network bandwidth. Try to sit and not move around with your camera on as this may distract the other attendees. Teams has a video on/off button, as shown in the following screenshot:

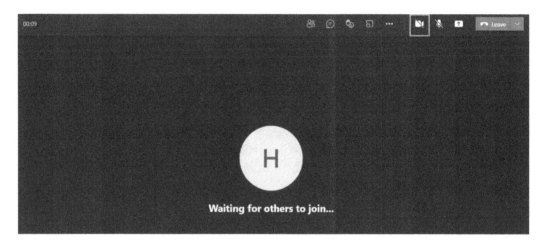

Figure 8.9 – Video on/off button

- **Do not talk over others**: Unlike an in-person meeting, it's sometimes difficult to distinguish between multiple voices when several people are speaking at the same time. This leads to confusion and can impact work productivity.

- **Use the chat window**: Consider, especially for large meetings, asking your questions in the chat window. Speaking might introduce confusion or people talking over one another. The Teams chat option for this is shown in the following screenshot:

Figure 8.10 – Chat option

- **Tag individuals in the chat**: Tag other attendees (using the @userid format) in the chat window for direct communication and to avoid unwanted responses:

Figure 8.11 – Mentioning a user in the chat

- **Meeting recording**: If a meeting is being recorded, the moderator should announce this and take consent from all the attendees. The meeting recording option is shown in the following screenshot:

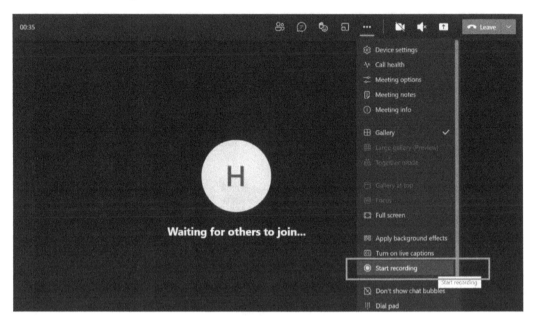

Figure 8.12 – Start recording option

For many, Teams is easier to work with compared to other tools with disintegrated services such as email, file shares, and phones. It has been observed that for new tools, user adaptation is slow, but for Microsoft Teams, the Teams community itself has guided new users to understand the tool. Microsoft has several best practices that can be followed to achieve the best of Teams' services. We'll check them out in the next section.

Microsoft Teams best practices

The following Microsoft Teams best practices assist users in taking advantage of this powerful collaboration tool. These recommendations assist in Teams governance and contribute toward a better user experience and maximizing productivity. We'll discuss the best practices to be followed in the upcoming sections.

Getting started

Microsoft has several recommendations to be followed by Teams. However, let's start with the first steps toward achieving an ideal collaboration environment:

- **Adjust App Settings**: For each device you are using, make sure you go through the settings to make sure they align with your workflow. For example, you can configure the video background settings for a more formal look while attending a video meeting.

- **Teams Training option**: The **Help** option (bottom left) of the Teams desktop app has a dedicated **Training** section. For new users, this is a recommended option to visit. The short videos, which range from a few seconds to minutes, help users understand the functionalities offered by Teams. To go to training, click on the **Help | Training** option:

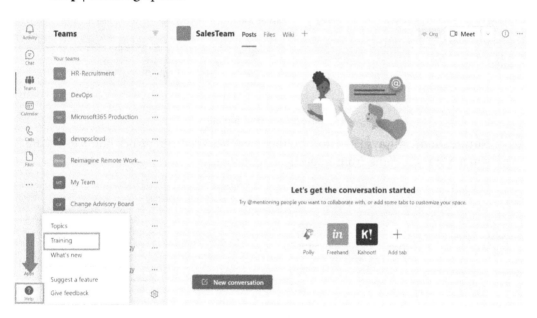

Figure 8.13 – The Help option

Click **Training** and choose a learning video, as shown in the following screenshot:

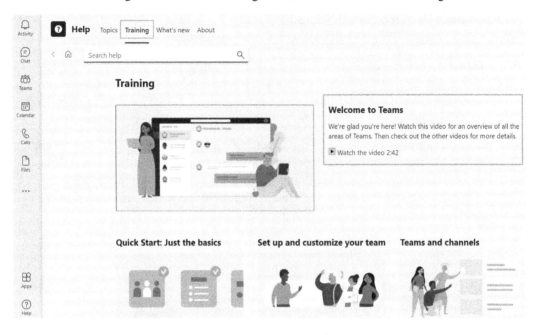

Figure 8.14 – Training tab

- **Notifications**: Always keep notifications switched on during work hours to ensure you never miss a ping from a colleague or manager:

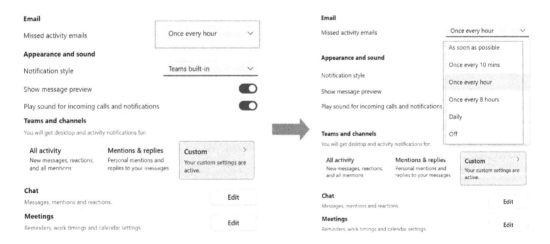

Figure 8.15 – Notifications

- **Quiet hours notifications**: On the Teams mobile app, the **Quiet hours** setting can help suppress notifications during set time durations, which can be hours or days. You can access this via the Teams mobile app by going to **Settings | Notifications**. From here, click **During Quiet time** and select **Quiet hours**, along with **Quiet days** (if needed):

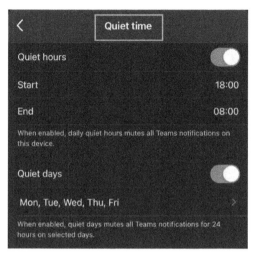

Figure 8.16 – Notifications

- **Status Messages and Out of Office**: It is recommended to set a status message in Microsoft Teams to let people know about your current availability. You can set the message from the profile area, and you can also set an out-of-office message from the same place:

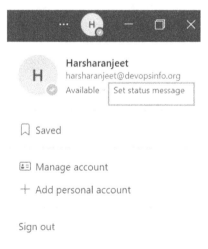

Figure 8.17 – Profile status

Chat

While collaborating using Teams, a set of best practices can help you get the most out of the tool. The best practices are as follows:

- **Adding Members to a Chat**: You have the option to add a new member to an existing chat so that they can catch up with the team. You can also select whether they can see the chat history or not.

- **Group Chat versus Channel Conversations**: Group chats are for when the whole channel does not need to be involved in the ongoing conversation. Always use the channel option for addressing all groups at once.

- **Choose text format from the Compose Box**: To highlight a message, you can choose a different format. There are options to alter the font's size, color, and many more things, as shown in the following screenshot:

Figure 8.18 – Text formatting option

- **Add a Subject to Your Message**: While you have the compose box expanded, you also have the option to add a subject to your message, with more description added on the body. This helps the message to standout in group chats.

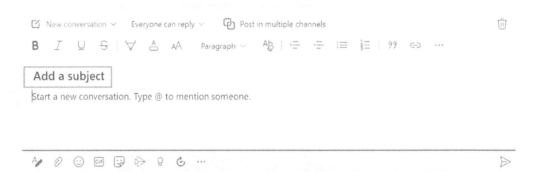

Figure 8.19: Choosing a subject for message

- **Email versus Teams Messages**: Email is a more formal way to communicate and at times, Teams can serve as a quick way to connect, more like an instant message service.

- **Reply versus Start a New Conversation**: The **Reply** option is selected when addressing an existing chat, while **New conversation** initiates a new chat, as its name suggests:

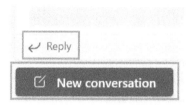

Figure 8.20 – Choosing the conversation option

- **Priority Notifications**: To mark a message as urgent, you can click the **!** icon in the toolbar to make it a priority (important or urgent). Users will receive a continuous notification until they read it:

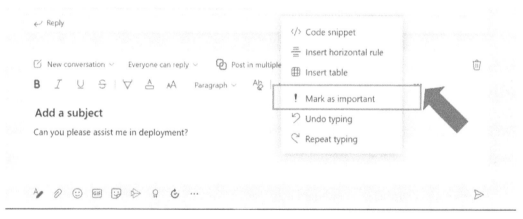

Figure 8.21 – Marking a message as important

- **Save a Message**: Existing messages can be saved for future reference, so this option can help you bookmark important messages. This option can be selected by clicking the ellipsis (…) and clicking on the **Save this message** option, as shown in the following screenshot:

Figure 8.22 – Saving a message

Shared files

The meetings/chats in Teams also include files being shared among users, and these files require proper handling and management. We'll look over this here:

- **Teams Files**: Each Team stores the files in a SharePoint Online document library where each channel gets a dedicated folder. It is best to keep the files in the designated channel to avoid data leakage.

- **File Management**: Teams files can be moved/copied between Teams or channels within a Team. These files are shared from OneDrive, and you can leverage the OneDrive **sync** client to keep the files offline.

- **File Version History**: Files are saved in versions and, if needed, files can be reverted to a specified version. To access the previous version, go to **Files | Open in SharePoint**. When you have located the file, click on the file's hidden menu button and choose **Version history**. In the pop-up window under the **Modified** column, click to **View** or **Restore**:

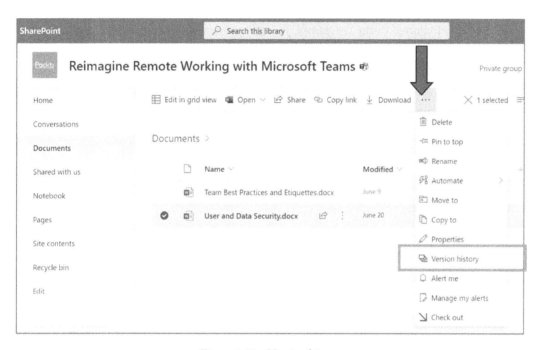

Figure 8.23 – Version history

- **File Size and File Path Limits**: Teams has a file upload limit of 250 GB and a 400 character limit on the file path, so it is recommended to control the file size and use short filenames.

> **Note**
>
> The file limits keep on updating. Please refer to the following link for the latest version:
>
> https://support.microsoft.com/en-us/office/
> restrictions-and-limitations-in-onedrive-and-
> sharepoint-64883a5d-228e-48f5-b3d2-eb39e07630fa.

Creating teams

Microsoft Teams allows users or moderators to create several teams for different departments, projects, or executives. These teams should also follow a set of recommendations, as follows:

- **Team Planning**: It is recommended to plan your team name, plan which members are to be included in the team, and plan the purpose of the team. Also, make it standard practice to add supporting apps for day-to-day tasks such as Planner, OneNote, Wiki, Approvals, and so on.

- **Wiki**: It is recommended to use the Teams Wiki to record any additional information about the Team. For example, a goal could be set for any team and each member can refer to the **Wiki** option for additional information:

Figure 8.24 – Wiki for additional information

- **Team Membership**: There is always an option to add people later, so start with the bare minimum and then expand as required. This saves you from needing to evict any unwanted people later.

- **@Mention New Members**: You should introduce newly added members. In addition to this, if a message is directed to a particular person, mention them.

- **Guest Membership**: The business can decide whether to add guest members or not. If you must add guests to Teams, avoid sharing sensitive information even before adding guests, as the chat history is visible to guests that are added later as well.

Teams channels

Teams is comprised of two types of channels: standard (available and visible to all) and private (private conversations with a specific audience). Channels are created on topics such as a department name, or just for fun. We must follow the recommendations for channels, as follows:

- **The Channel List**: The Teams channel list is always displayed in alphabetical order. To move a channel to the top of the list, start the channel name with a number:

Figure 8.25 – Order of channels

- **Channel Moderation**: For channels designed for general announcements, it is recommended to disable the **New conversation** option for members and reserve this for moderators.

- **The General Channel**: Use the **General** channel to make Team-wide announcements. The **General** channel is created automatically, and we do not have a delete option for it, as shown in the following screenshot:

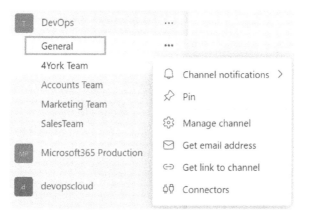

Figure 8.26 – Channel's email address

- **Send Emails to a Channel**: Each channel has an email address, which makes it handy to continue a conversation that started with an email. It is good practice to remove any headers or previous email history from the forwarded message. You can find the email address by clicking on the ellipsis (**…**) and then clicking on the **Get email address** option, as shown in the following screenshot:

Figure 8.27 – Get email address

- **Renaming Channels**: If you ever need to rename a channel, make sure that you rename the underlying folders as they do not get renamed automatically.

- **Private Channels**: Private channels are recommended when employees want a focused space to collaborate, and also when sensitive information cannot be shared in the shared channel. Membership for a private channel is managed by the channel owner. Removing a member from the team removes them from all private channels:

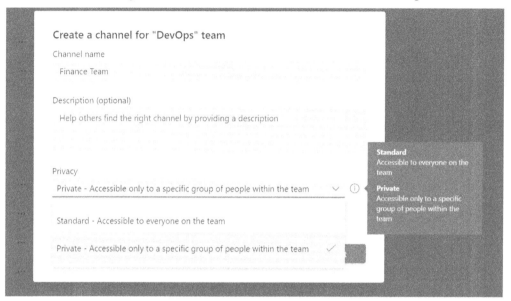

Figure 8.28 – Create a channel for the "DevOps" team

Teams brings many collaborative capabilities to your M365 subscription. And while this platform has the power to enhance the productivity and quality of communication across your organization, knowing and following best practices is key to running Teams efficiently. While etiquette and best practices can help you set up a near to perfect working environment, we should not forget that Teams also has certain limits, and the services cannot expand beyond those limits. We will explore those limits in the next section.

Teams limits and specifications

Microsoft Teams limits how many teams can be created, how many owners there are per team, and many more other features for teams and channels. Let's discuss the limits and specifications proposed by Microsoft:

- **Teams and channels**

    Teams has a finite limit on the number of teams and team memberships. Here are some applicable limits for Teams and channel creation:

Feature	Maximum Limit
Maximum number of teams a user can create	Subject to a 250 object limit
Maximum number of teams a user can be a member of	1,000
Maximum number of members in a team	25,000
Maximum number of owners per team	100
Maximum number of org-wide teams allowed in a tenant	5
Maximum number of members in an org-wide team	10,000
Maximum number of teams a global admin can create	500,000
Maximum number of teams an M365 organization can have	500,000
Maximum number of channels per team	200 (includes deleted channels)
Maximum number of private channels per team	30 (includes deleted channels)
Maximum number of members in a private channel	250
Maximum number of members in an Office 365 group that can be converted into a team	10,000

- **Messaging**

    Sending messages in Teams is one of the most used features. However, Microsoft has some limits on messages, as demonstrated in the following table:

Feature		Maximum Limit
Maximum number of people in a private chat		2,502
Maximum number of people in a video or audio call from chat		20
Maximum number of file attachments in the chat		10
Chat size		Approximately 28 KB per post
Message size in an email		24 KB
Maximum number of file attachments in an email		20
Size of each file attachment in an email		Less than 10 MB
Maximum number of inline images in an email		50

- **Channel names**

    While channel names identify their purpose, Microsoft has some conditions when it comes to naming them:

Type	Example
Characters not allowed	~ # % & * { } + / \ : <> ? | ' " , ..
Characters in these ranges are NOT allowed	0 to 1F 80 to 9F
Words not allowed	forms, CON, CONOUT$, NUL, COM1 to COM9, desktop.ini, _vti_, CONIN$, PRN, AUX, LPT1to LPT9
Cannot start channel names with	An underscore (_) or period (.), or end with a period (.)

- **Meetings and calls**

  Microsoft has a limit on attendees, as well the number of days it will keep the meeting recordings available to be downloaded:

Feature	Maximum Limit
Maximum number of people in a meeting (can chat and call in)	1,000*, 20,000 listen-only/view-only participants
Number of people in a video or audio call from chat	20
Maximum PowerPoint file size	2 GB
Maximum number of days Teams keeps meeting recordings available for local download	20 days

  *License Limitations

- **Teams live events**

  Teams also hosts live events for organizations. Though it is public still, it has some limits regarding the audience's size and running events in parallel, as per the following table:

Feature	Maximum Limit
Audience size	10,000 attendees
Duration of event	4 hours
Concurrent live events	15

- **Tags**

  Tags in Teams let users quickly and easily connect with a subset of people on a team. These tags can be created based on a role, location, project, and so on. These are the limits of tagging:

Feature	Maximum Limit
Maximum number of tags per team	100
Maximum number of suggested default tags per team	25
Maximum number of team members to assign to a tag	100
Maximum number of tags assigned to a user per team	25

Whether you're running a small business or a large multi-national company, Teams can assist in bringing your organization together via chats, voice calls, video conferences, file sharing, and more. By abiding by the Teams limits and specifications, it is possible to obtain a failproof environment for internal and external collaborations.

Summary

In this chapter, you've explored some of the ways to understand chat and online meeting etiquette that can help improve collaboration, productivity, and engagement with your colleagues, whether you work alongside one another or you work together virtually.

Working from home is the new work standard and in these trying times, companies are dependent on collaboration tools, so they expect their employees to be equipped with the basic know-how when it comes to using these tools. Following the best practices outlined in this chapter can help you get the most out of the tool.

In the next chapter, we will learn about how to automate day-to-day tasks that can be carried out in Microsoft Teams.

9
End User Automation

Every company aspires to business process automation. If your organization is already using Office 365, then you already have a few tools that can help you achieve business process automation. These tools allow end users to easily automate business processes and tasks without the need for coding knowledge.

In this chapter, we will go through a list of end-user automation tools that are available and can be integrated with Microsoft Teams. There are Microsoft Teams templates available by default, which help us to carry out automation tasks very easily with a few clicks. We will try to cover each topic with a classic example. By the end of this chapter, you will know how to automate recurring tasks with the available Office 365 toolsets and how to perform these tasks from Microsoft Teams. It's highly recommended that you practice along with either the same or similar examples so that you get comfortable in effectively utilizing these features and functionalities.

In this chapter, we will cover the following learning objectives:

- Managing approvals in Microsoft Teams with Power Automate
- Utilizing Power Virtual Agents for Microsoft Teams
- Using the Inspection solution for Microsoft Teams
- Building the next generation of collaborative apps for hybrid work

Technical requirements

To begin our practice, we recommend signing up for an Office 365 trial membership via the methods outlined in our main index, and your administrator must activate all the relevant Microsoft applications.

Managing approvals in Microsoft Teams with Power Automate

Microsoft Teams and **Power Automate** can be used to enhance effective communication through automation. Microsoft Teams can use Power Automate flows via the Power Automate app in Microsoft 365 or by integrating the Power Automate app into Teams. When the Power Automate app is added to Teams, flows generated with Power Automate will appear in Teams. Flows can be edited or created in Teams as well as in Microsoft 365's Power Automate app.

Installing Power Automate in Teams

The first task is to install the Power Automate app in Microsoft Teams. In order to do that, follow these steps:

1. Navigate to **Apps** – type in `power automate` and double-click on **Power Automate**. This Power Automate application is just a connector that integrates with Microsoft Teams and Power Automate in the backend to bring all the features and functionalities together in Microsoft Teams.

Figure 9.1 – Searching for Power Automate

2. On the next screen, we will be prompted with the following options:

    - **Add to a team** – Will add this application to a team channel of our choosing

    - **Add to a chat** – Will add this application to a chat

    - **Add to a meeting** – Will add this application to an existing meeting

Figure 9.2 – Add the Power Automate tab

3. In our example, we are using the **Add to a team option**. On doing that, we will be presented with the following screen. On this screen, we need to type a team or a channel name where we wish to set up Power Automate.

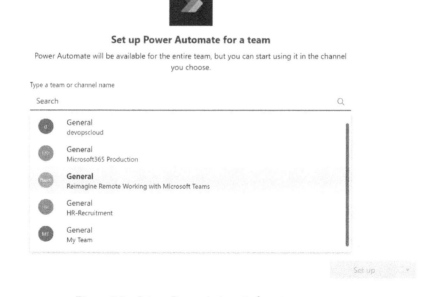

Figure 9.3 – Set up Power Automate for a team

4. Once we have selected the team, we will be presented with the following two options: **Set up a tab** or **Set up a bot**. In our example, we are trying to manage **Approvals** via Teams and **Set up a tab** is ideal in our scenario, so we have selected the **Set up a tab option**.

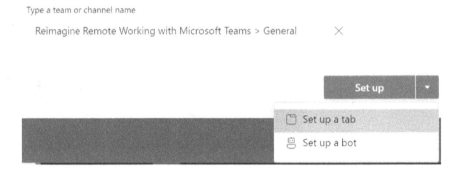

Figure 9.4 – Set up a tab

After completion, we will be presented with the next screen, which summarizes what Power Automate and Microsoft Teams can do for us.

Figure 9.5 – Save Power Automate and post to the channel

5. When we navigate to the team after Power Automate has been added, we'll see the following screen:

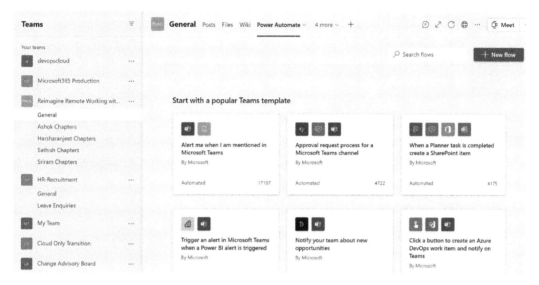

Figure 9.6 – Power Automate tab in the selected team's interface

6. In our example, we have chosen the following predefined template. Search here for templates that suit your needs:

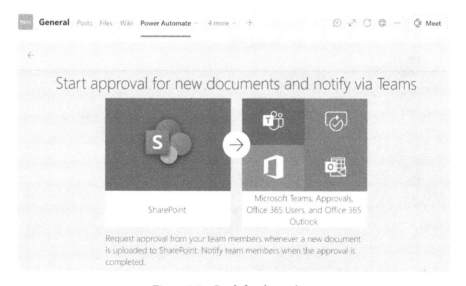

Figure 9.7 – Predefined template

When we scroll down, we see information on which applications this flow will connect to; we need to sign in to those applications.

Figure 9.8 – Sign in to Office 365 apps

7. After we click on all the individual plus signs, it changes them to a green check mark as shown in the next screenshot. We now need to click on **Continue**.

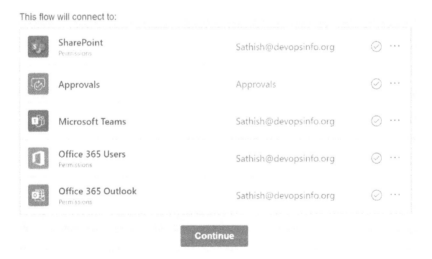

Figure 9.9 – Connect to Office 365 apps

Configuring Power Automate

Having completed the initial setup, it's now time for us to set up the configuration on the next screen that is presented to us:

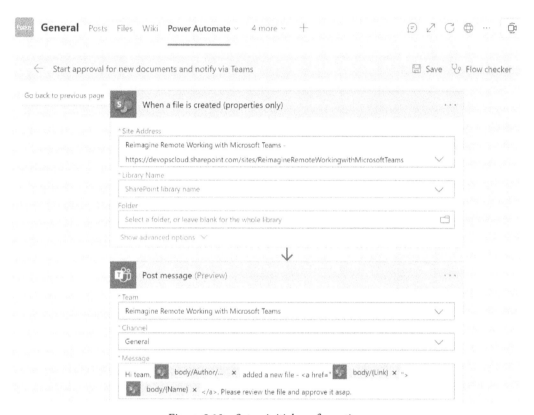

Figure 9.10 – Setup initial configuration

1. The first step is choosing the library name:

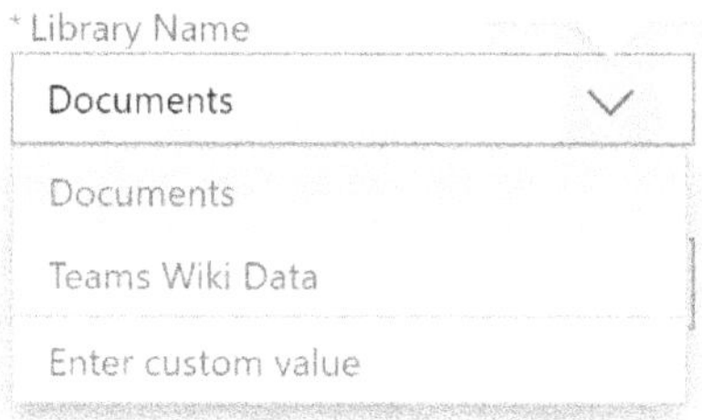

Figure 9.11 – Choose the correct library

2. The best part is that since it already has predefined templates, we don't have much work to do over here. All the fields are auto-populated and we only need to select the approver and add it in the **Assigned to** field. We can add more people in this field as well. Getting familiar with Power Automate flows can help us in building our own custom flows.

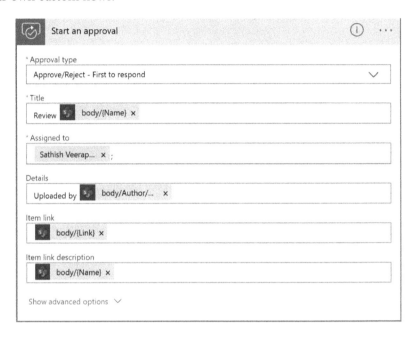

Figure 9.12 – Adding people to approve

3. Another great feature is the **Flow checker**, which can be used to check the flow before saving it. When we run the **Flow checker**, if there are any issues in the fields populated, we will see them as errors or warnings.

Figure 9.13 – Flow checker

4. A correct configuration will appear as in the following screenshot. In our example, when we run the Flow checker, it reports zero errors and warnings. If you encounter errors, then it's good to check your flow configuration.

Figure 9.14 – Flow checker validation

5. Finally, we can test the flow through **Test Flow**, from **Flow checker** which offers two options – **Manually** and **Automatically**:

-   **Manually**: Manually trigger the test yourself by doing the action that triggers the flow.

-   **Automatically**: We can use this only if we are using data from a previous test run. If this is the first time you have tested this flow, only the first option (**Manually**) is available.

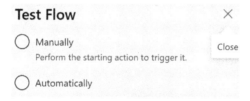

Figure 9.15 – Test Flow

6. After saving this flow, we see the successful summary of the flow that we have created. Also, there is an easy toggle switch that helps us to turn flows on or off.

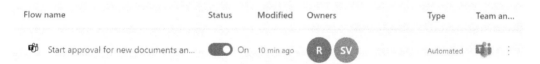

Figure 9.16 – Status of the flow

So, to test this scenario, I have uploaded a test document. After 10 seconds, I received the following message, requesting my approval:

Figure 9.17 – Notification to approve

Furthermore, when opening the approval notification window, we get the following screen. It's nice to see that it provides us with the option to add comments for the person who sent the request for the document approval to be uploaded.

Figure 9.18 – Approving the document

Finally, once the document is approved, we see the notification sent to the document uploader that the file upload has been approved.

Figure 9.19 – Final status notification

With just a few clicks we have managed to complete the approvals. We have seen one example demonstrating the business value of Power Automate integration with Microsoft Teams. Simply put, integrating Power Automate with Microsoft Teams enables educators to easily harness the power of automation to boost productivity and efficiency. We have reviewed the relationship between Power Automate and Microsoft Teams and how to utilize this technology for our daily business operations. Let's move on to our next topic, on how Power Virtual Agents can help us with automation from Microsoft Teams.

Utilizing Power Virtual Agents for Microsoft Teams

The **Power Platform** is a leading application that assists end users with automation via local applications that are provided. **Power Virtual Agents** is one such application; it is available within Microsoft Teams, allowing us to easily create our own chatbots that answer questions posed by other employees or team members.

The following are examples of scenarios in which we might want to create a Power Virtual Agents chatbot in Microsoft Teams:

- A **human resources** (**HR**) employee may create a bot that can answer questions about vacation balance, time off, and benefits.

- A person from facilities management may create a bot to answer questions that come through support services such as workspace availability, pantry availability/ stock, emergency operator numbers, and so on.

Power Virtual Agents enables us to build powerful chatbots that can respond to questions posed by customers, other employees, or visitors to our website or service.

Creating our bots

These bots can be easily created without the assistance of data scientists or developers. This section will walk you through the steps of making your chatbot available in Teams via the Power Virtual Agents portal and adding your bot to Teams via App Studio.

The first step is to add the Power Virtual Agents app in Microsoft Teams. In order to do that, follow these steps:

1. Navigate to **Apps**, search for `Power Virtual Agents`, and double-click to add it to Microsoft Teams.

Figure 9.20 – Searching for Power Virtual Agents

2. Once we have added Power Virtual Agents, we'll see the following introductory page:

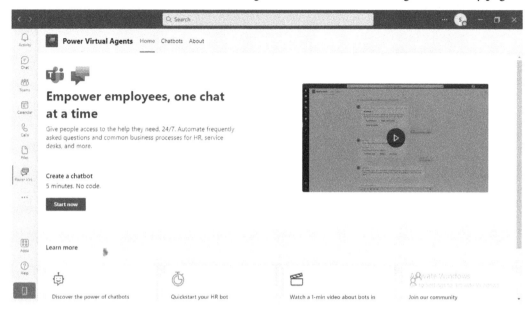

Figure 9.21 – Power Virtual Agents introduction

When scrolling down, we see the following information, which gives us quickstart templates. In our example, we are going to choose the second option, **Quickstart your HR bot**.

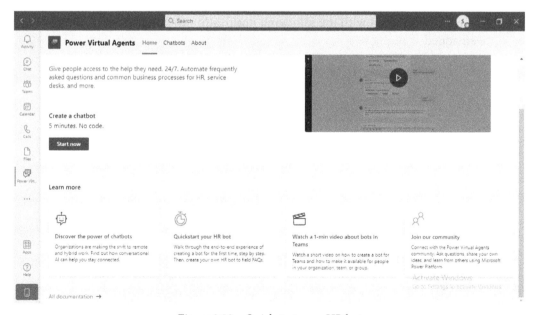

Figure 9.22 – Quickstart your HR bot

3. The first step is to click on **Start now** and choose the team where this bot will be available. Now that the bot is created, we can go ahead and start adding content to the bot.

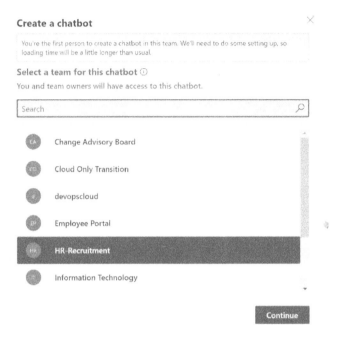

Figure 9.23 – Choosing the correct team

4. We will be prompted with the following notification the moment our bot has been added:

Figure 9.24 – Notification when the bot is added

5. On the next screen, we will be prompted to provide a name for the bot and choose the preferred language for this bot. Once you have chosen the name and language, click **Create**.

Figure 9.25 – Choosing the name and preferred language

6. Finally, we are presented with the next screen, which we need to start populating with the bot contents. Try not to panic on seeing these multiple options, as it's not too tricky to configure bots. It can take a minute or so to create the bot and get to this stage.

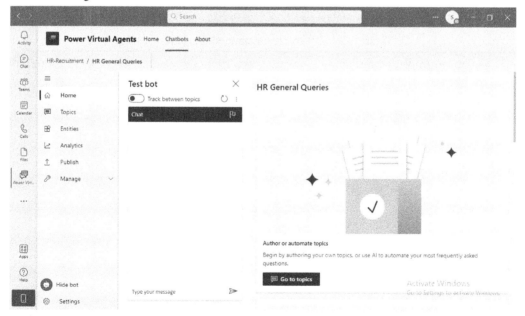

Figure 9.26 – Bot configuration

The first part is the test bot, which we can test by turning on the toggle switch and typing a test message as shown in the next screenshot *Figure 9.27*. After that, we are presented with a screen, over which when the mouse is hovered, gives us the option to change the messages as per our requirements:

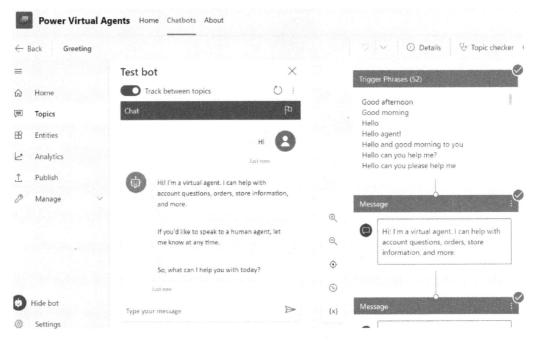

Figure 9.27 – Bot configuration modifying messages

7. In our example, we are going to create a new topic by selecting **New topic** at the top right of the view pane, as shown in the following screenshot.

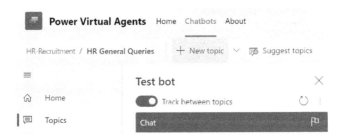

Figure 9.28 – Create a new topic

8. On the screen shown in the following figure, we are asked us to provide a name, friendly name, and description. In our example, we have provided `Employee time off` as the name, with the friendly name `Leave Balance Enquiry` and a short description about the functionality of this bot.

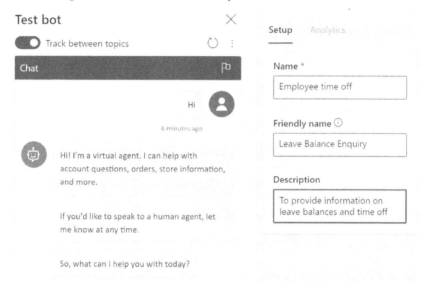

Figure 9.29 – Provide a name and description for the bot

9. On the next pane of the same screen, we need to create the trigger phrases. Trigger phrases are easy. Trigger phrases are ways that users will ask questions about a topic. Just type a question in the blank section and click on **Add**. You can see a few examples of added trigger phrases in the following screenshot:

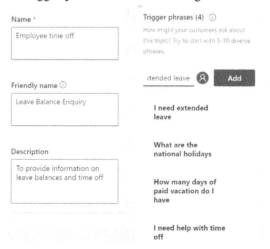

Figure 9.30 – Creating trigger phrases

10. Power Virtual Agents comes with built-in natural language capabilities. You only need to define a few trigger phrases and chatbots can answer similar questions raised by the end users' side to this bot. Finally, select **Save topic**.

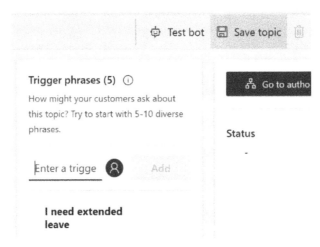

Figure 9.31 – Creating trigger phrases continued

11. On the next screen, click on Go to **authoring canvas** by hovering your mouse towards the right corner of this same view pane, to start building the conversation flow for this topic.

Figure 9.32 – Creating an Go to authoring canvas

12. The next screen brings us to this window. This is the question an employee will be asked when triggering the bot from their side. So, in our example, we have entered I can help with questions related to time off.

Figure 9.33 – Example question

13. Click on the plus sign and select the **Ask a question** textbox as shown in the next screenshot.

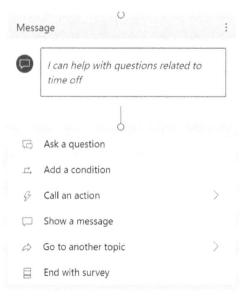

Figure 9.34 – Adding a question

14. Here in **Ask a question**, enter the text What information are you looking for?. This is the question the employee will be asked. On the next screen, add two options: **Paid vacation** and **National Holidays**. Additional options can be simply added with the **New option** plus sign that we can see in the screenshot.

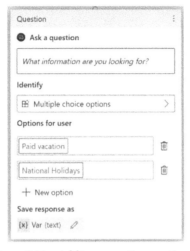

Figure 9.35 – Adding a question continued

15. Finally, we need to click on the pencil icon that we see in the **Save response as** field section and change the name from Var to TimeoffType and click on **Save**.

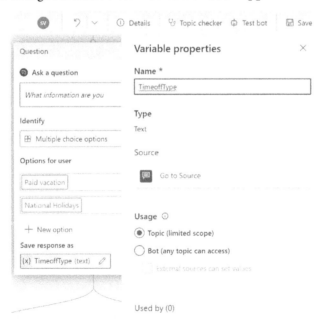

Figure 9.36 – Changing the name

16. We can now customize the responses for each option. We can have the bot direct employees to an internal HR website to look up paid time off policies for paid vacation.

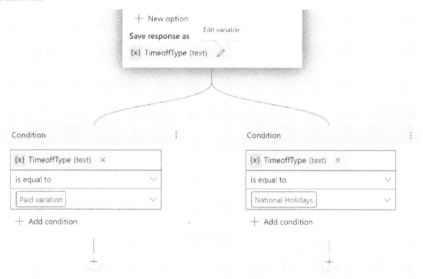

Figure 9.37 – Customizing the response

17. For the paid vacation, click on the plus sign and add a message node such as the following example:

```
For paid vacation time off, go to www.devopsinfo.org/
HR/PaidTimeOff to learn more on how to submit time-off
requests.
```

Figure 9.38 – Adding the message node

18. After we add the message node successfully, we get a message as shown in the next screenshot.

Figure 9.39 – Finally adding the message notification

19. Finally, click on **end the conversation** by using the **End with survey option**.

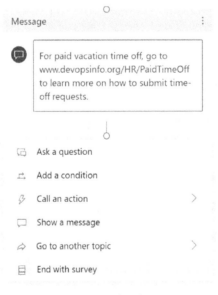

Figure 9.40 – End with survey

20. We get a screen like the following one, and this customer satisfaction survey is prebuilt for everyone to use in their topics.

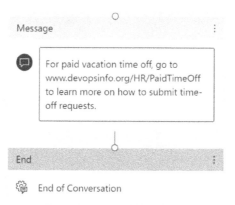

Figure 9.41 – Prebuilt survey

21. Similarly, in the **National Holidays** path, add a message node such as the following:

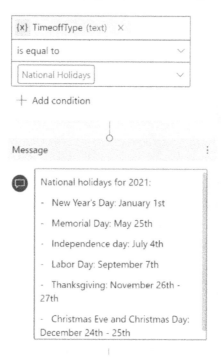

Figure 9.42 – Adding a message condition node

22. You can also end this flow with the same option as before: **End with survey**. Finally, the successfully created topics will appear, as shown in the following screenshot.

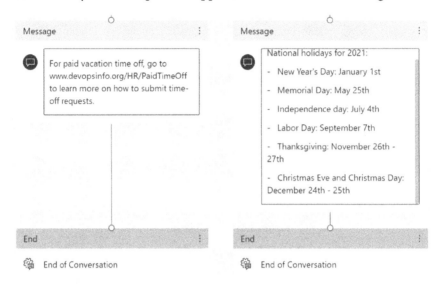

Figure 9.43 – Successfully created topics

When we navigate to Power Virtual Agents and select **My chatbots**, we can see the chatbot that we created in the previous demonstration.

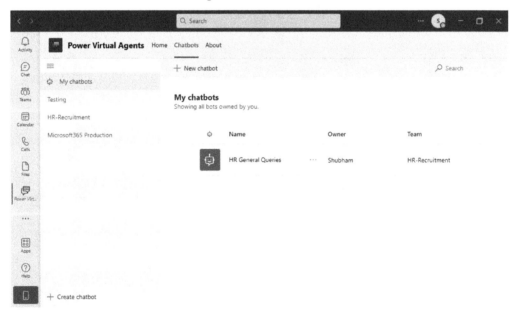

Figure 9.44 – Identify the chatbot

Testing our example

1. So, in our example, we entered I need time off information. After that, we could see the messages that we added to the topic while creating the bot, and the two options that are presented to the end user.

Figure 9.45 – Testing the chatbot

2. In our example, I'm just clicking on **Paid vacation** so that we'll get the information that we entered as a message during the creation of this bot.

Figure 9.46 – Testing the chatbot continued

3. We can enhance the topic to handle more complex queries by escalating them to HR experts. Finally, we need to publish this bot by clicking on the **Publish** icon in the top-right corner.

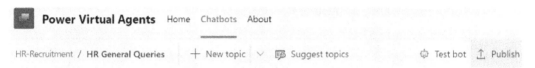

Figure 9.47 – Publishing the chatbot

After a few minutes, this bot will be available to all end users from the App Store. With no code and just a few clicks, we have successfully deployed a bot that will help us a lot in addressing end users' questions on leave balances. This will be of great benefit to the business; they save on time and additional resources for answering these basic-level, general questions. In this section, we've gone through Power Virtual Agents. We'll move on to the next topic, which is how the **Inspection** may aid us with Microsoft Teams.

Using the Inspection solution for Microsoft Teams

We can simply track and check our precious assets in the organization using the Inspection app in Microsoft Teams. The Inspection solution for Microsoft Teams is generic inspection software that can be used to inspect everything from a location to assets and equipment such as automobiles and machinery. This solution includes two apps, each designed for a different type of user:

*   A manager, who uses the **Manage Inspections** app to carry out the inspection.

*   Employees, who can use the **Inspection** app to carry out their regular inspections.

Here's how to get started with Inspection:

1. Navigate to **Apps.** Search for Inspection as shown in the following screenshot.

Figure 9.48 – Searching for Inspection

2. We will be presented with the following screen, where we need to click on **Add to a team**:

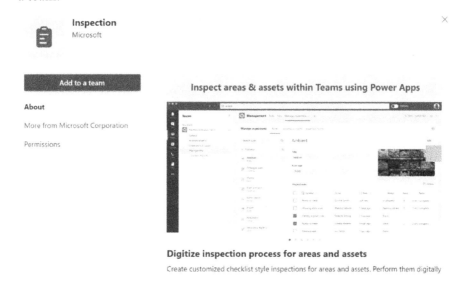

Figure 9.49 – Adding Inspection to a team

3. Here, we have selected a team and clicked on **Set up a tab**:

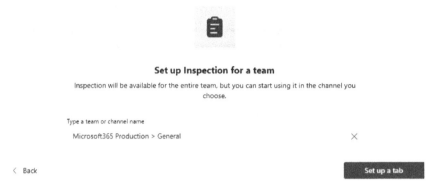

Figure 9.50 – Set up a tab

We will be presented with the following screen for the first time after we click on **Set up a tab**:

Figure 9.51 – Save the Inspection app to your channel

4. After clicking on **Save**, we will see the following information with the progress bar that tracks the installation:

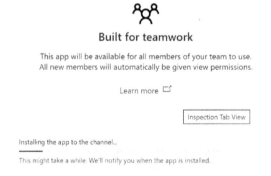

Figure 9.52 – Installation of the Inspection app to the Teams channel

5. After the installation process is complete, we will be presented with the following screen to provide permissions to use Microsoft Teams, Planner, and Office 365 Users. On this screen, we need to click on **Allow**:

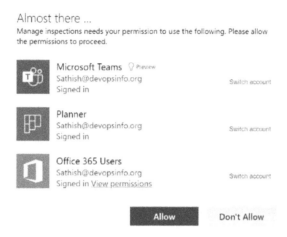

Figure 9.53 – To provide permissions to the Office 365 apps

6. After the permissions have been configured, we will see the following screen, where a suggestion to create a **Tasks** tab in Teams will pop up:

Figure 9.54 – Get started with Inspection with a Tasks tab

In our example, we already have tasks created in a few channels, so we are selecting the **I've a Tasks tab option**.

7. On the next screen, we will be prompted with the **Configure the inspection app** window, where we will be asked to select the team and choose the channel and the tasks that will be used to inspect from the inspection app.

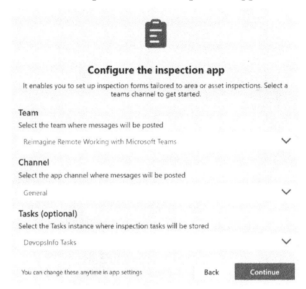

Figure 9.55 – Choosing the channel for inspection

8. Finally, we get the following welcome screen:

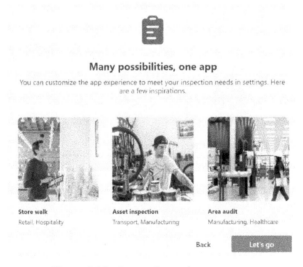

Figure 9.56 – Inspection welcome screen

9. When looking at the Teams channel where we added **Inspection** as a tab, navigate to **Inspection**, and here we have the complete overview of the inspection tasks that are present. These are the tasks that were previously created in Planner when creating new tasks:

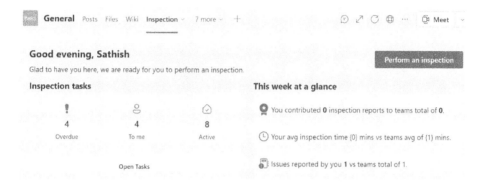

Figure 9.57 – Overview of Inspection tasks

10. When clicking on **Open Tasks**, we'll see all the tasks that are assigned and overdue, the number of which is shown below the **Inspection tasks** heading.

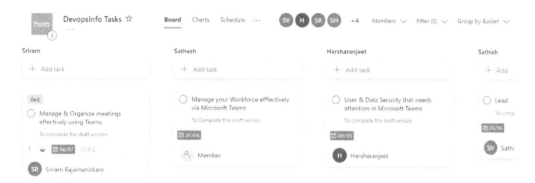

Figure 9.58 – Overview of Inspection tasks continued

11. When clicking on **Perform an inspection**, we'll get the following options. These are the default templates and the labels we have for the inspection:

Figure 9.59 – Performing inspection

12. Labels can be customized based upon our requirements – by selecting the **Manage inspections** tab at the top of the channel and by choosing **Location type**, we have the option to customize all settings based upon our requirements. There is also an option to **Add location type**.

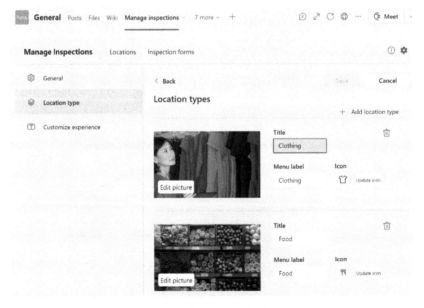

Figure 9.60 – Customization

13. In our example, we are going with the default **Food inspection** and **Morning Store Walk options**.

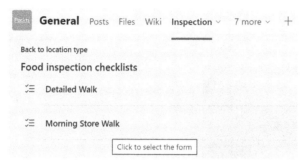

Figure 9.61 – Inspection example checklists

14. On the next screen, we have two checklists that are present for this template:

Figure 9.62 – Inspection example checklist entries

15. When clicking on **Clean and hygienic**, we see the options: **Ok**, **Issue**, and **N/A**:

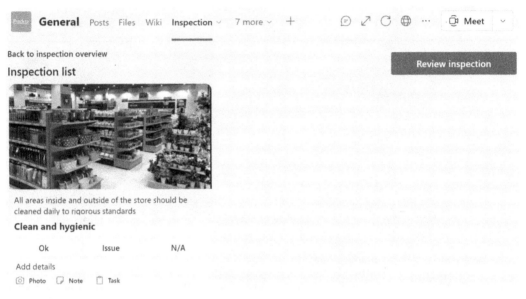

Figure 9.63 – Options in Inspection list

16. We also have the option to add a **Photo**, **Note**, or **Task**. We can add a task that automatically creates a Planner task in the team to complete.

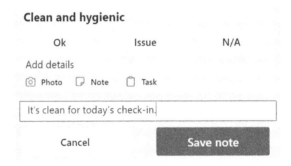

Figure 9.64 – Completing Inspection with comments

17. Finally, after reviewing two checklists, both of the inspections have a green tick and we now have the **Submit inspection** option.

Figure 9.65 – Submitting the inspection

18. On successful submission, we get the following screen, confirming that the inspection has been submitted successfully:

Figure 9.66 – Successful message on submitting an inspection

19. After performing all four default inspections, we get the following message as a summary when we click on the inspection.

Figure 9.67 – Performing the inspection

The Inspection app is a superb service maintenance tool for maintaining an asset or a specific area within a building or other place, which is enhanced by being able to provide notes when first-line employees do their daily routine maintenance check. The software includes inspection checklists that can be used to inspect multiple places. A store clerk, for example, could use this app to evaluate a portion of a retail store to ensure that it is ready for customers. Finally, let's get on to our last topic in this chapter, which provides us with options to build the next generation of collaborative apps for hybrid work.

Building the next generation of collaborative apps for hybrid work

Microsoft recently launched the **Developer Portal** for Microsoft Teams. The Developer Portal for Teams is currently in developer preview for the general public. The Microsoft Teams Developer Portal is the primary interface for configuring, distributing, and administering Microsoft Teams apps. You can collaborate on your project with others, set up runtime environments, and much more using the Developer Portal. In this topic, we will go over the options that can help us with Microsoft Teams.

The Developer Portal can be accessed by navigating to the URL `https://dev.teams.microsoft.com/home`.

After we log in, we are presented with the screen shown here:

Figure 9.68 – Developer Portal

Looking closely, we see there are two options provided to us: **Apps** and **Tools**

Apps

This is used to create an app for our internal application. There is an option to import an app directly from here as well.

Figure 9.69 – Apps overview in the Developer Portal

When going further into the **Apps** option by clicking on **New app**, we will find all the options required for creating our own custom apps, and for publishing them in the Microsoft Teams Apps section.

Since there are no real custom bots or apps we have created, in our example, we are just looking at the options that are present in the **Apps** section while creating the apps. Here in the **Basic information** section, we have the **App ID** that can be used in your code to use this app.

> **Important note**
> The **App ID** that is generated on the following screen is mandatory for creating a link between this app and the application in the backend usually used in the backend code.

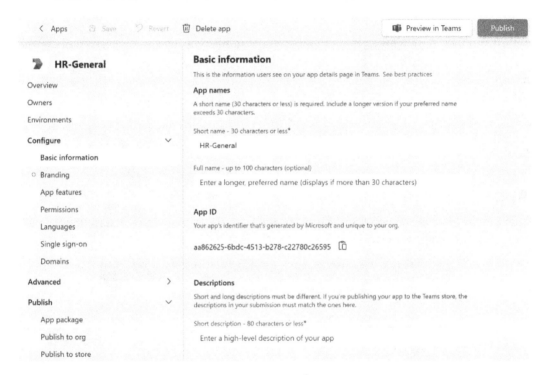

Figure 9.70 – Basic information

In the **Branding** section, we have the option to add an image icon of our own and customize the application further by adding an outline icon and accent color.

Figure 9.71 – Branding options

There are also the options to **Distribute** and **Preview in Teams**.

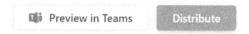

Figure 9.72 – Preview and distribute in Teams

In the **Distribute** section, we have the **Publish to store** and **Publish to org options**.

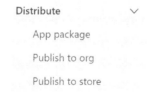

Figure 9.73 – Publish the package

By using the **preview and distribute** option, we can configure our app's capabilities and other important metadata based upon our requirements. The Developer Portal provides options for testing and debugging your app before it is published to the organization. Traditionally, this has been accomplished by creating an **app manifest**, which is a JSON file containing all the metadata required by Teams to display your app's content. This process is abstracted in the Developer Portal, which includes new features and tooling to help you be more successful.

Tools

Finally, we have the last option, **Tools**, which can be helpful to create and edit features that are associated with Microsoft Teams. For instance, all the bots that have been published in Microsoft Teams can be fully managed from here.

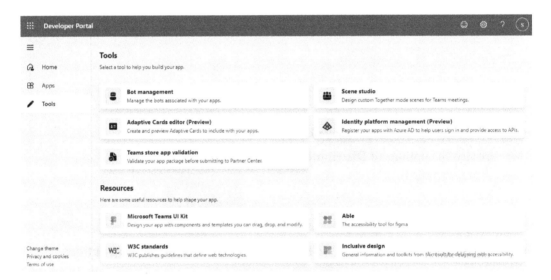

Figure 9.74 – Tools options

The most interesting part is that when we use **Scene studio**, we can create custom **Together Mode** scenes for Teams meetings.

Figure 9.75 – Creating custom Together Mode scenes

When we start customizing the **Getting started sample** scene, there are options to modify the number of participants, add a custom image, mirror participants, and autozoom to fit the participants as well.

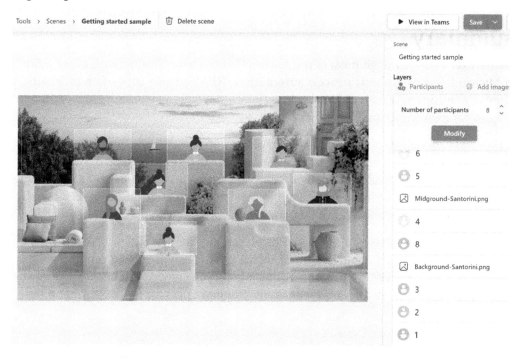

Figure 9.76 – Creating custom Together Mode continued

There are options to **View in Teams** and **Save**, as shown here:

Figure 9.77 – View in Teams and Save

When saving our scenes, we have the options to **Share** and **Export** our own custom-created Together Mode scenes to another tenant.

Figure 9.78 – Share and Export

With only a few clicks, we will be successfully able to create custom Together Mode scenes for our Teams meetings. The Developer Portal for Teams enables an intuitive design experience for developers to create bespoke scenes to make meetings more interesting and to tailor scenes to our organization.

Summary

We have now gone through most of the options that can benefit us in terms of automation in Microsoft Teams. **Robotic process automation** (**RPA**) is being used by an increasing number of businesses to streamline business processes, ranging from simple repetitive tasks to complex workflows.

Customers can use RPA to automate repetitive tasks and workflows. Businesses benefit greatly from these low-code and no-code applications that come with zero additional cost with an Office 365 subscription and Microsoft Teams because they save a significant amount of time on repetitive tasks and employees can invest their time in research and development in their workstreams.

With the tools we have seen in this chapter, you can now map workflow tasks, identify organizational bottlenecks, and determine which time-consuming tasks can be automated—all from within Microsoft Teams. I hope you enjoyed this chapter, and do not forget to read our next chapter on *Productivity Tips and Tricks* for more information.

10
Productivity Tips and Tricks

In this last chapter, we will go through the module that will help us learn some Microsoft Teams tips and tricks. Every week, Microsoft releases tips and shortcuts to help you be more productive and efficient with this powerful tool.

It will be useful to visit `https://www.microsoft.com/en-us/microsoft-365/roadmap?filters=Microsoft%20Teams` every week to see the new features being launched for the Microsoft Teams client.

Because this is a continual update, we'll include a few key takeaways in this chapter that might be extremely useful for anyone utilizing Microsoft Teams.

In this chapter, we will cover the following learning objectives:

- Creating a team – proper naming standards
- Background images in Teams
- Live captions in a Teams meeting
- Validating your network health during a Teams meeting
- Using Proximity Join to attend Teams meetings

After completing this chapter, you will be completely confident in using Microsoft Teams to collaborate efficiently with your colleagues and will have gained hands-on experience with a few techniques.

Technical requirements

To begin our practice, we recommend signing up for an Office 365 trial membership via the methods outlined in our main index, and your administrator must activate all the relevant Microsoft applications.

Creating a team – proper naming standards

In this topic, we will see the strategies that can be used and the decisions that can be made by an admin to create a team in Microsoft Teams. Firstly, in most cases, we do not need to create a team. Often, a team has already been created and we must join it. But if you do need to create a team, it's better to create one with some naming standards.

The following are some examples of team creation with some naming standards:

- Setting up a naming prefix or suffix for an organization with an organization code
- Setting up a naming prefix or suffix for a business unit and department, both with the business code and department code
- Setting up a naming prefix or suffix for the location with the location code
- Setting up a naming prefix or suffix for the process or project with the process or project code

Behind the scenes, when a team is created, an Office 365 group is created in the backend. A group naming policy can be used to ensure that groups formed by users in your business have a consistent naming strategy. A naming policy can assist you and your users in identifying the group's role, membership, geographic region, or creator. The naming policy is applied to all groups established across all workloads (such as Outlook, Microsoft Teams, SharePoint, Planner, Yammer, and so on). It's applied to the group name as well as the group alias. It's also applied when a user creates a group and when an existing group's name, alias, description, or avatar is changed.

The following features make up the group naming policy:

- **Prefix-Suffix Naming Policy**: To determine the naming convention of groups, you can use prefixes or suffixes (for example, "US My Group Engineering"). The prefixes/suffixes can be fixed texts or user characteristics such as [Department], which will be substituted depending on the user who is creating the group.

- **Custom Blocked Words**: You can submit a list of blocked words that are unique to your company and will be blocked in user-created groups (for example, "CEO, Payroll, and Human Resources").

- **Examples**:

  Policy = "GRP [GroupName] [Department]"

  User's department = HR

  Created group name = "GRP Recruitment HR"

Supported **Azure Active Directory (Azure AD)** attributes are [Department], [Company], [Office], [StateOrProvince], [CountryOrRegion], and [Title].

To enforce this naming standard, admins need to configure this setting from their side by logging into the Azure AD portal, navigating to **Overview**, and clicking on **Groups,** as shown in the following screenshot:

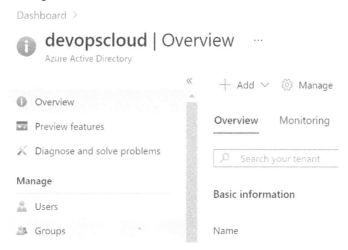

Figure 10.1 – Logging into the Azure AD portal and click on groups

On the next screen, click on **Naming policy**.

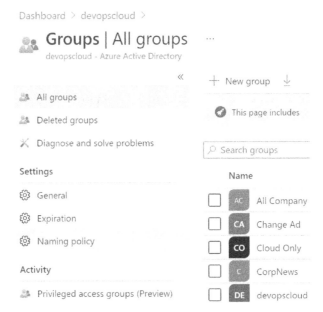

Figure 10.2 – Navigate to Naming policy

When navigating to **Naming policy**, there are two options.

The first tab is Blocked words. To prohibit Microsoft 365 groups from being given profane or reserved names and aliases, you can provide a list of words you want to block. You can examine and/or update the existing list of prohibited words by downloading the .csv file.

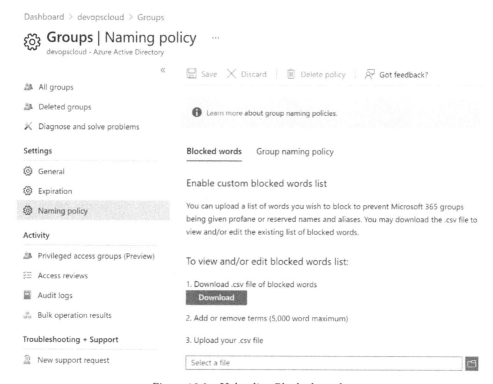

Figure 10.3 – Uploading Blocked words

The next tab is **Group naming policy**, which allows us to add a prefix or suffix for better naming conventions.

Under **Current policy**, choose whether you want to require a prefix, suffix, or both, and select the appropriate checkboxes.

Choose between **Attribute** and **String** for each line and then specify the attribute or string.

When you have added the prefixes and suffixes that you need, click **Save**.

In the prefix, we have two values to choose from based on our requirements. Either choose an **Attribute** (a value that is already available in user properties such as department, company, or office) or a **String**, which can be a constant value for all users.

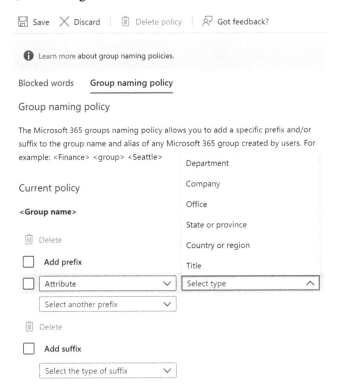

Figure 10.4 – Using Attribute

In **Attribute**, for illustration, we can select **Country or region**, which will automatically populate the country or region name in front of the team name as a prefix. Alternatively, we can select the department, office, or state, depending on how we are designing the group creation strategy.

Blocked words   **Group naming policy**

Group naming policy

The Microsoft 365 groups naming policy allows you to add a specific prefix and/or suffix to the group name and alias of any Microsoft 365 group created by users. For example: <Finance> <group> <Seattle>

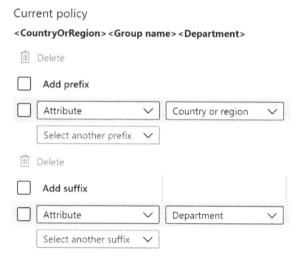

Current policy

<Group name>

🗑 Delete

☐ **Add prefix**

☐ | Attribute   ∨ | | Select type   ∧ |
   | Select another prefix   ∨ |

Department

Company

Office

State or province

Country or region

Title

Figure 10.5 – Choosing the required attribute

The same options are applicable for the suffix. Once we populate the required prefix and suffix, the current policy will be shown, as seen in the next screenshot, where it adds the country as a prefix in the middle group name, and in the suffix, it adds the department name.

Current policy

<CountryOrRegion><Group name><Department>

🗑 Delete

☐ **Add prefix**

☐ | Attribute   ∨ | | Country or region   ∨ |
   | Select another prefix   ∨ |

🗑 Delete

☐ **Add suffix**

☐ | Attribute   ∨ | | Department   ∨ |
   | Select another suffix   ∨ |

Figure 10.6 – Adding a suffix

After we click on **Save**, the group naming policy will be applied for Microsoft Teams team creation.

Figure 10.7 – Saving the naming policy

With only a few clicks, an administrator can create a standard naming convention for Microsoft Teams team creation. And that's all it takes to enforce a policy while creating a new team that helps people to identify the team based on the naming convention. Let's move on to the next topic of background images in Teams.

Background images in Teams

Using custom background images in video meetings and calls has been available in Microsoft Teams for more than a year. This allows us to participate in video meetings and video calls from anywhere, including while traveling, or from a cluttered room in our house. In this video, we will look at how to change your background in Teams.

The first important thing to know is that changing background images in Teams is possible only from the Microsoft Teams desktop client, iOS, and iPad devices. At the time of writing this book, this option is not available from the Teams web app browser client.

You can either blur your background or replace it totally with whatever image you want in your video meeting or call if you want to change what appears behind you.

For example, before joining a meeting, we can select the preferred devices, turn on the camera, and click on **Background filters**.

Figure 10.8 – Enabling Background filters

Here, we have options to choose an existing image or add new images by using the **Add new** option at the top of the **Background settings** page.

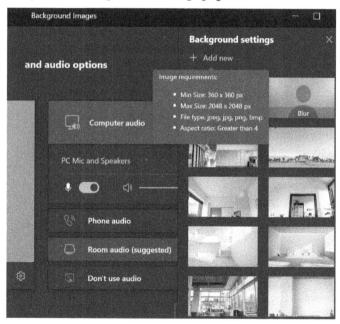

Figure 10.9 – Choosing the right image

We can get more backgrounds from the Microsoft website: `https://www.microsoft.com/en-us/microsoft-teams/background-blur`.

For example, I have added an image by downloading one from the Microsoft website and adding it to this meeting. You can see in the next screenshot that it has totally masked the actual background image with the image that we uploaded.

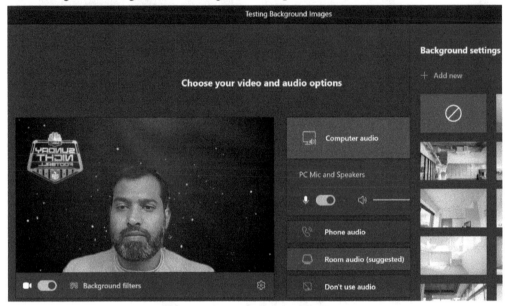

Figure 10.10 – Background image preview example

If you have accidentally already started a meeting with a messy room in the background, you can always click on the three dots and select the **Apply background effects option**. This will bring us to the same screen where we are allowed to change the images.

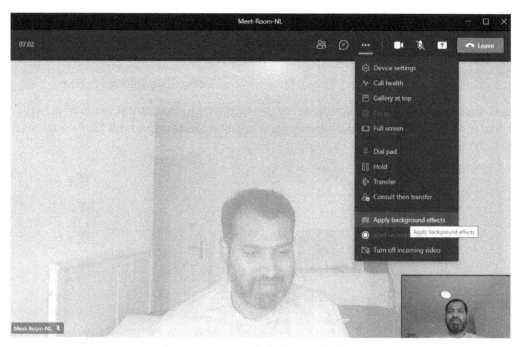

Figure 10.11 – Apply background effects

> **Important Note**
>
> For now, Linux users are not able to use this feature.
>
> Background effects won't be available to you if you're using Teams through optimized **virtual desktop infrastructure (VDI)**.

That's everything for Teams background images, so let's proceed to the next topic: how to use live captions in a Teams meeting.

Live captions in a Teams meeting

We will learn how to use live captions in a Teams meeting in this topic. Live captions provide us with something similar to subtitles, which show what the participants in a video call are saying. Teams live captions work only on the desktop application, and we must have the **new meeting experience** feature enabled on the Microsoft Teams desktop client.

The first action required is for an admin user to enable this functionality from the Teams admin center. To do that, log in to the Teams admin center, and navigate to **Meeting policies** using the following link:

```
https://admin.teams.microsoft.com/policies/meetings/edit
```

Next, turn on the **Allow transcription** toggle switch. One important point to note here is that the transcription is available only for scheduled meetings and not for peer-to-peer audio/video calls at the time of writing this book.

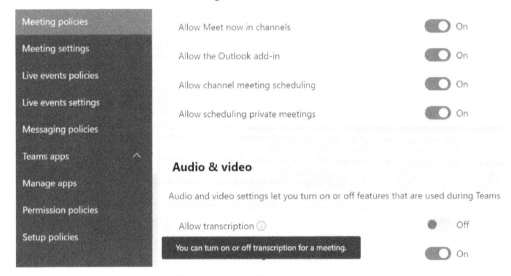

Figure 10.12 – Allow transcription

To test this behavior, I have scheduled one test meeting and sent a meeting invitation for it. After we have joined the meeting, we click on the three dots at the top of the meeting and enable **Turn on live captions**. Once this has been done, the live captions will start working for this meeting.

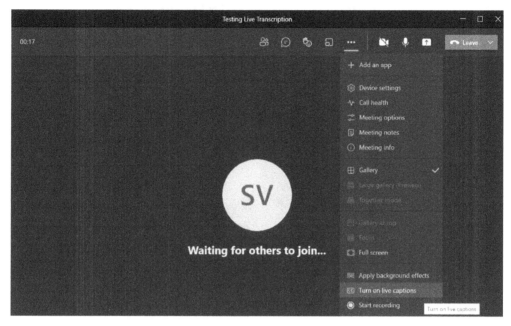

Figure 10.13 – Turn on live captions

Once the live captions feature is turned on, we also get a notification message that says live captions are turned on and enabled in English.

Figure 10.14 – Live captions notification

When speaking a few test words, we can see the transcriptions are being recorded live without any delay. To increase the accuracy of captions, the **Microsoft Automatic Speech Recognition (ASR)** technology service, which generates Teams meeting captions, may use the subject, invitation, participant names, attachments, and recent emails of the participants.

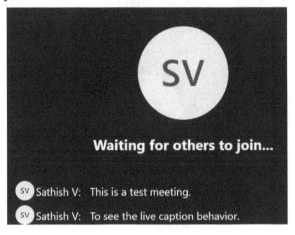

Figure 10.15 – Example transcription during a live meeting

When the remote participant "Smith" speaks, we can see their voice is being converted into the transcript in the following screenshot.

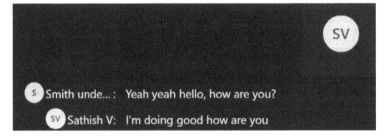

Figure 10.16 – Transcription of a remote participant

This is a fantastic feature for people with hearing impairments. With the Microsoft Artificial Intelligence service's ASR technology, the live captions are accurate most of the time, with only the occasional mistake. This is a great feature of Teams and comes with no additional cost. Now we will hop on to the next topic to check for fundamental network validation during a Teams meeting.

Validating your network health during a Teams meeting

Microsoft Teams is built so that it can work effectively even in low-bandwidth scenarios. But there are cases where we will experience poor audio/video quality during a Teams meeting.

When end users experience poor call quality, they can use a few strategies to assist their internal support staff, as well as Microsoft, by debugging such circumstances when they open an incident with Microsoft.

We will look through a few options that can be helpful in troubleshooting such scenarios. The main thing to remember is that when we experience such issues, it's always highly recommended to reproduce the situation and perform the following actions.

A live call can be now monitored with the option called **Call health** from the Teams client.

This can be checked when a live call is happening by clicking on the three dots at the top and by selecting the **Call health** option.

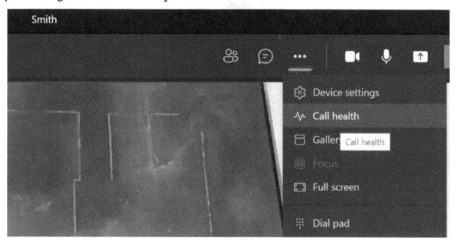

Figure 10.17 – Choosing Call health

When clicking on the call health details, network information regarding the call will be shown.

On the first screen, it will show the general network information of the Teams client sending the data and receiving the data. The most interesting part is that we see packet loss at the bottom of the screen as well. It's highly recommended to take a screenshot of the affected call, which you can provide to the support team. The performance will also be related to local internet connectivity.

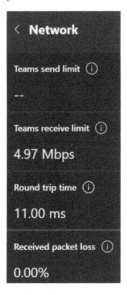

Figure 10.18 – Showing network information

When going to the next screen, we see the audio information. This information will be helpful when we are dealing with a choppy audio experience during a meeting or a call.

Figure 10.19 – Audio information

On the next screen, we see the options that will be helpful for the support team when people report freezing during video calls. A video call consumes most of the bandwidth and this information will help the support team to identify the problem. The video call information provides more details on how many pixels the video frames were sent in and the bitrate. Also included is the type of the video codec.

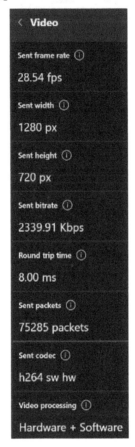

Figure 10.20 – Video information

There are cases where people may report that the screen freezes while performing screen sharing. To help with those scenarios, Microsoft provides the following information:

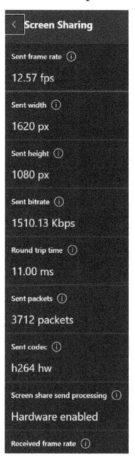

Figure 10.21 – Screen sharing information

An alternative solution is, when a Teams call is going on, to open the Task Manager by holding *Ctrl + Shift + Esc*.

When the Task Manager is opened, click on **Open Resource Monitor**.

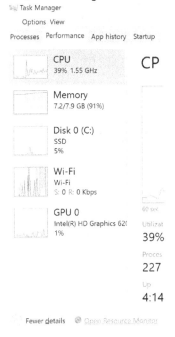

Figure 10.22 – Opening Resource Monitor

When the Resource Monitor is opened, navigate to the **Network** tab and select only **Teams.exe,** as shown in the next screenshot.

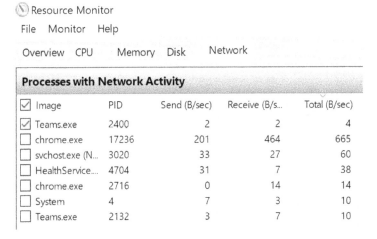

Figure 10.23 – Selecting Teams.exe

Then, on the next screen, there is **Network Activity**, which provides information on what IP addresses Teams is communicating with, and the total number of bytes consumed in sent and received bytes.

Network Activity			106 Kbps Network I/O		0% Network Utilization
Filtered by Teams.exe, Teams.exe, Teams.exe, Teams.exe, Teams.exe					
Image	PID	Address	Send (B/sec)	Receive (B/s...	Total (B/sec)
Teams.exe	2400	52.114.76.113	280	304	584
Teams.exe	2400	Spro_Meet1.home	0	272	272
Teams.exe	2400	52.114.251.234	35	55	89
Teams.exe	2400	52.114.74.119	57	0	57
Teams.exe	2400	52.114.249.161	17	17	34
Teams.exe	2400	52.114.249.169	17	17	34
Teams.exe	2400	52.114.249.90	31	0	31
Teams.exe	2400	52.114.249.224	31	0	31
Teams.exe	2400	52.114.77.98	2	2	4

Figure 10.24 – Network Activity

On the next screen, you will find **TCP Connections**, with more information on packet loss and latency. It also provides information on which local address the Teams client communicates from. Ideally, Teams traffic must not flow through the TCP stream. Although Teams audio and video calls can be established successfully via TCP, we might experience bad call quality. If it does flow through TCP, report this to the network team with the evidence you get from this procedure. Ask them to allow the required port ranges for Teams defined in the Office 365 URL and IP ranges section in the Microsoft documentation.

TCP Connections							
Filtered by Teams.exe, Teams.exe, Teams.exe, Teams.exe, Teams.exe							
Image	PID	Local Address	Local ...	Remote Address	Remot...	Packet Loss (...	Latency (ms)
Teams.exe	2400	192.168.1.64	49288	52.114.32.8	443	0	225
Teams.exe	2400	192.168.1.64	52384	52.114.76.113	443	0	73
Teams.exe	2400	192.168.1.64	50024	52.114.249.169	443	0	28
Teams.exe	2400	192.168.1.64	50008	52.114.249.161	443	0	28
Teams.exe	2400	192.168.1.64	55909	52.114.77.98	443	0	23
Teams.exe	2400	192.168.1.64	56860	52.114.77.98	443	-	-
-	-	192.168.1.64	50029	52.114.251.234	443	-	-
Teams.exe	2400	192.168.1.64	50009	52.114.251.234	443	-	-
-	-	192.168.1.64	50030	52.114.254.162	443	-	-

Figure 10.25 – TCP Connections

Lastly, we have information on **Listening Ports**, which provides more details on the ports that audio and video streams are communicating from.

Listening Ports					
Filtered by Teams.exe, Teams.exe, Teams.exe, Teams.exe, Teams.exe					
Image	PID	Address	Port	Protocol	Firewall Status
Teams.exe	2400	192.168.1.64	50014	UDP	Allowed, not restricted
Teams.exe	2400	192.168.1.64	50015	UDP	Allowed, not restricted
Teams.exe	2400	192.168.1.64	50026	UDP	Allowed, not restricted
Teams.exe	2400	192.168.1.64	50027	UDP	Allowed, not restricted
Teams.exe	2400	IPv6 unspecified	59600	UDP	Allowed, not restricted
Teams.exe	2400	IPv4 unspecified	59600	UDP	Allowed, not restricted
Teams.exe	2400	IPv6 unspecified	63873	UDP	Allowed, not restricted
Teams.exe	2400	IPv4 unspecified	63873	UDP	Allowed, not restricted

Figure 10.26 – Listening ports

We have now covered enough information from the end user perspective to collect details and provide information to the support team for further analysis of any issues with Microsoft Teams call quality. Let's have a look at the last topic, **Proximity Join**, which is really helpful in Microsoft Teams meetings.

Using Proximity Join to attend Teams meetings

Proximity Join allows you to connect to a Teams meeting room from your phone or other device by utilizing Bluetooth. Ad hoc, spontaneous meetings account for most interactions between coworkers. Proximity Join enables you to find and join nearby available Microsoft Teams rooms. This can be beneficial for any ad hoc meetings and adding a nearby meeting room that is free and available.

Let's check out Proximity Join in a few steps. To start testing Proximity Join, I have opened the Teams client on my Android device. I've then navigated to **Calendar** and initiated one meeting by clicking on **Join**.

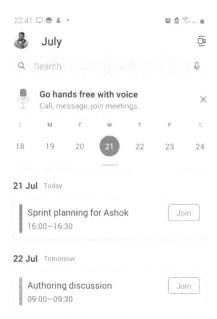

Figure 10.27 – Calendar view from an Android device

The moment we click on **Join**, we are prompted with the following screen in the Android client. You will notice that there is a small arrow right next to **Join now**. Click on this drop-down arrow.

Figure 10.28 – Selecting the drop-down arrow

On clicking on the dropdown next to **Join now**, we are presented with the following two options. The first one is **Audio Off** and the second one is **Join and add a room**. An important point to remember here is that Bluetooth *must* be turned on on your mobile device and the meeting rooms will have Bluetooth enabled by default.

Figure 10.29 – Joining options

On the next screen, the Microsoft Teams client provides us with the option to **Search for rooms** and **Add a room**. It also provides us with suggestions on any nearby rooms that are free and available to be used for this meeting.

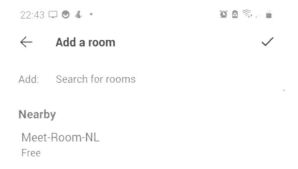

Figure 10.30 – Searching for a room

Here, all we need to do is to pick an available room and click on the checkmark in the top-right corner.

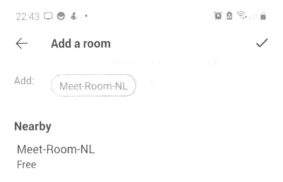

Figure 10.31 – Choosing an available room

This finally brings the ring notification on the meeting room display panel with the name of the person who has invited this meeting room to a Teams meeting.

Figure 10.32 – Notification on the meeting room device

Once we click on **Join**, we see the meeting room has successfully joined the Microsoft Teams meeting.

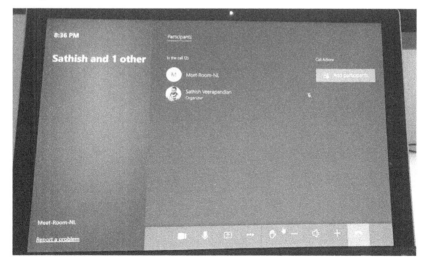

Figure 10.33 – Successfully joined meeting

Proximity join is a great feature that makes Teams meetings more enjoyable through meeting rooms.

Summary

Tips and tricks are essentially shortcuts or ways to make something easier to do. I hope you enjoyed this chapter and that you will try to apply these concepts in your daily Microsoft Teams usage. Microsoft Teams is a constantly changing Microsoft program that has seen widespread adoption in recent years. On March 14, 2017, Microsoft introduced the service globally. When compared to other Microsoft products such as Microsoft Outlook, the product has seen a significant improvement. Microsoft has put a lot of money into this fantastic collaboration platform, and we can expect more new features in the future.

Packt.com

Subscribe to our online digital library for full access to over 7,000 books and videos, as well as industry leading tools to help you plan your personal development and advance your career. For more information, please visit our website.

Why subscribe?

- Spend less time learning and more time coding with practical eBooks and Videos from over 4,000 industry professionals

- Improve your learning with Skill Plans built especially for you

- Get a free eBook or video every month

- Fully searchable for easy access to vital information

- Copy and paste, print, and bookmark content

Did you know that Packt offers eBook versions of every book published, with PDF and ePub files available? You can upgrade to the eBook version at packt.com and as a print book customer, you are entitled to a discount on the eBook copy. Get in touch with us at customercare@packtpub.com for more details.

At www.packt.com, you can also read a collection of free technical articles, sign up for a range of free newsletters, and receive exclusive discounts and offers on Packt books and eBooks.

Other Books You May Enjoy

If you enjoyed this book, you may be interested in these other books by Packt:

Hands-On Microsoft Teams

João Ferreira

ISBN: 978-1-83921-398-4

- Create teams, channels, and tabs in Microsoft Teams
- Explore the Teams architecture and various Office 365 components included in Teams
- Perform scheduling, and managing meetings and live events in Teams
- Configure and manage apps in Teams
- Design automated scripts for managing a Teams environment using PowerShell

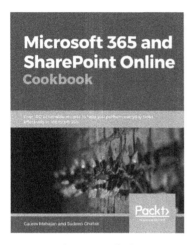

Microsoft 365 and SharePoint Online Cookbook

Gaurav Mahajan , Sudeep Ghatak

ISBN: 978-1-83864-667-7

- Get to grips with a wide range of apps and cloud services in Microsoft 365

- Discover ways to use SharePoint Online to create and manage content

- Store and share documents using SharePoint Online

- Improve your search experience with Microsoft Search

- Leverage the Power Platform to build business solutions with Power Automate, Power Apps, Power BI, and Power Virtual Agents

- Enhance native capabilities in SharePoint and Teams using the SPFx framework

- Use Microsoft Teams to meet, chat, and collaborate with colleagues or external users

Packt is searching for authors like you

If you're interested in becoming an author for Packt, please visit `authors.packtpub.com` and apply today. We have worked with thousands of developers and tech professionals, just like you, to help them share their insight with the global tech community. You can make a general application, apply for a specific hot topic that we are recruiting an author for, or submit your own idea.

Share Your Thoughts

Hi!

We Sathish, Harsharanjeet, Ashok & Sriram, authors of *Reimagine Remote Working with Microsoft Teams*, really hope you enjoyed reading this book and found it useful for increasing your productivity and efficiency in Microsoft Teams.

It would really help us (and other potential readers!) if you could leave a review on Amazon sharing your thoughts on *Reimagine Remote Working with Microsoft Teams*.

Go to the link below or scan the QR code to leave your review:

`https://packt.link/r/1801814163`

Your review will help us to understand what's worked well in this book, and what could be improved upon for future editions, so it really is appreciated.

Best wishes,

Sathish Veerapandian   Harsharanjeet Kaur   Ashok Madhavarayan   Sriram Rajamanickam

Index

M

www.ingramcontent.com/pod-product-compliance
Lightning Source LLC
Chambersburg PA
CBHW081502050326

40690CB00015B/2889